A Tasty Way to a H
Healthy Reci
Nutritional Information & \

CW00404617

Margareta Wikiuna

1

Table of Contents

Introduction

I was apparently a fussy eater at the very beginning of my life. I have no memories of this. All I remember is that I loved the food my mother put on the table. She was a great cook who cooked everything from scratch.

Food was a big thing in my family when I was growing up.

And food has continued to be a big thing throughout my life – I'm a chef - accompanied by a huge appetite. I had a miraculous metabolism to start with and got away with eating a lot of just about anything without putting on weight.

It didn't take that long though before my body started to protest about what went in, and then the weight started to creep up.

I've always had an interest in nutrition and the more my body complained, the more interested I got. This started my quest for food that was both tasty and healthy. I love big, bold flavours and now I wanted to combine that with healthy ingredients – to find a tasty way to a healthy life!

Health and weight maintenance – where to start?

Improving digestion is the cornerstone to good health and a well-functioning metabolism.

For your body to be able to absorb and make use of the nutrients in the food you eat, the food first has to be broken down into smaller particles. This is done by chemical compounds called enzymes.

Protein is broken down into amino acids; complex carbohydrates into simple sugars and fat into fatty acids and glycerol.

Enzymes turn the food we eat into fuel for every single cell in our bodies, be it a muscle cell, a brain cell, an immune cell or a blood cell. Further enzymes within these cells turn the fuel into useable energy that makes our heart beat, our nerves fire and all other bodily functions take place.

Your body needs nutrients – a wide variety of vitamins and minerals - to make these enzymes. If the food you eat is nutrient-poor, you will become enzyme-deficient - making it even harder for your body to make use of what little nutrients there are in the food.

You can increase your enzyme potential by eating raw food such as vegetables as raw food contains quite a lot of enzymes. It is important though, to chew properly to activate these enzymes.

Digestion starts in your mouth and chewing your food well is really important. Chewing release saliva, a watery liquid which contains enzymes that start the breakdown of carbohydrates.

A good starting point with healthy eating is to take a closer look at carbohydrates – see Low-GL carbohydrates - page 533. Your body needs them, it's the safest form of fuel for your body. There's a lot of different carbohydrates though, and some are better than others for both your health and your weight.

Some of the best carbohydrates are non-starchy vegetables, such as spinach, broccoli, tomatoes, peppers, cabbage and lettuce. **All non-starchy vegetables are very low in calories, rich in healthy nutrients and all contain fibre.**

My advice is to include non-starchy vegetables with most meals – and to include a lot of it! It is good for your health and it is good for controlling your weight. But tasty and healthy food is so much more than just these vegetables.

I also believe that you should allow yourself a treat from time to time so I have included some delicious cake recipes as well as a recipe for raw chocolate truffles.

Well, let's get cooking - go explore and try out the recipes in this book.

Happy Cooking!

Margareta Wiklund

Breakfast Recipes

Bircher Muesli

If you want a really tasty and healthy start to your day, try this Bircher muesli.

My problem with it is that once I have done a batch of it, I can easily dip into it several times a day. I find it wonderfully addictive.

There are worse things to be addicted to though - this is healthy stuff we're talking about, and it's quite filling as well.

It is a great breakfast to have in the fridge if you are short of time in the morning and easy to take with you if you don't eat before you leave to go to work. It needs an overnight soaking but all you have to do in the morning is add some yogurt and "Bob's your uncle".

There is no one single recipe for Bircher muesli. I make it without any fresh berries or fruit as I make a big enough batch to last me for several days. I add fresh berries when I'm eating it.

What I do add is a mix of seeds - sunflower seeds, pumpkin seeds, whole un-hulled sesame seeds, chia seeds - and nuts, such as Brazil nuts, walnuts, almonds and pistachio nuts.

Seeds and nuts are really healthy – containing lots of vitamins and minerals as well as being good sources of protein. Seeds and walnuts are also rich in the polyunsaturated essential fats Omega 3 and Omega 6.

These types of healthy fats are absolutely vital for our health - vital for both our bodies and our brains - and a lot of people are deficient in Omega 3 and Omega 6.

I used to add a bit of dried fruit but the sugar content in dried fruit is incredibly concentrated so I stopped adding it. I add ground cinnamon instead.

Fruit juice also has a high concentration of sugar but out of all juices, apple juice is the best. I use cloudy 100% pure apple juice for my bircher muesli.

You might think that I am picky but I also buy organic oats. Oats contain gluten but not "gliadin", which is a specific sub-set of gluten and what causes allergic reactions.

Some people with gluten intolerance can eat oats, as long as they are organic - most non-organic commercial oats are processed in facilities that also process wheat.

The tastiest oats I have used for both this muesli and porridge are organic wholegrain, rolled jumbo oats.

For 4-6 people:

100g, 3½oz, 1 cup, oats

75g, 2 3/4oz, 0.6 cup, mixed seeds and nuts, roughly chopped

1 teaspoon ground cinnamon

250ml, slightly more than a 1 cup, pure, unsweetened apple juice

Juice from ½ a lemon

1. Mix all the ingredients together in a bowl. Cover the bowl and leave in the refrigerator overnight.

2. The next morning, add 100ml natural yogurt (I use Greek-style yogurt) to the muesli and mix well. Any left-overs will easily keep in the fridge for 3-4 days.

Adding fresh berries to each portion will make this really nutritious. Fresh berries have the lowest sugar content of all fruit and are full of healthy antioxidants. Or you can add some grated or chopped apples to each portion.

Blueberry Pancakes

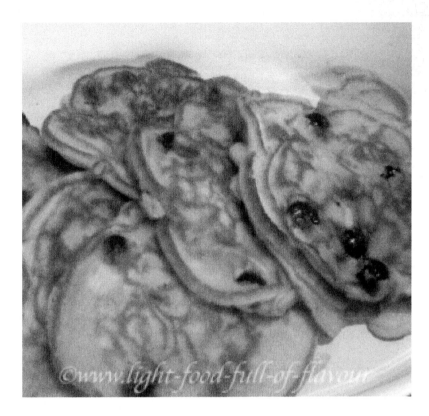

These American-style blueberry pancakes make for an indulgent breakfast on a day off when I've got time on my hands and friends around me.

I once worked as the cook on a small cruise-boat up in Scotland. I served a different breakfast every morning on each six-day long cruise.

The galley on the boat was minuscule and you had to be really organised when there was a lot of things going out at the same time – like a full Scottish breakfast which I always got out of the way on the first morning.

Making pancakes was much easier to do in that galley.

Pancakes in any shape and form will never be enough for me personally as the only thing to eat for breakfast. On the boat we always served cereals, mueslis and porridge as well as fresh fruit and toast.

For me these blueberry pancakes are simply the cherry on top of a tasty and healthy breakfast.

Confession: When I was testing my recipe below – having tweaked it after a couple of earlier attempts – I was on my own and absolutely starving. I actually polished off the whole lot in one go.

This will make about 8 pancakes:

100g, 3½oz, 0.7 cup self-rising flour

½ teaspoon bicarbonate of soda

½ teaspoon salt

1 tablespoon caster (superfine) sugar

100g, 3½oz, ½ cup, ricotta or cottage cheese

2 eggs

75ml, 1/3 cup, milk

100g 3½oz, ½ cup, blueberries

olive oil and butter for frying

1. In a bowl, mix together the flour, bicarbonate of soda, salt and sugar. In a separate bowl, mix together the ricotta (or cottage cheese), eggs and milk. Add the egg, cheese and milk mixture to the flour mixture and, using a large spoon, stir together to make a batter. Add the blueberries.

2. Grease a small frying pan with half a teaspoon of butter and a little olive oil over a medium heat. Spoon a small ladle of batter into the pan and cook for 1-2 minutes on each side (use two spatulas to turn over), until each side is nicely browned and slightly puffed up. Repeat until you have used up all the batter.

I eat these blueberry pancakes as they are or with a mix of fresh berries. But, if you don't mind the increase of calories, you can also serve them with some maple syrup.

Smoothie Recipes

Mixed Berries, Pomegranate Juice and Soya Milk Smoothie

This is a super-healthy, super-delicious and quite filling smoothie. I came up with the idea when I was writing about food that could help you lose weight.

All the ingredients in this smoothie are, apart from their apparent ability to help you lose belly fat, full of healthy nutrients.

Make sure you buy 100% natural pomegranate juice. I buy frozen berries to use for smoothies as it is both convenient and undoubtedly cheaper than buying fresh berries.

For 3 -4 people as part of a breakfast

200g, 7oz, 1½ cups, mixed berries – like blueberries, blackberries, strawberries and raspberries

200ml, 7floz, 0.9 cup, pomegranate juice

200ml, 7floz, 0.9 cup, soya milk, light or ordinary

Defrost the berries if using frozen ones and mix everything in a blender.

Mango, Raspberry and Blueberry Smoothie

When a smoothie is only going to be a part of a breakfast, I often make smoothies with nothing but a mix of fruit. Really, I just mix whatever fruit I've got available at the time but I do like to get some type of exotic fruit in there, mango being a clear favourite.

For 2 people as part of a breakfast:

1 ripe small mango - peeled and cubed

3 heaped tablespoons raspberries

3 tablespoons blueberries

Juice of 1 large orange

Juice of ½ a lime

Blitz all the ingredients in a blender and ENJOY!

Green Breakfast Smoothie

If you really can't face eating much at breakfast time, try this super-healthy and tasty green breakfast smoothie. Or make it and take it with you to work.

I have personally got far too big an appetite to settle for nothing but a smoothie for breakfast, but this one contains all the goodness of a really healthy breakfast.

There is avocado, rich in heart-healthy monounsaturated fat and full of vitamin E; spinach, rich in antioxidants, iron, different vitamins and many other nutrients; seeds and nuts, rich in protein, antioxidants and other nutrients, and on and on the list goes.

I get a bit of an allergic reaction when eating ordinary kiwi fruit so I use kiwi gold fruit instead in this green breakfast smoothie of mine. But obviously, either of them will do.

For 2 people:

1 ripe avocado, peeled and de-stoned

2 kiwi fruits, peeled

2 handfuls fresh baby spinach

1 teaspoon finely grated ginger

1 tablespoons pumpkin seeds

5 almonds

5 walnuts

Juice of 1 lime

Juice of 1 orange

1 teaspoon honey (optional)

200 ml, 7floz, 0.9 cup, natural yogurt (or use soya/coconut yogurt)

Blitz all the ingredients in a blender and ENJOY.

Antioxidant Booster Smoothie

Here's a smoothie that could make you glow and go that extra mile – a smoothie that is packed with seriously antioxidant rich ingredients. These ingredients also have a high nutritional value.

I got the idea for this smoothie when I was reading up on the nutritional value of beetroots. Several studies have apparently shown that eating beetroots or drinking beetroot juice can increase your stamina.

Just what I need in the morning – extra energy!

And then I thought about other antioxidant rich vegetables and fruit that would go well with the beetroot and came up with the following recipe.

All of the ingredients are nutritional powerhouses, and raspberries and spinach are also rich sources of dietary fibre which help to make you feel fuller for longer.

For 2 people:

250g, 9oz, 1.3 cups, cooked beetroots (beets) in natural juice, roughly chopped

100g, 3½oz, 1 cup, raspberries

1 tablespoon goji berries – or just add some more raspberries

2 large handfuls fresh spinach leaves

Juice of 2 large oranges

Blitz all the ingredients in a blender and ENJOY!

Oat-So-Good Breakfast Smoothie

Don't have the time or the appetite for porridge in the morning? Make this smoothie with oats and linseeds (flax seeds) in it and take it with you to work or school.

Oats contain a fibre called beta-glucan which has been shown to lower blood cholesterol. All in all, oats contain more soluble fibre than any other grain and eating fibre-rich food helps to make you feel fuller for longer.

Oats also contain magnesium which helps boost energy levels.

You will need to soak the oats and the linseeds overnight in some of the pomegranate juice. But all you have to do in the morning is place all the ingredients in a blender and whiz together.

I've also added almonds to this smoothie. Almonds are a rich source of vitamin E, B-vitamins, dietary fibre, calcium, iron and magnesium.

For 1 person:

3 heaped tablespoons oats

1 tablespoon linseeds (flax seeds)

200ml, 7floz, 0.9 cup, 100% natural pomegranate juice

1 medium-sized banana

3 heaped tablespoons raspberries

3 heaped tablespoons blackberries or blueberries

10 almonds, roughly chopped

4 tablespoons natural soya yogurt or plain yogurt

1 level teaspoon honey (optional)

Soak the oats and linseeds overnight in half of the pomegranate juice. In the morning, place the soaked oats and linseeds and the rest of the ingredients in a blender and whiz together. Enjoy!

Chia Breakfast Pot with Coconut and Apple

It's really easy to make this chia breakfast pot. And it's tasty. And healthy!

You need to make it in advance though – minimum two hours - to allow the seeds to soak up the liquid you add them to.

I prepare it in the evening and leave it in the fridge overnight. All I do in the morning is add some fresh berries and some nuts to each portion.

This is a breakfast dish full of healthy nutrients – and it is an ideal thing to take with you if you are not eating anything at home before leaving for work. Any leftovers will keep in the fridge for the next day.

Chia seeds are rich in omega-3, fibre, antioxidants, calcium, iron and vitamins. These seeds can be absorbed by your body in their natural state – unlike flax seeds (linseeds) which will go straight through your body unless you grind them first or chew them really well.

Cinnamon and turmeric are two equally healthy spices.

To make it more filling, top your chia breakfast pot with some yogurt – either natural Greek or soya yogurt – as well as berries and some nuts.

Fresh berries are full of antioxidants and are the best type of fruit to eat if you are watching your weight.

I top my pot with some walnuts as well. While all nuts and seeds are full of healthy nutrients, walnuts are among the healthiest ones.

Chia Breakfast Pot for 4 people:

50g, 1 ¾oz, ¼ cup chia seeds

1 level teaspoon cinnamon (see above)

½ teaspoon ground turmeric

1 apple, coarsely grated

½ - 1 teaspoon honey, preferably raw (optional)

200ml, 7floz, 0.9 cup coconut milk

200ml, 7floz, 0.9 cup cold water

To serve:

Fresh berries – like strawberries blueberries or raspberries

Nuts/seeds – like walnuts, pistachios and/or pumpkin seeds

Yogurt (optional)

1. Mix together the chia seeds cinnamon and turmeric in a bowl. Add the grated apple and honey (if using) and stir through before adding the coconut milk and water to the bowl. Mix everything together thoroughly.

2. Divide the mixture between 4 bowls or glasses. Cover each bowl/glass and place them in the fridge for minimum 2 hours – or leave them overnight

3. Serve each portion with a dollop of yogurt (optional), fresh berries and nuts of your choice.

Scrambled Eggs

I LOVE EGGS! And I love all the wonderful things you can make with them, like scrambled eggs - which I flavour with a variety of things and only indulge in occasionally. The things that I add to the eggs are undoubtedly a bit calorific.

Eggs are good for you. They are a great source of protein, relatively low in calories (a medium egg contains around 78 calories) and contain a lot of nutrients - including many different vitamins.

I wouldn't dream of cutting out the egg yolk for the sake of lowering the calories in eggs. Apart from the glorious taste, **the yolk is the most nutritious part of the egg**.

And there is no need to worry about the cholesterol in eggs - it doesn't have a significant effect on our blood cholesterol.

Scrambled eggs should, as far I am concerned, have a creamy texture. It really is such a simple thing to cook, but I have had so many cardboard-like versions in hotels, cafés and restaurants that I've stopped ordering it.

I read an article about a famous British chef who said that when he interviewed chefs to employ in his restaurants, he started off by asking them to make him scrambled eggs.

I add a variety of cheeses, vegetables and herbs to my eggs. I then cook them very quickly over quite a high heat. And because it's so quick, I make sure that everything else that I'm serving for the breakfast is ready and on the table.

For 4 people:

8 medium-sized eggs - preferably organic, or at least free-range - whisked together in a bowl

Suggestions for flavourings:

1. 50g, 1¾oz, 1/3 cup, feta cheese + 1 tablespoon olive oil + a good pinch of dried herbs (oregano and thyme, for example, or mixed dry herbs). Mash it all together and add it to the eggs. Season with salt and pepper.

2. 75g, 2¾oz, 1/3 cup, soft goats' cheese + 4 chopped spring onions (scallions). Crumble the goats' cheese and add to the eggs together with the chopped spring onion. Season with salt and pepper.

3. 1-2 tablespoons of Philadelphia Cheese, or similar soft cheese + 1 tablespoon chopped fresh chives. Add it all to the eggs and season with salt and pepper.

Melt a teaspoon of butter in a non-stick frying pan and add the egg mixture. Keep stirring over quite a high heat and remove the frying pan as soon as the eggs have a creamy but not runny texture.

Breakfast Bread Toppings

I love good bread, especially sourdough bread. My personal favourite is moist rye sourdough bread of the Danish type. Super-Yum!

My breakfast bread toppings can be anything from scrambled eggs to ripe avocado.

I often eat sourdough bread with hummus and sliced avocado. I absolutely love it!

Avocado and hummus are both really nutritious, and as long as you don't overdo it - no more than 1/2 an avocado and a couple of tablespoons of hummus - neither of them will affect your weight very much.

Make it even healthier and tastier by adding sliced raw red pepper (bell pepper) as well.

Other ideas for breakfast bread toppings:

Filled Pitta Bread

I sometimes toast wholemeal (whole wheat) pitta bread and fill it with hummus, dark green leaves (water cress, spinach, arugula), sliced avocado and red pepper (bell pepper). It's a bit messy to eat but Oh So Tasty!

Feta and Cottage Cheese Topping

100g, 3½oz, ½ cup cottage cheese

25g, 1oz, ¼ cup, feta cheese, crumbled

Black pepper

Watercress or chopped chives

Red or yellow pepper (bell pepper), sliced

Mix together the cottage cheese with the feta cheese and season with a bit of black pepper. Divide the mixture over slices of bread and top with watercress or chopped chives and red or yellow pepper (bell pepper).

As an alternative, you could swap the pepper (bell pepper) for smoked salmon.

This is a really tasty soybean topping for bread.

Edamame beans - immature green soya beans (soybeans) – are considered to be a source of complete protein and are low in saturated fat while jam-packed with dietary fibre. I personally make sure that the edamame beans I use are not from a GM-crop.

50g, ¼ cup cooked soya beans (soybeans), roughly mashed (use a potato masher)

3 tablespoons cottage cheese

2 tablespoons grated Parmesan cheese

A small handful of parsley leaves

A squeeze of lemon juice

Salt and pepper

Mix the mashed soya beans with the cottage cheese, Parmesan cheese, parsley and lemon juice and season with a little bit of salt and pepper.

If you want to take this a step further and make it even healthier and tastier, top with sliced avocado and red or yellow pepper (bell pepper).

Fried Mushrooms on Toast with Lemon Thyme Feta Cheese

I love the idea of brunch, of having time in the morning to work up an appetite for a meal that is sitting between breakfast and lunch. This recipe for fried mushrooms on toast with lemon thyme feta cheese is a perfect meal for a brunch.

It is a recipe from Shelagh Ryan that I have made some slight changes to. I used chestnut and meaty shitake mushrooms but you can use any mushrooms of your liking.

Mushrooms are rich in essential nutrients while low in calories.

Unless you are on a dairy-free diet, I suggest frying the mushrooms in a mix of olive oil and butter. Otherwise, simply skip the butter and add some more olive oil to the frying pan.

If you can't get hold of lemon thyme, use ordinary thyme and add the zest of a lemon.

I prefer to use sourdough bread or some other really good bread for the toast.

Fried mushrooms on toast for 4 people:

100g, 3½oz, 0.75 cup feta cheese, crumbled

1½ tablespoon olive oil

2 teaspoons fresh lemon thyme leaves - or use plain fresh thyme leaves + grated zest from a lemon

Black pepper

500g, 1lb2oz, mixed mushrooms (see above), sliced

1 garlic clove, crushed/minced

1 tablespoon olive oil + half a tablespoon butter

Salt and pepper

4 slices sourdough bread - or other good bread

Watercress and/or rocket (arugula) leaves

Red peppers (bell peppers) - I buy the sweet, pointed varieties

1.In a bowl, mix together 1½ tablespoon olive oil with the fresh lemon thyme leaves and some black pepper. Add the crumbled feta cheese and mix together.

2.Add 1 tablespoon olive oil and half a tablespoon of butter to a frying pan over a medium high heat. Once the oil and butter is hot, add the sliced mushrooms and crushed/minced garlic to the pan and toss to coat the mushrooms with the oil and butter. Season with some salt and pepper and fry for about 3-4 minutes – stirring every now and then – until the mushrooms start to brown and all the liquid from the mushrooms has evaporated.

3.Toast the bread and once ready, top each slice of bread with watercress/rocket leaves, followed by the fried mushrooms and the crumbled feta. Add some sliced peppers to each plate.

Gluten-Free Bread with Nuts, Seeds and Quinoa

It is hard to say what I have missed the most since finding out that I am intolerant to wheat, gluten, dairy, eggs and three different types of nuts. Bread is pretty high up on the list though.

Before cutting it out, I mostly ate sourdough bread – preferably dark rye sourdough bread. Just seeing such bread in a good bread shop makes me drool.

But guess what, I have found a way to make super-tasty gluten-free bread with quinoa flakes, seeds and nuts. It pretty much tastes like the rye bread I love - I am hooked!

It requires a fair bit of resting time before being baked in the oven but it is super-easy to make. All you have to do to make this gluten-free bread is mix all the ingredients together and pour the mix into a bread-tin.

I have used a recipe from Ella Woodward but I have made some changes to it – including resting time before baking and baking method.

There is no yeast in this bread and the only flour I am using is the flour you get from blending quinoa flakes, walnuts and pumpkin seeds together. To this you add sunflower seeds, chia seeds and psyllium husks.

The psyllium husks (a source of dietary fibre) are vital to this gluten-free bread recipe as the husks bind the mixture and make the bread less crumbly. You will find it, and all the other ingredients, in health food shops and sometimes in well-stocked supermarkets.

I have chosen to add five chopped, organic dried apricots to my bread. The sugar content in dried fruit is high, but as I put in so few, it won't cause much damage.

Try buying organic ones if you can. Naturally dried apricots have a dark "brownish" colour. As producers are afraid that this will turn off buyers they treat the dried apricots with sulphur dioxide to give them the colour apricots have when fresh.

I use a bread-tin which is 22cm (9 inches) long x 11cm (4¼ inches) wide and 6cm (2½ inches) deep – **but it might be better to use a larger one (see below)**.

To make 1 gluten-free bread-loaf:

90g, 3 ¼oz, 1 cup walnuts

100g, 3½oz, 1 cup quinoa flakes

150g, 5¼oz, 1½ cups pumpkin seeds (you use 100g, 3½oz, 1 cup to make the flour and the rest go in to the mixture whole)

70g, 2½oz, ½ cup sunflower seeds

40g, 1oz, ½ cup psyllium husks

2 tablespoons chia seeds

1 teaspoon ground sea or rock salt

5 dried organic apricots, chopped (optional)

600ml, 21floz, 2½ cups water

Cover the baking tin with baking parchment. Place the walnuts, quinoa flakes and 100g, 3½oz, 1 cup of the pumpkin seeds into a food processor and blend for a couple of minutes until you have a fine flour.

Add this to a bowl together with the remaining pumpkin seeds, sunflower seeds, psyllium husk, chia seeds, salt and chopped apricots. Mix together before adding the water and mixing everything together thoroughly.

3.Pour the mixture into the baking tin and smooth out the top with the back of a spoon. Let it sit out on a counter for either a day, or overnight, before baking.

4.Pre-heat the oven to 180C/Fan 160C/350F/gas mark 4. Place the baking tin in the oven and bake for 40 minutes. Remove the bread from the tin and place it upside down (without the baking parchment) directly onto the oven rack and bake for further 30 minutes.

If you pierce the bread with a sharp knife, the knife should ideally be dry when you pull it out. Now I am going to confess that I have never achieved this even

though I have baked the bread for even longer most times.

It doesn't matter to me – I toast each slice anyway.

Footnote: I had my first intolerance test about 5 years ago. I did another test this year (2019) in the hope of a change as I had mostly kept away from the food I was intolerant to. No such chance - apart from the nuts. Instead I'm now intolerant to soya as well! Sigh. I am not entirely strict when travelling or at work as a chef. But the one thing that really affects me if I eat it more than occasionally is any food containing gluten.

Turkish Menemen

Turkish menemen is a delicious spiced tomato and red pepper (bell pepper) dish with eggs cooked on top.

It might not be something you would eat before running off to work but it is a perfect dish to eat as a late breakfast on a day off – or as a light lunch. I serve it with lots of peppery rocket (arugula) leaves and watercress and some really good bread.

You'll find similar dishes in other countries – such as Mexican huevos rancheros and a Middle Eastern dish called shakshouka which are both mostly eaten as breakfast.

For 4 people:

2 tablespoons olive oil

1 teaspoon fennel seeds

1 teaspoon cumin seeds

½ teaspoon mustard seeds

1 red onion, peeled and finely chopped

Thumb-sized piece of ginger, peeled and finely chopped

2 cloves of garlic, crushed

1 large red chilli (or more if you really want to kick-start the day), finely chopped

1 large red pepper (bell pepper), diced

400g, 14oz, 2¼ cups, ripe tomatoes, diced, or use the same amount of tinned chopped tomatoes

Salt and pepper

4 organic or free-range eggs

To serve:

2 handfuls chopped parsley

Plain or Greek yogurt

Watercress and/or rocket (arugula) leaves

1.Heat the oil in a frying pan over a medium high heat. Add the fennel, cumin and mustard seeds and fry for a couple of minutes until the spices are aromatic.

2.Add the chopped onion, ginger, garlic and chilli to the frying pan. Continue to fry for 5-7 minutes, until the onion has softened. Add the chopped red pepper and tomatoes.

Season with salt and pepper, stir, cover with a lid and simmer for about 10 minutes until the sauce has thickened a little.

3.Check the seasoning, then crack the eggs on top and leave the sauce to simmer gently until the eggs are cooked to your liking.

Place the frying pan in the middle of the table and let everyone help themselves and add as much parsley and yogurt as they want plus watercress/rocket and bread.

Porridge Ideas

©www.light-food-full-of-flavour.com

Porridge is good for you!

You won't find me eating it plain but by adding a few things - like flax seeds (linseeds), cinnamon, cardamom, chopped almonds and some berries or chopped banana/apple - it becomes a super-healthy and mega-tasty breakfast that leaves me with a big smile on my face.

Or I make my portion into an extra healthy-and-tasty plate of food by stirring in a teaspoon of coconut oil as well as half a teaspoon of cinnamon into the cooked porridge. I top it all off with loads of seeds - flax, chia, sesame, sunflower and pumpkin seeds - and a good handful of berries.

Here's the scientific part:

Oats contains beta-glucan which has been shown to lower blood cholesterol and slow down carbohydrate uptake. Oats also gives us silica, a trace mineral believed to be vital for good quality skin, and contain magnesium which helps to boost energy levels.

Flaxseeds (linseeds), Chia seeds, sesame seeds, sunflower seeds and pumpkin seeds contain high levels of dietary fibre as well as an abundance of micronutrients. Flax and chia seeds are the richest plant source of essential omega-3 fats, which are essential for a healthy brain, heart, joints and immune system.

Sesame and sunflower seeds contain the other type of essential fat, omega-6 fats - which are just as important for the body as omega-3 fat.

Tip: Your stomach will not dissolve whole flax seeds – you can either grind them yourself in a food processor, coffee grinder or blender or you can buy them already ground up. Be aware of that ground flax seeds have a short shelf life and need to be stored in an air-tight container in the fridge.

Cinnamon is good for you in many different ways. Several studies have shown that by adding ½ teaspoon of cinnamon to your diet per day, you can lower your bad cholesterol. Other studies have shown that cinnamon may help type 2 diabetics to control blood sugar levels.

Please note: if you are eating cinnamon on a daily basis then it is very important that you eat the right type of cinnamon. The most common cinnamon is made from the cassia bark and contains a naturally occurring toxin. True or real cinnamon does not. True/real cinnamon comes mostly from Sri Lanka (former Ceylon).

Cardamom is a digestive (and super-yummy) spice. It improves circulation and boosts energy.

Almonds are also known to lower bad cholesterol. Whole almonds with the skin on provide the most heart healthy benefits. These nuts are a rich source of vitamin E and they also contain high quality protein and are rich in dietary fibre, B vitamins, essential minerals and monounsaturated fat.

Adding fresh berries will make this a really nutritious breakfast. Fresh berries have the lowest sugar content of all fruit and are full of healthy antioxidants.

Or you can add some chopped banana or some grated apple to each portion – both are of course also highly nutritious but only eat a small amount of banana if you are watching your weight, or want to lose weight.

And after all this scientific hoo-ha, all you need to make 1 portion of porridge is:

40g, 1½oz, 0.4 cup, of oats (I buy organic oats)

275ml, 9¾floz, 1.2 cups, of water or milk

Place in a pan and cook and stir for 6 minutes.

I do personally cook with water and eat it with either milk or unsweetened almond milk.

Quinoa and Apple Porridge with Cinnamon

A porridge with a difference – a quinoa and apple porridge with cinnamon which is tasty and oh so healthy.

The expression "super-food" might have been over-used but quinoa is worthy of that title. It contains plenty of high-quality protein, is low in calories and rich in essential fats, calcium, iron, minerals and vitamins such as B-vitamins and vitamin E.

Essential fats Omega 3 and Omega 6 are the brain's best friend – they are essential for proper brain function. So it's a good idea to start your day with food that includes a lot of seeds (quinoa is technically a seed) and nuts.

While oats contain gluten, quinoa does not so it is a good alternative for those with gluten intolerance. Having said that, it is a specific part of gluten called gliadin which is apparently what causes an allergic reaction, and gliadin is not found in oats.

You might be able to eat oats even if you have gluten intolerance but buy organic oats in such case. Oats can be contaminated with gliadin if it has been processed at mills that also handle wheat.

I know, it sounds picky but if you have gluten intolerance it's better to be safe than sorry.

I am adding ground omega 3-rich flax/linseeds to this quinoa and apple porridge. You can buy already ground flax/linseeds, or you can grind whole seeds in a food processor or blender.

Serve the porridge with some nuts – such as walnuts, almonds, pecan, pistachio and Brazil nuts – some extra chopped apple and either plain almond milk, milk or natural yogurt. If you are able to eat oats, you could eat the porridge with oats milk.

For 2 people:

110g, 3¾oz, 0.6 cup, white quinoa

1 level tablespoon crushed flax/linseeds

1 teaspoon ground cinnamon

1 apple, peeled and coarsely grated

290ml, 10floz, ½ pint, water

To serve:

1 apple, chopped

Mixed nuts

Plain almond milk, milk, oat milk or yogurt

1.Start by rinsing the quinoa under plenty of cold water. Drain in a sieve and add to a pot together with all the other ingredients and bring to a boil. Lower the heat and leave to simmer for 15 minutes – stirring every now and then.

2.Divide the quinoa and apple porridge between two plates and top with chopped apple and nuts. Serve with plain almond milk, milk, oats milk or yogurt.

Quinoa Pop Muesli with Cocoa Nibs

What do you eat for breakfast? I get this question a lot since I found out I was intolerant to eggs, dairy, wheat and gluten.

I am a breakfast person so I've had to come up with alternatives - this quinoa pop muesli with cocoa nibs is a super-tasty and healthy gluten-free alternative.

And what are quinoa pops, you might ask? Quinoa can be popped, a bit like popcorn. They won't get anywhere near the size of popcorn but the taste is fantastic. You can do this yourself but I buy organic quinoa pops from a health food shop.

I eat a lot of quinoa – whether it is cooked quinoa, or quinoa pops. Quinoa is technically a seed and is rich in nutrients and contains healthy essential omega fats. Quinoa is also rich in protein so it helps to fill you up.

I add four different seeds and raw cocoa nibs to this muesli. Yes, really – I sometimes eat chocolate for breakfast.

Raw cocoa nibs though, are nothing but coarsely ground nibs from cocoa beans which have been sun-dried and gently fermented – there is nothing else added so don't expect the smooth taste of chocolate. I actually think they taste a bit like coffee.

Raw cocoa nibs are rich in antioxidants, different minerals and fibre - but is also a stimulant as it contains theobromine, which can have a similar effect on your body to caffeine.

In an ideal world, you would grind all the seeds I add to this quinoa pop muesli as this makes the nutrients in the seeds more easily absorbed. I like a bit of crunch though, so the only seeds I grind are the sesame seeds.

Sesame seeds are rich source of selenium, a mineral which may help to protect us against certain types of cancer and premature ageing. It may also be essential for the thyroid gland, which controls the body's rate of metabolism.

Quinoa pop muesli

There is no need to exact with the measurements. You can use either an American cup measure or an ordinary tea mug/cup. I keep the muesli in a sealed jar in the fridge – which is the best place to store most seeds.

1 cup/tea mug quinoa pops

½ cup/tea mug sesame seeds

½ cup/tea mug sunflower seeds

½ cup/tea mug pumpkin seeds

2 heaped tablespoons chia seeds

2 heaped tablespoons raw cocoa nibs

Mix together all the ingredients and store the muesli in an air-tight container.

I eat 3 tablespoons of this muesli together with either berries or a chopped apple and coconut yogurt. You can swap the coconut yogurt for plain yogurt or soya yogurt.

You could also add some ground flax seeds (linseeds) to the muesli.

Vegetarian Recipes

Courgette and Pesto Lasagne

This courgette and pesto lasagne is always popular when I make it at work. It is quite easy to make as well and apart from the cheese, relatively light.

To make it as light as possible, I use cottage cheese and feta cheese but if you want it to be more indulgent, use ricotta cheese instead of the cottage cheese.

My pesto is as healthy as it is tasty. I make it with a mixture of basil, spinach, rocket/arugula leaves, walnuts, sunflower seeds, garlic and parmesan cheese.

It is a great way to incorporate super healthy dark green leaves, such as spinach and rocket/arugula, as well as super healthy garlic, walnuts and sunflower seeds.

You can use this healthy pesto with pasta as well, preferably wholegrain pasta.

Note: you can either use both spinach and rocket/arugula for the pesto, or just one of them. Spinach is somewhat more nutritious than rocket/arugula but has quite a bland taste. I like to mix the two as rocket/arugula packs a punch taste-wise.

For 4 people:

1 kilo courgette, thinly sliced

Extra virgin olive oil

For the pesto:

25g, 1oz, basil

100g, 3 1/2oz, mix of spinach and rocket/arugula - or use only one

1 handful walnuts

1 tablespoon sunflower seeds

2 garlic cloves - crushed/minced

2 tablespoons grated parmesan cheese

1/2 teaspoon sea salt

1/4 teaspoon black pepper

2 tablespoons extra virgin olive oil

For the cheese mix:

300g, 10 1/2oz, cottage cheese

100g feta cheese - crumbled

1/2 teaspoon sea salt

a pinch of black pepper

Grated parmesan to sprinkle over the top

1.Preheat the oven to 220C/fan200C/425F/gas mark 7. Cover a baking tray with parchment (baking) paper and place the sliced courgettes in a single layer on top of the paper. Brush both sides with some olive oil. Roast for about 12 minutes, until golden on one side. Take out the tray and turn over each slice and put the tray back in the oven for about 8-10 minutes, until golden. Remove the tray from the oven.

2.While the courgettes are roasting, place all the ingredients for the pesto in a food processor and pulse for about 10-15 seconds until it comes together. Mix together the cottage cheese and feta cheese in a bowl and season with salt and black pepper.

3.Line a lightly greased casserole dish with one third of the courgettes. Spread out half of the pesto over the courgettes and top with half of the cheese mixture. Top with half of the remaining courgette slices, then the rest of the pesto and cheese mix. Top with the remains courgette slices, sprinkle with some grated parmesan cheese and place the dish in the oven.

Bake for 12-15 minutes until golden. Serve with a mixed salad.

Gluten-Free Socca Pancakes with Sweet Potato and Chickpea Stir-Fry

Pancakes with a difference, gluten-free socca pancakes which are made with gram (chickpea) flour, water and olive oil - making them dairy-free as well.

I add spices to the batter as well to give these pancakes more oomph!

In this recipe, I have chosen to serve my socca pancakes with a spicy sweet potato and chickpea stir-fry. As I had also made a batch of oven-roasted tomato sauce the day before, I added a dollop of this on top. Total Yum!

You could just add some tomatoes to the stir-fry instead of the oven-roasted tomatoes. I've added them to this recipe.

For the gluten-free socca pancakes:

150g, 5 ½oz, 1.1 cup gram (chickpea) flour

250ml, 9floz, 1.1 cup cold water

2 tablespoons olive oil

½ teaspoon sea salt

½ teaspoon ground ginger

½ teaspoon turmeric

Pinch of dried chilli flakes

For the stir-fry:

2 tablespoons coconut oil, or use olive oil

½ teaspoon mustard seeds

1 small red onion, finely chopped

2 heaped teaspoons finely grated ginger

2 garlic cloves, crushed/minced

2 heaped teaspoons ground coriander

2 heaped teaspoons ground cumin

¼ teaspoon dried chilli flakes

Sea salt and black pepper

1 large sweet potato, peeled and coarsely grated

10 halved small tomatoes – like cherry or plum tomatoes

400g, 14oz, 2 ½ cups, tin/can cooked chickpeas, rinsed

A handful of fresh coriander (cilantro), roughly chopped

To serve:

Watercress or rocket (arugula) leaves

1.Start by making the batter for the socca pancakes. Add the gram flour, water, olive oil, spices and salt to a bowl and whisk until you have a smooth batter. Leave to rest for at least 15 minutes.

2.Add the coconut (or olive oil) to a large frying pan over a medium-high heat. Once the oil is hot, add the mustard seeds and as soon as they start to crackle and pop, add the chopped onion, and minced ginger and garlic, ground coriander (cilantro), cumin and chilli flakes to the pan. Season with some sea salt and black pepper and stir-fry for about 5 minutes.

3.Add the grated sweet potato and tomatoes - continue to stir-fry for another 5 minutes. At the end, add the cooked chickpeas. Turn off the heat.

4.To make the gluten-free socca pancakes – add a teaspoon of coconut oil to a frying pan over a medium-high heat. Wait until the oil is really hot before adding a small lade-full of batter to the pan. Cook for about 2-3 minutes – until bubbles appear – then flip and cook the other side for about 2 minutes. Place the pancake on a plate and repeat with the rest of the batter.

5.Once the pancakes are ready, quickly re-heat the stir-fried mix. Add the fresh coriander (cilantro). To serve, top the pancakes with watercress or rocket leaves followed by some of the stir-fry.

Vegetarian Curry with Chickpeas, Lentils and Sweet Potato

A lot of people ask for vegetarian chilli recipes and sweet potato recipes – this recipe fits the bill for both. It's also a vegetarian curry recipe that will satisfy even a carnivore - it is SO delicious and on top of it, really filling and low in fat.

I once travelled around in India for three months. I arrived as a former vegetarian who'd gone back to being a meat-eater and quickly went back to being a vegetarian once I saw how they dealt with raw meat and fish – out in the open, in the heat and with quadrillion flies buzzing around.

I can't speak for the methods of the higher-end restaurants. I went to the local street vendors and the food-shacks along the roads which all served wonderful vegetarian food. Funnily enough, the only time I got sick was when I went to a restaurant up in the Himalayas which catered for westerners serving Western-style food.

I found this vegetarian curry recipe in a Woman&Home food magazine but I have changed it a bit and have added a few things to make it even more delicious and nutritious.

I serve this with quinoa which is gluten-free and rich in protein, vitamins and minerals - including calcium – which makes it an excellent choice for vegans and people with lactose and gluten intolerance. And apart from all the goodness – I just love the taste of quinoa.

For 4-6 people:

1 large red onion, peeled, halved and finely sliced

2 tablespoons coconut oil (healthiest and tastiest), or use groundnut or vegetable oil

1 teaspoon each of: ground coriander, fennel seeds, ground cumin, turmeric, garam masala, black pepper and ground cinnamon

1 tablespoon finely grated fresh root ginger

2 cloves of garlic, finely chopped

2-3 red chillies (depending on how hot you like it), deseeded and finely chopped

Salt and pepper

150g, 5½oz, ¾ cups, red lentils

1 small butternut squash, peeled de-seeded and chopped into bite-size pieces

2 large sweet potatoes, peeled and cut into chunks

10-15 small ripe tomatoes, left whole

800ml, 1½ pints, 3½ cups, water

400g tin, 14oz, 2 cups, cooked chickpeas, drained and rinsed

100g, 3½oz, 3½ cups, fresh baby spinach

Juice of a lemon

A handful of fresh coriander, chopped

200g, 7oz, 1 cup, quinoa

500ml, 18floz, 2¼ cups, hot vegetable stock

1. Cook the onion in the oil in a large saucepan over a medium heat until softened. Add the spices, fresh ginger, garlic and chilli, season with salt and pepper, stir well and cook for a few minutes.

2. Add lentils, butternut squash, sweet potato, tomatoes and the water. Stir and bring to the boil then simmer until lentils are thick and mushy – around 30 minutes.

3. Halfway through the cooking time of the curry, get the vegetable stock boiling in a large pan. Add the quinoa, return the stock to a boil, stir well and then lower the heat to a simmer. Cook for approximately 15 minutes, drain in a colander before tipping the quinoa back into the pan. Allow to stand for a few minutes before fluffing with a fork.

4. Add the chickpeas and spinach to the curry. Stir well until the spinach has wilted and the mixture is properly hot. Add

the lemon juice and coriander. Serve the vegetarian curry with the quinoa.

Oven-Roasted Tomato Sauce/Soup

I LOVE the taste of oven-roasted tomatoes and the following recipe is great for making a rich, seductive oven-roasted tomato sauce that is wonderful to eat with pasta. Or thin the sauce out with a bit of water and you'll get a totally stunning tomato soup. I'm talking proper showstopper here!

I once walked up through Spain and into France. Okay, I didn't start at the very bottom of Spain. I started in the mountains inland from Malaga and kept on walking through the interior of Spain, mostly up and down mountains.

On this walk – it took me 4 weeks to reach the French border - I ate the most amazingly sweet and tasty tomatoes. In the Andalucía region, where they produce some of the most stunning olive oils I've ever tasted, I ate tomatoes on toast for breakfast in the cafés.

Tomatoes, along with carrots, benefit from being cooked. Tomatoes contain the red pigment lycopene, a super-nutrient, and cooking/processing tomatoes increases the concentration of lycopene in the tomatoes.

Use this oven-roasted tomato sauce recipe as a blueprint only, as there is no need to be exact. The only thing that matters is that you use ripe, fragrant tomatoes.

Oven-roasted tomato sauce:

500g, 1lb2oz, 3 cups, ripe tomatoes cut into pieces (small tomatoes halved)

1 red onion, finely chopped

2-3 garlic cloves finely, chopped

2 tablespoons sun-dried tomato puree (if you can't get hold of it, use plain tomato puree)

1 tablespoons olive oil

2 tablespoons balsamic vinegar

3/4 teaspoon sea salt

Freshly ground black pepper

1.Preheat the oven to 200C/fan 180C/400F/gas mark 6. Mix together all the ingredients in a roasting pan and roast in the oven until the tomatoes start to blister (around 30 minutes). Give the mixture a stir mid-way through.

2.Remove from the oven and place the roasted vegetables in a non-metallic bowl and cover the bowl with cling film. Allow to infuse for at least 30 minutes, longer if you can. I usually leave it for 1-2 hours - quite frankly the longer the better as this will intensify the taste.

3.If you want a smooth sauce - or are making a tomato soup - remove the cling film and once the mixture has cooled down to room temperature, blitz the mix in a blender.

If it is too thick for a soup, simply add some water until you get the desired consistency. Reheat and check the seasoning before serving.

I love to eat this oven-roasted tomato sauce with a bowl of pasta and some crumbled feta or grated Parmesan cheese and some torn basil leaves on top. I personally prefer to use either wholemeal (whole-wheat) pasta or pasta made of pulses, a much healthier alternative to white pasta and REALLY ta**sty.**

Puy Lentils with Roasted Beetroot and Sweet Potato

An utterly gorgeous and deeply satisfying dish which is bursting with earthy flavours from the puy lentils and the sweeter, full-on flavours of the beetroot (beet), sweet potato, butternut and red onion.

I adore beetroots (beets) but I know they are a bit of a divider.

Apart from the glorious taste, beetroots are also really healthy.

They are a rich source of antioxidants and also contain potassium, magnesium, iron, vitamins A, B6 and C and folic acid, as well as protein, carbohydrates and soluble fibre.

Lentils are packed with nutrients and are rich in protein and fibre, which will make you feel full for longer.

To make this an incredibly nutritious meal, serve it with a green salad full of dark green leaves.

For 4-6 people

4 medium sized raw beetroots (beets), peeled and each beetroot cut into 6 wedges

4 thyme sprigs

2 tablespoons olive oil

1 medium butternut squash, peeled, deseeded and cut into chunks

3 medium-sized sweet potatoes, peeled and cut into chunks

12 ripe small tomatoes

1 large red onion, peeled, halved and then cut finely

1 tablespoon olive oil

2 tablespoons balsamic vinegar

250g, 9oz, 1 cup, puy lentils

A handful chopped parsley

100g, 3½oz, 2/3 cup, feta or goats cheese

1. Heat the oven to 200C/ 400 F/ gas 6. Toss the beetroot, thyme and some sea salt and pepper in the oil in a roasting tin and roast in the oven for 15 minutes.

2. Add the butternut and sweet potato to the roasting tin with beetroot and mix well. Return to the oven for a further 30 minutes. While the vegetables are roasting in the oven,

gently fry the red onion in the oil for about 10 minutes. Add the balsamic vinegar and turn up the heat for a couple of minutes to reduce the vinegar. Put to the side.

3. Cook the lentils according to pack instruction. I cook them in vegetable stock for 20-22 minutes before draining them.

4. Add the tomatoes to the other vegetables and return the roasting tin to the oven for a further 10 minutes.

5. Tip the lentils into a bowl and stir through the parsley, the fried red onion and some seasoning. Divide between 4 plates, top with the roasted vegetables and crumble over either some feta or goats cheese.

Vegan Banana Pancakes with Coconut and Cinnamon

It's very easy to make these delicious vegan banana pancakes.

I have been making them a lot, as part of my breakfast, since coming back from a stay at a Sri Lankan Ayurveda and yoga retreat.

The food at this amazing retreat (Sen Wellness Sanctuary) was mostly vegan/vegetarian and the inspiration for my recipe comes from food they served at the retreat.

Coconut, in different forms, plays a big role in Sri Lankan cuisine. I have continued to use it a lot myself since coming back to Scotland and I can only say that this type of healthy fat has had a positive effect on my body.

I lost weight while away and have continued to keep the weight off since coming home.

While I can't get hold of whole coconuts in my neck of the woods on the Scottish West coast, I can buy fresh pieces of raw coconut which I grate myself.

If you are buying desiccated coconut, look out for natural varieties.

The flours I am using for the vegan banana pancakes are oat flour and brown rice flour.

Vegan Banana Pancakes: this will make approximately 8 small pancakes

50g, 1 3/4oz, oat flour

50g, 1 3/4oz brown rice flour

15g, 1/2oz ground almonds

1 heaped tablespoon grated (desiccated) coconut

1/2 teaspoon ground cinnamon

1/4 teaspoon salt

1 medium-sized ripe banana - mashed (use a fork)

100ml - 110ml, about 12 tablespoons, cold water

coconut oil for frying

1.Add all the ingredients, apart from the coconut oil, to a bowl and mix. You should end up with a quite thick batter.

2.Add half a tablespoon coconut oil to a large frying pan over a medium-high heat. Once the oil is hot, add a tablespoon of the batter to the pan and use the spoon to spread it out before adding another spoonful of batter, and so on. I can fit 3 pancakes into my pan.

3.Fry for 2-3minutes - until nicely browned - before flipping the pancakes over and fry for a further 2-3 minutes. Once ready, transfer the pancakes to a plate and keep warm. Add some more coconut oil if needed and continue until you have used up all the batter.

I eat these vegan pancakes with **coconut sambal** - grated coconut mixed with finely chopped red onion, crushed/minced garlic, black pepper, some cayenne pepper, salt and fresh lime juice.

Sri Lankan Vegetable Curry

The inspiration for this Sri Lankan vegetable curry comes partly from my recent travels to this beautiful country, and partly from my introduction to Ayurveda whilst there.

An amazing Ayurvedic doctor told me what kind of food was best for my body type. I was happy to discover that this meant eating mostly moderately spiced food - including lots of different spices.

It doesn't take long to actually cook this Sri Lankan vegetable curry. Once you have prepared the ingredients, you just add them to a pot and let it all simmer for about 15 minutes.

One of the preparations involve making your own curry powder mixture, which is also easy to do.

There is no one single recipe for curry powder. The recipe I've come up with includes several different spices that are often used, and which all have different health benefits.

I don't include chilli in the mixture - I add that separately to the dish instead, along with turmeric. I don't want chilli to be the dominant spice - I want to be able to taste all the different spices I'm using.

By dry-roasting the whole spices, like I do in this recipe, you bring out more flavour from the spices.

This will make more curry powder than you need for this recipe. Store the rest in an air-tight container in a cupboard or in the fridge.

Curry Powder Mixture:

4cm, 1.5 inch, piece of cinnamon bark - crumbled, I use real, Sri Lanka (Ceylon) cinnamon

4 tablespoons coriander seeds

2 tablespoons cumin seeds

the seeds from 6 cardamom pods (you can use the outer husk for a herbal tea)

1/2 teaspoon fennel seeds

1/2 teaspoon fenugreek seeds

4 cloves

1 teaspoon black pepper corns

Heat up a frying pan over a medium-high heat and once hot, add all the spices to the pan. Keep stirring the spices for 2-3 minutes until they release their fragrance. Place the spices in either a pestle and mortar or a spice grinder, and grind to a fine powder.

To make the Sri Lankan Curry:

As you can see from the colour of the finished dish at the top, I use beetroots (beets) as one the ingredients for the Sri Lankan vegetable curry. Yep, it colours everything else purple!

I love beets and they are super healthy. When I was in Sri Lanka they would cook the beetroots in a separate curry and serve it alongside other curries.

You don't have to use the specific vegetables that I use in mine. If you want to leave out the beets, then just add some more of another vegetable. (By the way - I had half a small butternut squash at home so I added that + one medium sweet potato.)

The green vegetable I use in this curry is okra, which is a common vegetable in Sri Lanka. You can replace it with chopped tenderstem broccoli (broccolini) or green beans.

1 small red onion - finely chopped

thumb-size piece of ginger - grated

3 garlic cloves - crushed/minced

2 heaped teaspoons curry powder

3/4 teaspoon chilli powder

1 level teaspoon ground turmeric

1 teaspoon salt

small hand-full of dried curry leaves - crushed

2 medium-sized beetroots (beets) - chopped into batons

1 small butternut squash (or use 2 sweet potatoes) - peeled, halved and de-seeded and then chopped into bite-size pieces

200g, 7oz, okra (or use tenderstem broccoli or green beans - chopped

400ml, 13 1/2floz, coconut milk

200ml, 7floz, water

Add all the ingredients to a pot and stir. Bring the mixture to a simmer, cover with a lid and a simmer for about 15 minutes.

I serve this curry with quinoa and some grated coconut on top.

Sweet Potato Rosti

Allow me to introduce you to some incredibly yummy sweet potato rosti cakes – grated potato cakes.

They are easy to make and perfect to eat as a light lunch or supper together with a big salad. I like to serve them with either a tomato-chilli jam or a tomato salsa/sauce.

I find that it is incredibly handy to have some kind of tomato salsa or sauce in the fridge. When I want something that is quick to make, I simply cook some spaghetti (wholegrain spelt spaghetti in my case) and top it off with some tomato sauce/salsa and either grated parmesan or crumbled feta cheese.

An easy and quick way to make a tomato sauce is to gently fry half a chopped red onion and a couple of crushed garlic cloves in a bit of olive oil for about 5 minutes.

Increase the heat a little and add chopped fresh tomatoes (250g, 9oz)/ or a tin of chopped tomatoes together with a good splash of balsamic vinegar and a tablespoon of tomato puree.

Season with salt and pepper, stir and let it all simmer for a further 10 minutes. If you've got some fresh basil, add that as well.

For the sweet potato rosti:

600g, 1lb 3½oz, sweet potatoes, peeled

1 small red onion

4 spring onions (scallions) chopped

2 large eggs

100g, 3½oz, feta cheese, crumbled

Salt and pepper

Olive oil for frying

1.Pre-heat the oven to 220C/Fan 200C/425F/gas mark 7. In a bowl, grate the sweet potatoes and red onion. Add the chopped spring onions (scallions), eggs and feta cheese, Season with salt and pepper and mix everything together.

2.Line a baking tray with baking parchment. Add a bit of oil to a frying pan over a medium high heat. Using a tablespoon, place a spoonful of the mixture into the frying pan and flatten it out into a thin cake – depending on the size of your frying pan, you can fry 3-4 cakes at the same time. Fry for about 2 minutes before carefully turning over and fry for a further 2 minutes. Transfer the fried potato cakes to the baking tray and continue to fry the rest of the mixture.

3.Once you have used up all the mixture, place the baking tray with the fried rosti in the oven and bake for 5 minutes.

Aubergine (Eggplant), tomato and Chilli Lasagne

While I personally find lasagne made with pasta a bit heavy, this lasagne is both light and healthy.

This is another one of my many vegetarian chilli recipes that even a carnivore will be bowled over by.

I admit that until recently I wasn't a big fan of aubergines (eggplants). I'd eat them if someone else had cooked them, but I didn't really use them myself.

This changed when a client I cooked for declared a love for them. As I don't want to deny people the food they love, I set about exploring ways to cook this vegetable and was pleasantly surprised to find I quite liked them myself.

These vegetables are notoriously over-fond of oil and soak it up as if there was no tomorrow. My way of avoiding oil-soaked, soggy ones is to slice them lengthways, place the slices on baking trays lined with baking parchment and brush them lightly with olive oil. I then bake them in a fairly hot oven.

I came up with the idea for this lasagne when I was cooking for a vegetarian friend who loves this vegetable but who tries to avoid wheat. I simply made a batch of my tomato chilli jam and made a kind of lasagne using aubergines instead of pasta. She absolutely loved it.

I served it together with a salad that included soya beans (soybeans) to make sure she got enough protein as well.

For 4 people:

Go to "tomato chilli jam" (**Salsa and Sauce Recipes**) to get the recipe for this. Then continue as follows.

4 large or 6 smaller aubergines (eggplants)

Olive oil

Salt and pepper

A batch of tomato chilli jam, made with 1 kilo, 2 1/4lb, 6 cups of tomatoes

100g, 3½oz, 1/2 cup, feta cheese

1. Heat the oven to 220C/fan 200C/425F/gas mark 7. Start by cutting the aubergines lengthways into quite thin slices. Line 2 baking trays with baking parchment and place the slices on the trays. Brush each slice with a little bit of olive oil on both sides. Season with salt and pepper. Bake in the

oven for 20--25 minutes – turning them over half-way through – until the slices are nicely browned. Once done, turn down the oven to 200C/fan 180C/400F/gas mark 6.

2. Assemble the lasagne by placing some aubergine slices at the bottom of a lightly oiled oven-proof dish. Cover the slices with some of the tomato chilli jam and repeat the layers until you have used up all the slices and tomato jam. Crumble over the feta cheese and bake in the oven for about 15-20 minutes, until it's piping hot, bubbling and golden.

Broad Beans (fava beans) and Eggs on Sourdough Bread

Together with a salad, these mashed broad beans (fava beans) on sourdough bread becomes an incredibly tasty and healthy lunch or dinner.

There are not many things that I buy frozen – peas, broad (fava) beans, soybeans and berries being the exception. Unless you have them growing in your garden, frozen peas and those two beans don't come much fresher than this as they are often frozen a couple of hours after being picked.

I find it very therapeutic to pod the beans, and the reward you get when you eat something like this makes it worth the while. I do personally prefer to use sourdough bread but in Britain this is not something that you find easily.

Most bread that you find on supermarket shelves is mass produced and contains improvers, enzymes, stabilisers, emulsifiers and preservatives to make the bread stay soft and without deterioration for up to a week, which is completely unnatural.

Oh dear, once I get started on bread it's hard to stop me as this is something I am very passionate about. If you refrain from eating bread because you think you have wheat intolerance, try eating sourdough bread - or other properly made bread with very little yeast and none of the above mentioned horrors. You might be pleasantly surprised to find you can eat this without a problem.

For 2 people:

250g, 2 cups, shelled frozen broad (fava) beans

Small handful each of parsley and basil

2 tablespoons olive oil

1 tablespoon lemon juice

2 tablespoons freshly grated parmesan cheese

Salt and pepper

2-4 organic eggs, depending on how many you want per person

2 large slices of sourdough or some other good bread

1. Cook the beans in a pan of simmering water for 2-3 minutes. Drain and then cool the beans under cold running water to stop them from cooking any further. Once cool, peel

off the skin of each bean (the skin slips off easily when you pinch the ends).

2. Crush the broad beans lightly with a potato masher or fork. Bash the parsley and basil in a pestle and mortar and add to the broad beans together with the olive oil, lemon juice and parmesan cheese and season with salt and pepper.

3. Poach the eggs in a shallow pan of barely simmering water for 2-3 minutes.

4. Meanwhile, toast the bread. Divide the broad bean mix over the top of the bread and put 1 or 2 poached eggs on top of this. Scatter over some more grated parmesan cheese.

Beetroot and Chickpea Burgers

Vegetarian burgers, like these beetroot and chickpea burgers, can be just as tasty as ordinary ones.

I am using grated raw beetroot (beet) in the burgers together with mashed cooked chickpeas. Beetroots are really nutritious. They are a rich source of antioxidants and also contain potassium, magnesium, iron, vitamins A, B6 and C and folic acid, as well as protein, carbohydrates and soluble fibre.

Chickpeas also contain soluble fibre, a type of fibre which is good for regulating blood sugar and which helps you feel full.

Like all pulses, chickpeas are low in fat and a rich source of protein.

I cook the burgers in the oven, which is the healthiest way to cook – not to mention the least messy! By placing them on baking parchment you don't need to use any fat either - making these beetroot and chickpea burgers really low in calories as well.

I serve the burgers with caramelised red onion and peppers (bell peppers) and sweet potato wedges.

While sweet potatoes are incredibly healthy and low GI food, they do contain a large amount of carbohydrates. It is a good idea to only eat a small amount of sweet potatoes if you are watching your weight or want to lose weight.

Butternut squash and pumpkin contain fewer carbohydrates. Add some wedges of either vegetable if you wish.

And to make this a really healthy meal, serve together with a salad containing a mix of dark green leaves.

For 4 people:

Burgers:

275g, 9¼oz raw beetroot (beet), peeled and coarsely grated

400g, 14oz, 2.6 cups cooked chickpeas (I buy cooked organic chickpeas)

4 spring onions (scallions), chopped

100g, 3½oz feta cheese, crumbled

1 egg – preferably organic or free-range

½ teaspoon sea or rock salt - I use Himalayan pink rock salt

¼ teaspoon black pepper

2 medium-sized sweet potatoes, each cut into 4 wedges

1 tablespoon olive oil

1 medium-sized red onion, peeled, halved and finely sliced

1 tablespoon balsamic vinegar

Salt and pepper

2 peppers (bell peppers), 1 red + 1yellow/orange – sliced

1.Preheat the oven to 200C/Fan 180C, 400F/gas mark 6. Place the sweet potato wedges in an oven-proof dish and toss them in a little bit of olive oil. Cook in the oven for 30 minutes

2.While sweet potatoes are cooking, cover a baking tray with baking parchment. Mash the cooked chickpeas with a potato masher or a fork and place in a bowl. Add the grated beetroot, chopped spring onion (scallion), feta cheese, egg, salt and pepper. Mix together and form 4 burgers and place the burgers on the prepared tray. When the sweet potatoes have been in the oven for 30 minutes, place the tray with the burgers in the oven as well and cook for a further 10 minutes.

3.Place 1 tablespoon of olive oil and the sliced onion in a pot and cook gently over a low heat for about 7 minutes – stirring every now and then. Increase the heat, add the balsamic vinegar and some salt and pepper and continue to cook for another minute. Add the peppers and cook for a further minute. Remove from the heat.

Serve the burgers with sweet potato wedges, caramelised onion and peppers and a mixed salad.

Spicy Indian Fritters (Pakoras) with Sweet Potato

I love Asian-style vegetarian food, like these utterly delicious spicy Indian fritters (pakoras).

Traditional pakoras are usually made with ordinary potatoes but I wanted mine to be healthier so I am using sweet potatoes instead. Pakoras are gluten-free as the vegetables in these fritters are bound together with chickpea (gram/besan) flour.

This recipe will make 8 spicy Indian fritters. You can serve them with raita (see recipe below) or with my tomato chilli jam.

I brown the fritters in a frying pan before placing them on a baking tray and finishing them off in the oven.

1 tablespoon coconut oil

1 medium-sized red onion, finely chopped

2 garlic cloves, crushed/minced

thumb-sized piece of fresh ginger, peeled and finely grated

2 teaspoons ground coriander

1 teaspoon ground cumin

¼ teaspoon each of ground chilli powder, ground cloves, ground turmeric, black pepper and ground cinnamon

1 teaspoon sea salt

150g, 1 cup chickpea (gram) flour

1 large sweet potato, 350g, coarsely grated

75g, 1 tightly packed cup spinach, chopped

a large handful fresh coriander (cilantro), leaves and stalks, chopped

50 ml, 0.2 cup cold water

Raita:

150ml, 3/4 cup, natural Greek-style yogurt

¼ cucumber, finely chopped

1 clove of garlic, crushed/minced

10 mint leaves, finely chopped

juice of ½ lime

pinch of sea salt and black pepper

Preheat the oven to 220C, Fan 200C, 425F, gas mark 7. Add the coconut oil to a large frying pan over a medium-hot heat and add the onion, garlic and ginger to the pan. Keep stirring for about 3 minutes. Add the ground spices and the salt to the pan and keep stirring for a further 2 minutes. Turn off the heat and place the pan to the side to let the mixture cool down.

1.Add the chickpea flour, grated sweet potatoes and chopped spinach and coriander (cilantro) to a large bowl and mix together. Once the onion and spinach mix has cooled down add this to the bowl as well together with the cold water and mix everything together.

2.Cover a baking tray with baking parchment. With your hands, form 8 patties and place them on a plate. Add some more coconut oil to a large frying pan over a medium-high heat. Once the oil is hot, fry four of the patties one minute on each side, until nicely browned, before placing the fritters on the baking tray. Do the same with the remaining four patties.

3.Place the baking tray in the pre-heated oven and cook for five minutes. If you are serving the fritters with raita, simply mix together all the ingredients for the raita in a bowl.

Serve the pakoras with your choice of accompaniment.

Indian Falafels

Do try these Indian falafels - they take a bit of time to make but they are super delicious and worth every minute of work that you put in.

I decided to flavour the falafels with garam masala, which is a warm spice blend rather than a fiery one. There is no one single recipe for a garam masala blend – the recipes vary from region to region in India, and quite often from family to family.

I've used a ready-made garam masala blend in this recipe and have combined it with some turmeric (if you add too much of turmeric it can make a dish bitter). Turmeric is a spice though, with a lot of medicinal benefits.

I like to serve these Indian falafels together with lots of rocket and coriander leaves, my tomato chilli jam and natural, Greek-style yogurt. If you want a more substantial meal, serve it with toasted pitta bread as well.

For 4 people:

1 tablespoon coconut oil, or use vegetable oil

1/2 red onion, finely chopped

2 heaped teaspoons garam masala

1/2 teaspoon turmeric

150g, 5½oz, either sweet potato or butternut squash, coarsely grated

Large handful fresh coriander (cilantro), stalk and leaves

400g, 14oz, 2½ cups, tin of cooked chickpeas, rinsed and drained

70g, 2¾oz, 1½ cups, fresh breadcrumbs (I make my breadcrumbs from sourdough bread)

1 egg, organic or at least free-range

Salt and pepper

2-3 tablespoons oil (same as above)

1. Heat a tablespoon of oil in a frying pan. Add the chopped onion and cook, stirring, over a medium heat for 5 minutes. Add the spices, stir and cook for a further minute. Remove the frying pan from the heat and let the spiced onions cool down to room temperature.

2. Place the grated sweet potato or butternut squash, spiced onions, fresh coriander (cilantro), chickpeas, breadcrumbs and egg in a food processor. Season with salt and pepper and pulse to a coarse paste.

3. Form 20 walnut-size balls with your hands and place them on a tray. Place the tray in the fridge and chill for 30 minutes.

4. Preheat the oven to 200C/fan 180C/400F/gas mark 6.

5. Remove the falafels from the fridge. Cover a baking tray with baking parchment. Heat the remaining oil in a frying pan and quickly fry the falafels over a medium high heat until they are brown all over. Depending on the size of your frying pan, you may have to do this in batches. Place the falafels on the baking tray, place the tray in the oven and cook for 10 minutes until they are cooked through.

Thai-Style Curry Sauce

I want to give you an incredibly versatile and utterly delicious Thai-style curry sauce. You can add vegetables for a vegetarian curry, or add fish and/or prawns for a seafood curry, or chicken to make a chicken curry.

The choice is yours.

This is a fantastic sauce to have in the freezer as you can whip up a gorgeous curry in no time. You make your own paste – it's not difficult – but once that is done this curry sauce comes together very quickly.

It might look like a lot of ingredients but I have deliberately chosen quite common ingredients, leaving out more specialized ones. As Asian-style food is so popular in so many countries these days, you should be able to find it in most supermarkets.

The only fat I am using in this Thai-style curry sauce is coconut fat – coconut oil for the paste and coconut milk for the sauce.

You can replace the coconut oil in the paste with vegetable oil if you can't get hold of it. Coconut oil is so common in Britain today that it is sold in well-stocked supermarkets as well as health food shops.

To make a vegetarian curry you could oven-roast diced vegetables - such as squash, carrots and sweet potatoes – and add them to the curry sauce once they are nearly cooked. At the same time, you could add vegetables such as sliced sugar snaps, broccoli florets, sliced peppers (bell peppers) and halved cherry tomatoes and cook for a further 3-4 minutes.

To make a fish/prawn curry, add bite-size pieces of firm white fish and/or raw prawns to the sauce together with some sliced sugar snaps and peppers (bell peppers) and thinly sliced carrot sticks. Bring the curry back to a boil, lower the heat and simmer for about 3-4 minutes until the fish/prawns are cooked through. The vegetables should still be crunchy.

To make a chicken curry, add **thinly sliced**, skin-less chicken breasts or chicken thighs to the curry sauce. Once the sauce comes back to a boil, lower the heat, stir to separate the chicken slices and allow simmer for about 7 minutes. Add some sliced sugar snaps and peppers (bell peppers), stir, bring back to a simmer and cook for a further 3 minutes.

You can top either of these curries with some fresh coriander (cilantro) leaves, Thai basil and chopped spring onion (scallion).

If you are watching your weight or want to lose weight, avoid eating the curry together with white rice or things like naan bread. Quinoa is a much better choice – both for your weight and your health.

Tip: if you can't find un-waxed lemons and limes, make sure you scrub them really well with a clean scrubbing brush under running water. And when grating the zest, don't be too forceful. You only want the very outer layer of the fruit, not the bitter pith, the inner white part.

Thai-style curry sauce for 4-6 people

For the paste:

2 tablespoons coconut oil (melt it first if it is solid)

1 small red onion, chopped

3 garlic cloves, crushed/minced

Thumb-size piece of ginger, finely grated

2-3 large red chillies - depending on how hot you like it (I use 2) - deseeded and finely chopped

2 teaspoons ground coriander

1 teaspoon ground cumin

¼ teaspoon black pepper

Finely grated zest of 1 un-waxed lemon

Finely grated zest of 1 un-waxed lime

1 tablespoon tomato puree

1 teaspoon honey

The stalks of a small handful of fresh coriander (cilantro) - you can use the leaves for garnish

¾ teaspoon ground turmeric

For the sauce:

All of the paste

400ml, 13½floz, 1¾ cups, coconut milk

150ml, 5floz, ¾ cup, water

2 tablespoons Thai fish sauce

1 tablespoon lime juice

1.Start by making the paste. Place all the ingredients, apart from the turmeric, in a blender/food processor and blitz to a smooth paste.

2.Place a wok or large frying pan with high sides over a medium heat. Add all of the paste and the ground turmeric to the pan. Stir and fry for about 2 minutes. Add the coconut milk, water and Thai fish sauce to the pan, stir, bring to a boil, then lower the heat and allow the curry sauce to simmer gently for about 10 minutes.

The Thai-style curry sauce is now ready. Once you have added and cooked whatever ingredients you have chosen for a curry – finish it off by adding the lime juice and check the seasoning. Add a bit more fish sauce if you think it needs more salt.

Cauliflower Rice

Cauliflower rice - what a revelation!

I never used to like cauliflower. But cauliflower seems to have become trendy recently. People swap unhealthy white rice for healthy cooked, grated cauliflower and claim you can't tell the difference between the two.

There are all these different methods of cooking – grate and steam or cook briefly, or grate and fry, adding this, that and the other.

Hmm, it still didn't sound very attractive to me, it was still cauliflower. But my curiosity took over and I had to try.

Wow! Double-wow! Super-delicious! I'm most definitely a convert to cauliflower cooked this way. No, it doesn't taste like rice but it tastes fantastic and can easily replace rice for a variety of dishes.

It's the perfect accompaniment to a curry - to most types of Asian-style food actually.

To avoid losing all the healthy nutrients in the cauliflower, only fry it for a couple of minutes and fry in ultra-healthy and tasty coconut oil (this oil really adds to the taste of the rice). This will give you an al-dente texture.

Although I love fresh coriander/cilantro myself, I know that some people can't stand the taste of it. If you are one of them you can use some chopped parsley or some finely chopped spring onion (scallion) instead.

It's a good idea to prepare the ingredients for the cauliflower rice in advance as it cooks so quickly. Cook it at the last minute once the food you are serving it with is ready.

For 4 people:

2 tablespoons coconut oil for frying

1 large head of cauliflower - coarsely grated. I use the coarse side of an ordinary handheld grater which I place over a large bowl.

Either the finely grated zest of an un-waxed lime - or the juice of half a lime

A large handful of fresh coriander (cilantro) - roughly chopped

Some sea salt and black pepper

1.Add the coconut oil to a wok or a large frying pan over a medium high heat.

2.Once the oil is hot, add the grated cauliflower to the pan and season with some sea salt and black pepper. Use two spatulas and keep stir-frying the cauliflower rice for about 2 minutes (it will be al-dente).

3.Take the pan off the heat and stir in the chopped coriander (cilantro) and lime zest or juice. Serve immediately.

Buckwheat Sweet Potato Crepes

If I had a café, these buckwheat sweet potato crepes would be one of the dishes I would have on the menu. The crepes are awesome on their own but together with this vegetable stir-fry they are sublime.

I got inspired when I saw an Ella Woodward recipe for sweet potato pancakes - though hers were of the sweet variety containing lots of honey and cinnamon.

I wanted to use buckwheat flour and make mine savoury and a bit spicy.

Contrary to what the name suggests, buckwheat has nothing to do with wheat: the grains are fruit seeds from the rhubarb family which are gluten-free.

I am using oats milk for these crepes though. Oats contain gluten but not gliadin, a specific subset of gluten which is apparently what causes gluten intolerance. If you want these crepes to be completely gluten-free, swap the oats milk for rice milk.

For the buckwheat sweet potato crepes – this will make 8 crepes:

1 medium sweet potato - about 220g, 8oz – peeled and diced

250ml, 9floz, 1.1 cups oats milk

200g, 7oz, 1.4 cups, buckwheat flour

1 level teaspoon ground coriander (cilantro)

1 level teaspoon ground cumin

¾ teaspoon sea salt

Coconut oil, or use vegetable oil, for frying

For the vegetable stir-fry:

2 tablespoons coconut oil – or use vegetable oil

1 small red onion, chopped

Thumb-size piece of ginger, finely chopped

1 garlic clove, finely chopped

1 red chilli, deseeded and finely chopped

Half a small cauliflower, cut into thin florets

10 Brussels sprouts, trimmed, halved and finely sliced

1 large red pepper, deseeded and sliced

3 spring onions (scallions), sliced

3 tablespoons tamari soy sauce – or use light soy sauce

Watercress, or use rocket (arugula) leaves

1.To make the crepes, boil or steam the diced sweet potato until soft, about 10 minutes. Once cooked, allow the sweet potato to cool down before placing them in a blender with the oats milk, buckwheat flour, coriander, cumin and salt. Blend until you have a smooth batter.

2.Place a small amount of oil in a non-stick frying pan over a medium-high heat and allow the oil to get hot before adding about 3 tablespoons of batter to the frying pan. Use the back of the spoon to smooth out the batter into a quite thin, round-shaped crepe. Fry for about a 1 minute – 1 ½ minute before flipping it over. Fry the other side for about the same length of time, until the crepe is nicely browned on both sides.

3.Place the crepe on a plate and continue to fry until you have used up all the batter. Cover the crepes and keep them warm.

4.For the stir-fry, place the oil in a large frying pan or wok over quite a high heat. Add the onion, ginger, garlic and chilli and fry for 30 seconds. Add the cauliflower florets, sliced Brussels sprouts and peppers to the pan/wok and continue to fry for another minute. Finally, add the spring onions and soy sauce to the pan/wok and fry for a further 30 seconds. Remove the pan from the heat.

To serve, place a small handful of watercress or rocket leaves on each pancake and top with some of the stir-fried vegetables.

Spinach Tomato Ricotta Bake

I will happily eat this spinach tomato ricotta bake both warm and cold. You can serve it, together with a mixed salad, as a light lunch or supper – or take it with you on a picnic.

It is also perfect for taking with you for lunch as it is so delicious cold. Together with a nice piece of bread (sourdough if you can get hold of it) and a side salad it will make for both a healthy and filling take-away lunch.

I am using ricotta cheese and a mixture of Parmesan and feta cheese in the mixture for the bake. You can swap the ricotta for cottage cheese - I would use a full-fat variety in such case - and use solely Parmesan or feta cheese instead of a mixture of the two.

I know I keep going on about this but, do buy nice fragrant tomatoes rather than cheap, bleak tasteless ones – it makes such a difference to whatever dish you are using them for. And, to be really picky, tomatoes should NOT be stored in the fridge as this will do no favours to the flavour of the tomatoes.

When it comes to feta cheese, I only use the ones made with goat and sheep milk. Parmesan cheese on the other hand is expensive and when using it in food, I sometimes buy the somewhat less expensive but still very tasty Grana Padano cheese.

Spinach tomato ricotta bake:

200g, 7oz, fresh spinach

250g, 9oz, ricotta cheese (or use cottage cheese)

4 eggs – organic or free-range

75g, 2 ¼oz, ¾ cup, mixture of grated Parmesan cheese and crumbled feta cheese

3 spring onions (scallions) chopped

Salt and pepper

200g, 7oz, ripe tomatoes (like cherry or plum tomatoes), halved

1.Pre-heat the oven to 220C/fan 200/425F/gas mark 7

2.Start by putting the fresh spinach in a colander and slowly pour over a kettle of boiled water to wilt the spinach. Rinse with a lot of cold water immediately afterwards. When the spinach is cold, squeeze out as much water as possible with your hands. Finely chop the spinach and leave to the side.

3.Crack the eggs into a bowl and add the ricotta, Parmesan and feta cheese. Season with salt and pepper and mix together. Stir in the chopped spinach and spring onions (scallions) to the mixture.

4.Pour the mixture into a baking dish and lay the tomato halves on top. Bake in the oven for about 15 minutes – until set and golden.

Coconut Dhal

I make this coconut dhal quite often. It is reasonably quick to make and so tasty– it is proper Asian-style comfort food.

To make it into a really healthy meal, serve it with oven-roasted vegetables – such as squash, pumpkin, carrots and sweet potatoes and/or some steamed green vegetables.

When I'm on my own, I often add nothing but raw watercress and red peppers (bell peppers) to my portion of coconut dhal. Raw watercress is truly super-healthy and the seriously peppery taste of watercress goes really well with this spicy dish.

Raw vitamin C-rich peppers add crunch and yet more taste to this dish - but I go for the long pointed peppers as I find that they have so much more taste.

I add both mustard seeds and turmeric to this dhal. These spices are rich in curcumin, which is a really powerful antioxidant.

I also add a pinch of dried asafoetida. It is a spice that aids digestion and reduces flatulence, so it's a good thing to add to dishes with beans and lentils in them! Some supermarkets sell it but if you can't find it there, try shops that specialise in Asian food.

For 4 people:

300g, 10½oz, 1.3 cups, red lentils

2 tablespoons coconut oil - or use groundnut or vegetable oil

1 teaspoon mustard seeds

½ teaspoon cumin seeds

1 large red onion, finely chopped

2 garlic cloves, crushed/minced

2 - 3 red chillies – depending on how spicy you like it - deseeded and finely chopped

1 teaspoon ground ginger

1 teaspoon ground coriander

1 teaspoon ground turmeric

A pinch of asafoetida (optional)

12 -16 small ripe tomatoes – like cherry or plum tomatoes – halved

400ml, 13½floz, 1¾ cups, coconut milk

400ml, 13½floz, 1¾ cups water

Salt and pepper

1.Start by rinsing the lentils under plenty of cold water. Drain in a sieve and leave to the side. Add the oil, mustard and cumin seeds to a pot over a medium-high heat. When the seeds start to "crackle and pop", add the chopped onion to the pot and stir and cook for about five minutes.

2.Add the crushed garlic, chopped chillies, ground ginger, coriander, turmeric and asafoetida (if using) to the pot and continue to cook for a further minute.

3.Add the rinsed lentils, tomatoes, coconut milk and water. Season with some salt and pepper, stir and bring to a simmer.

4.Simmer for about 20 minutes – it is important that you stir it from time to time or it will stick at the bottom of the pot - until the lentils are tender. Taste and check the seasoning before serving.

Aubergine Green Bean Tagine

You don't have to be a vegetarian to love this full-flavoured aubergine green bean tagine.

I got the inspiration for this dish from a friend who lived in Lebanon for quite a few years. She made something similar for me one time, but she only used green beans. I thought this would go ever so well with added aubergine (eggplant).

For a really tasty and nutritious vegetarian feast, you could serve the tagine with oven-roasted carrots and/or butternut squash and sweet potatoes, tzatziki and a side salad – to which I would add spinach, dark leafed lettuce and red and yellow peppers (bell peppers).

I make tzatziki with 250ml (a little bit more than a cup) Greek yogurt, 1 tablespoon olive oil, 2 crushed garlic cloves, 1/3 of a cucumber – peeled, halved, deseeded and cut into thin half-moons - salt and pepper and some shredded fresh mint.

You could also fry or grill slices of halloumi cheese to go with the aubergine green bean tagine.

For 4 people:

2 tablespoons olive oil

1 medium-sized red onion

4 garlic cloves, finely chopped

2 heaped teaspoons ground coriander (cilantro)

2 heaped teaspoons ground cumin

1½ teaspoon ground allspice

½ teaspoon ground cinnamon

1 large or 2 small aubergines (eggplants), diced

400g, 14oz, 2¼ cup, chopped tomatoes – or use the same amount of fresh, ripe tomatoes, diced

2 tablespoons tomato purée

400ml, 13½floz, 1¾ cups water

250g 9oz, slightly more than 1 cup, green beans

Salt and pepper

To serve:

Parsley, chopped

Feta cheese (buy a good one made with sheep's and goat's milk – it makes all the difference)

1.Heat the oil in a large pot or casserole dish over a medium high heat. Place the chopped onion in the pot and fry gently for 5 minutes, without browning the onion. Add the chopped garlic and ground spices and continue to fry – continuously stirring – for another minute.

2.Add the diced aubergine (eggplant) and quickly mix it together with the other ingredients in the pot. Add the chopped tomatoes, tomato puree, water and green beans to the pot. Season with salt and pepper, stir and mix everything together.

3.Bring to a simmer, cover the pot or casserole dish with a tight fitting lid and simmer gently for around 35 minutes – lift the lid and give the tagine a stir mid-way through. Remove the lid and continue to simmer for 3-5 minutes – until the sauce has thickened a little and the aubergine (eggplant) is soft. Check the seasoning to see if you need any more salt and/or pepper.

Serve with chopped parsley and crumbled feta cheese on top.

Carrot and Soybean Fritters

I'm not sure if I can call these carrot and soybean fritters with feta cheese for fritters as I make mine without any flour. As well as having a thing about sugar in savoury food, I have another thing about flour in fritters.

I don't add any breadcrumbs either, which means that my fritters are a little bit tricky to turn over. They taste sensational though.

Using cooked and mashed edamame beans, immature green soya beans (soybeans), adds a lot of protein and soluble dietary fibre to the fritters. You'll find soya beans in the frozen section in supermarkets.

If you fry fritters in a frying pan you will have to use a fair bit of oil. I prefer to place mine on a baking tray covered with baking parchment and cook them in a relatively hot oven. Not only is this a much healthier and fat-free way of cooking, it's a lot less messy. And I am still calling them fritters!

I serve mine with oven-roasted tomatoes and onions. Add a mixed salad to the carrot and soybean fritters and this will make for a light and healthy lunch or dinner.

For 4 people:

400g, 14oz, 2¼ cups, small tomatoes, like cherry or plum tomatoes, halved

½ large red onion, chopped

1 tablespoon olive or rapeseed oil

2 tablespoons balsamic vinegar

Salt and pepper

Fritters:

100g, 3½oz, 0.9 cup, cooked edamame beans (green soybeans), roughly mashed (use a potato masher)

300g, 10½oz, 3 cups, coarsely grated carrot

½ large red onion, finely chopped

4 spring onions, chopped

½ red pepper (bell pepper), chopped

Handful parsley leaves, roughly chopped

3 eggs

100g, 3½oz, ¾ cup, feta cheese, crumbled

Salt and pepper

1.Preheat the oven to 220C/Fan 200C/425F/gas mark 7. Mix together the tomatoes, onion, oil and balsamic vinegar in a roasting pan. Season with salt and pepper and roast in the oven until the tomatoes start to blister (around 30 minutes). Give the mixture a stir mid-way through.

2.Cover a baking tray with baking parchment. In a bowl, mix together all the ingredients for the fritters. Season with salt and pepper and mix thoroughly. Divide the mixture with a large spoon into 8 portions on the baking tray.

3.Place the baking tray in the oven and cook the fritters for 4 minutes. Take the tray out of the oven and using two turners, or large spoons, carefully turn over the fritters. Don't fret if they fall apart a bit, they are easy to reshape with the utensils you are using. Place the tray back into the oven and cook for a further 3-4 minutes – until the fritters start to get a nice brown colour.

Serve the carrot and soybean fritters with the oven-roasted tomatoes and a salad.

Sweet Potato Quinoa Bake

I cook food from all over the world. This sweet potato quinoa bake is my take on a Lebanese dish called "kibbeh". My version is a really tasty, light and healthy dish.

Sweet potatoes are highly nutritious and have a low GI-rating. Quinoa has a high protein content and is therefore a good choice for vegetarians.

Actually, all the ingredients in this dish are highly nutritious.

I serve this sweet potato quinoa bake with tomato chilli jam and yogurt with fresh mint.

Note: Pomegranate molasses – used in this dish and other Middle Eastern dishes - has a sweet-tart flavour. It is sold in many supermarkets but if you can't find it there, try specialist shops that sell Middle Eastern food.

For 4 people:

1 kilo, 2 ¼lb sweet potatoes, peeled and diced

½ teaspoon chilli flakes

2 tablespoons olive oil or rapeseed oil (canola oil)

100g, 3½oz, ½ cup, quinoa

600ml, 20floz, 2½ cups, vegetable stock

2 medium-sized red onions, peeled and chopped

Salt and pepper

2 tablespoons unsalted shelled pistachios, roughly chopped

4 spring onions (scallions), sliced

½ tablespoon pomegranate molasses

4 handfuls fresh spinach leaves, sliced

Pomegranate seeds (optional)

1.Pre-heat the oven to 200C/fan 1800C/400F/gas mark 6. Place the diced sweet potato in a roasting tray. Add the oil, chilli flakes, a bit of salt and pepper and toss until well combined. Place the tray in the oven and roast for around 25 minutes – stir midway through – until tender.

2.Get the stock boiling, add the quinoa, stir and simmer without a lid for 15 minutes. Drain in a colander.

3.While the quinoa is simmering, place 1 tablespoon of oil and the chopped onion in a frying pan. Gently fry the chopped onion for around 10 minutes, stirring frequently to make sure the onion doesn't burn. Once the onion is really soft, take the frying pan off the heat and mix in the pistachio nuts, spring onion, pomegranate molasses and season with some salt and pepper.

4.Use a potato masher to mash the oven-roasted sweet potato. Mix in the quinoa with the sweet potato mash. Spread out half of this mix in a lightly oiled oven-proof dish. Divide the onion mix on top, followed by the spinach and then the rest of the sweet potato and quinoa mix.

5.Place the sweet potato and quinoa bake in the oven and cook for around 15 minutes, until piping hot and slightly browned.

If using, scatter some pomegranate seeds over each portion.

Beans in Tomato Sauce

Happy memories - these delicious beans in tomato sauce reminds me of the time when I lived in Greece – in a small village up in the hills on the island of Crete.

I cooked this dish a lot – using butter (Lima) beans, olive oil made from my neighbour's olives and herbs growing wild outside. I always ate it with some gorgeous feta cheese.

When I cooked this dish in Greece, I always used dried beans that I soaked overnight and cooked the next day. Nowadays I must admit that I often use cooked, tinned beans – an organic variety if I can find it.

If you want to use dried butter (Lima) beans - once you've soaked them over-night and rinsed them – cook them for an hour before adding them to the tomato sauce and simmer for a further 30-40 minutes, until the beans are really soft.

I add herbs to my tomato sauce – fresh or dried or a mixture of both, whatever I've got at hand. You can add fresh herbs like oregano, thyme, basil and a little bit of rosemary – or use mixed dried herbs.

You can use tinned tomatoes but buy the best variety you can find. The same goes for fresh tomatoes – look out for ripe, ruby red, fragrant tomatoes.

To make this a super-tasty and ultra-healthy meal, I serve these beans in tomato sauce with oven-roasted butternut squash and sweet potato wedges, tenderstem broccoli (broccolini), a really good feta cheese and a salad.

I've said it before, and I'll say it again - when buying feta cheese, make sure it says that it's made from sheep and goat's milk – there are some bad imitations out there made from cow's milk.

For 4-6 people:

1 medium-sized butternut squash, or pumpkin, cut into thin wedges

2 large sweet potatoes - cut into thick wedges (they cook quicker than the squash)

A bit of olive oil

Salt and pepper

For the tomato sauce:

1 tablespoon olive oil

1 small red onion, finely chopped

3-4 garlic cloves, finely chopped

800g, 1lb12oz, ripe small tomatoes, chopped – or use the same weight of tinned/canned tomatoes

1 tablespoon sun-dried or plain tomato purée

1 heaped teaspoon mixed dried herbs, like "Herbes De Provence"

1 tablespoon balsamic vinegar

Salt and pepper

2 x 400g, 14oz, tin/can of butter (Lima) beans, thoroughly rinsed Tenderstem broccoli (broccolini), or broccoli

Feta cheese

1.Pre-heat the oven to 220C/Fan 200C/425F/gas mark 7. Start by making the tomato sauce. Place the olive oil in pot over a low heat. Add the chopped onion and garlic and stir and cook for about 10 minutes, until the onion is really soft but not browned.

2.Add the chopped tomatoes, tomato puree, herbs and balsamic vinegar to the pot and season with some salt and black pepper. Bring to a simmer - stirring every now and then – and let it simmer over a low heat for 30 minutes. Add a bit of water if it gets too thick.

3.Cover an oven-tray with baking parchment. Place the squash and sweet potato wedges on the tray and brush them with a bit of olive oil and season with salt and pepper. Place the tray in the pre-heated oven and cook for about 35 minutes, until the wedges are nicely browned and soft.

4.Add the beans to the tomato sauce and simmer for a further 10 minutes. Taste and check the seasoning.

5.Steam or boil the broccoli. Serve the beans in tomato sauce and vegetables with feta cheese.

Sweet Potato Halloumi Stacks with Guacamole

You don't need to be a vegetarian to love these sweet potato halloumi stacks with guacamole. They are delicious

You can do the sweet potato and the halloumi on the barbeque if you've got one going. But it is equally easy to do it in the kitchen.

I cut the sweet potatoes into 2.5cm, 1in, thick disks. If you are going to pop them on a barbeque you need to pre-boil these discs for about 10 minutes – or until they are nearly done. Dry them off on kitchen towel before brushing them with some olive oil and finish them off on the barbeque.

I cook the sweet potato in the oven and quickly fry the halloumi cheese when everything else is ready - just before I am ready to serve.

For the halloumi cheese, you can either do the quick version and simply brush the cheese slices with a bit of olive oil before grilling or frying. Or you can take this dish to an even higher level and marinate the slices with grated ginger, crushed garlic, lemon zest and oil before grilling.

Serve these sweet potato halloumi stacks with a big salad.

For 4 people:

2 large sweet potatoes, peeled and cut into 2.5cm, 1in thick discs

Olive oil

Halloumi cheese, cut into finger-thick slices (you want as many slices as you have   sweet potato discs)

If you are going to marinate the cheese:

1 heaped teaspoon finely grated fresh ginger

1 garlic clove, crushed

Grated zest of 1 un-waxed lemon

2 tablespoons olive oil

For the guacamole:

2 avocados

1 small red onion, finely chopped

1-2 red chillies (depending on how hot you like it) – deseeded and finely chopped

Juice of 1 lime

12 ripe small tomatoes, quartered

A good pinch of salt and pepper

1.Pre-heat the oven to 200C/fan 180C/400F/gas mark 6 (to barbeque the sweet potato, see above). If you are marinating the halloumi cheese, mix together all the ingredients for the marinade, pour this mixture over the cheese slices, cover and leave to the side.

2.Cover a baking tray with baking parchment. Toss the sweet potato discs in some olive oil and spread them out on the baking tray. Place the tray in the oven and cook for about 25 – 30 minutes – until they are cooked through.

3.While the sweet potato is cooking, make the guacamole. Peel, de-stone and cut the avocados into cubes. Place the avocado cubes and all the other ingredients for the guacamole in a bowl and carefully mix it all together.

4.Once the sweet potato is ready, place a large frying pan over a medium high heat and fry the cheese slices for about 30 seconds before turning them over and frying for a further 30 seconds. It's enough to brush the cheese with some olive oil if you have not marinated the halloumi slices.

5.Divide the sweet potato discs between four plates and top each disc with cheese slice and a dollop of guacamole. Serve immediately together with a salad.

I could eat this gorgeous vegetarian stir-fry anytime of the day. I absolutely love it!

I have chosen to use chickpeas, sweet potato, Brussel sprouts and beetroot for this particular one but you can add any vegetables that you like – such as sliced broccoli, cauliflower and carrots.

Unlike normal stir-fries where you cook the food on a high heat, my vegetarian stir-fry is cooked gently. Like with any stir-fry though, it is good to have all the vegetables chopped up and ready.

I do use already cooked chickpeas and beetroot in natural juice. I buy organic varieties of both and only add them at the end – just long enough to get them heated through.

I cube the sweet potatoes and cook them in the oven before adding them to the stir-fry. If you want to use raw beetroot, dice the beetroot and cook in the oven together with the sweet potatoes.

This stir-fry contains a fair amount of starchy vegetables - sweet potatoes and beetroot - and chickpeas, rich in both carbohydrates and protein. I like to serve it with non-starchy vegetables, such as broccoli or green beans.

To add an extra boost of highly nutritious non-starchy vegetables to the stir-fry, stir in some kale towards the end of frying.

For 4 people:

2 medium-sized sweet potatoes

3 tablespoons coconut oil

1 small red onion, chopped

A thumb-size piece of ginger, finely chopped

2 teaspoons ground coriander

2 teaspoons ground cumin

¾ teaspoon turmeric

¼ teaspoon dried chilli flakes

Salt and pepper

10 Brussel sprouts, trimmed and finely sliced

400g, 14oz, 2½ cups, cooked chickpeas

200g, 7oz cooked beetroot, diced - or use raw beetroot

2-3 spring onions (scallions) sliced

1.Pre-heat the oven to 200C/fan 180C/400F/gas mark 6. Peel and dice the sweet potato, place it in an oven dish and toss with a tablespoon of coconut or olive oil. Cook in the oven for about 20 minutes – until soft.

2.While the sweet potatoes are cooking, add the coconut oil and chopped red onion and ginger to a large frying pan over a low-medium-high heat and fry for 5 minutes. Add the spices, season with some salt and pepper and fry for a further minute before adding the finely sliced Brussel sprouts. Cook for another couple of minutes.

3.Stir through the chickpeas, diced beetroot and sweet potato. As soon as everything is warm, take the pan off the heat. Add the sliced spring onion (scallion) to the stir-fry.

Sourdough Bread with Tomatoes

The inspiration for this sourdough bread with tomatoes comes from breakfasts I ate when walking up through the interior of Spain.

In the region of Andalucía, the cafés served toasted bread to which you added freshly grated tomatoes, olive oil and some salt. So simple and so delicious!

I add chopped parsley and crushed garlic to my grated tomatoes - along with some olive oil, salt and pepper - then put the mixture on top of toasted sourdough/other good bread and pop it under the grill.

This sourdough bread with tomatoes is utterly moreish and perfect to eat with soup and/or a salad.

And I know that I go on about this on other pages of my website, but do try to get hold of some properly baked bread. Almost all bread sold in the supermarkets is made with factory-produced flour from which most of the nutrients have been removed and a lot of additives have been added.

For 4 people:

3 large ripe tomatoes

1 garlic clove, crushed

2 tablespoons chopped parsley

2 tablespoons olive oil

Salt and pepper

4 large slices of sourdough or other really good bread

1. Turn on the grill of your oven. Cut the tomatoes in half. Using the coarse side of a grater, grate the inside of each tomato half over a bowl, discarding the skin.

2. Mix together the grated tomato, chopped parsley, crushed garlic, olive oil and season with salt and pepper.

3. Place the bread slices on a baking tray and toast under the grill, turning each slice over and making sure they don't burn. Take out the bread from the oven and divide the tomato mixture on top of the bread slices. Place the baking tray under the grill once more for about 1 minute, until the tomato mixture is properly hot but not burnt.

See another type of tomato-topped bread on the next page.

Another Type of Tomato-Topped Bread

I use ripe, small tomatoes and cut them in half. I then fry them for a couple of minutes in a little bit of olive oil, add a good splash of balsamic vinegar and some salt and pepper and fry it all for a further couple of minutes.

I serve it on toasted bread with some shredded basil leaves and Parmesan cheese shavings (use a potato peeler to make these shavings) on top. This goes really well with a nice bowl of soup.

Swedish Pancakes

I LOVE pancakes! I make Swedish pancakes the same way my mother made hers - with loads of eggs.

I find that pancakes bring out the child in most of us. It's the milk and the eggs, in my humble opinion, which bring out that warm, fuzzy and comforting feeling in your tummy.

Although I also love American-style pancakes, with added baking powder, there is something very special about the way we make them in Sweden – thin with lots of eggs.

These thin pancakes are great to use for making filled savoury crepes. I also use them at times for making canapés.

Making Swedish pancakes for others is an act of love as far as I am concerned - not because they are difficult to make, but because you are stuck in front of that stove frying one pancake after another.

Having been brought up by the world's best pancake maker - my mother - brings a lot of pressure. But here goes.

4 medium-sized eggs

480ml, 17floz, 2.1 cups, full-fat milk

90g, 3¼oz, 0.65 cups plain flour

½ teaspoon salt

1 tablespoon butter + some more for frying

1.Crack the eggs into a bowl and add the flour, salt and 1/3 of the milk. Whisk vigorously – best thing to use is an electric whisk – until you have a lump-free batter. Add the rest of the milk and whisk a bit more. If you have the time (I rarely do), leave the pancake mix in the fridge for half an hour before frying the pancakes.

2.Melt the butter in a large non-stick frying pan and add the melted butter to the pancake batter whilst whisking. You only need to use a small amount of butter, ¼ of a teaspoon, for frying each pancake.

3.The frying pan needs to be quite hot and the butter should be turning brown before adding a small ladle of pancake batter to the pan. Swirl the pan around until you get a thin even pancake. Fry for about one minute, until you can see that it's nicely browned (just lift up a corner), before carefully flipping the pancake over. Fry for another minute. Transfer to a plate and continue with the next pancake, and the next one, and...

They are worth it though!

For a dairy, egg and gluten-free variation of pancakes, try my buckwheat and sweet potato crepes. I eat these crepes for breakfast sometimes – topped with some feta cheese and watercress.

Indian Dal

I'm using yellow split peas for this Indian dal. Yellow split peas are high in protein and fibre while low in fat.

I partly grew up on these peas. Every Thursday night my mother served a traditional Swedish meal consisting of her home-made yellow pea soup followed by her sublime pancakes.

It's funny how we use the same kind of ingredients in such a different way in different countries. While it's common to add cardamom to Indian food – I'm using it in this dish – in Sweden people add it to cakes and buns.

I love Indian dal. I ate a lot of different version on my travels in India. It is comfort food, food that leaves me with a warm and cosy feeling inside - just like my mother's Thursday dinners did once upon a time.

I like to add lots of different vegetables to whatever dal I'm making - to make more of a meal of this dish. This recipe will make quite a lot of dal. If you serve it with quinoa or rice it will easily be enough for 6 people.

I serve this Indian dal with lots of steamed green beans - tossed with a bit of oil and lemon zest – and natural yogurt with chopped fresh coriander.

For 4-6 people:

400g, 14oz, 1¾ cups, yellow split peas

1 litre, 1¾ pints, 4 ½ cups, water

1 heaped teaspoon ground ginger

4 cardamom pods

2 whole cloves

2 tablespoons vegetable oil

1 teaspoon mustard seeds

1 teaspoon cumin seeds

½ teaspoon dried chilli flakes

2 teaspoons ground coriander

1 teaspoon turmeric

1 teaspoon cinnamon

1 small red onion, finely chopped

2 medium-sized carrots, finely diced (the carrots take the longest to cook so need to be diced quite finely)

½ small butternut squash, diced

1 small aubergine (eggplant), diced

400g, 14oz, 2¼ cups, can chopped tomatoes

300ml, 10floz, 1¼ cups water

Salt and pepper

1.Start by rinsing the yellow split peas thoroughly under plenty of running cold water, until the water runs clear. Place the peas in a pot and cover with 1000ml, 4½ cups, fresh cold water.

2.Open the cardamom pods and take out the seeds. Place the seeds together with the cloves in a pestle and mortar. Grind to a fine powder and add to the pot with the peas together with the ground ginger. Stir well and bring to the boil. Skim off any scum that rises to the surface and reduce the heat. Simmer the peas for 40-45 minutes – until most of the water has evaporated and the lentils are tender.

3.While the peas are simmering, heat the oil in a large pot over a medium heat and add the mustard seeds, cumin seeds and dried chilli flakes. As soon as the seeds start to "crackle and pop", add the remaining spices and the chopped onion.

4.Stir and cook for 3-4 minutes before adding the carrots, butternut squash and aubergine. Keep on stirring and cook for a further couple of minutes. Add the chopped tomatoes and water to the pot, season with salt and pepper, stir and bring to a simmer.

5.Leave to simmer for 40 minutes (add some more water if it gets too dry), stirring every now and then to prevent the vegetables from burning at the bottom of the pot. When the yellow split peas are cooked, add them to the pot with the vegetables. Stir and continue to cook for a further 10 minutes. Check the seasoning and add a bit more salt and pepper to taste.

Halibut with Spicy Mash and Samphire

Halibut is the largest flatfish in the ocean and I am using it for this halibut with spicy mash and samphire dish.

Halibut is undoubtedly a bit of a treat as it is quite an expensive type of fish. It has a firm and meaty texture and is really delicious.

It's very important though, not to over-cook it as that really ruins the taste of it. I have all the other parts of this dish ready before I cook the fish.

Halibut is a good source of certain vitamins and minerals, including selenium which is an important antioxidant.

I like to serve this fish with a spicy butternut squash and sweet potato mash, tenderstem broccoli (broccolini) and top with salty and very healthy samphire.

Samphire is a sea vegetable and it is a very good source of many important minerals, including calcium and magnesium, vitamins and fibre.

For 4 people:

1 small butternut squash, peeled, halved, de-seeded and diced

2 medium-sized sweet potatoes, peeled and diced

1 tablespoon Extra virgin olive oil

1 teaspoon sea salt

1/4 teaspoon black pepper

1/4 cayenne pepper

3 spring onions (scallions), chopped

Tenderstem broccoli, or use ordinary broccoli - as much as you like as this is a super-healthy, low-calorie vegetable

50g, 1 3/4oz, samphire

4 halibut fillets, skin on

1 tablespoon olive oil

1 tablespoon butter

1.Start by pre-heating the oven to 200C/Fan180C/400F/Gas mark 6. Place the diced butternut squash and sweet potatoes in an oven-proof dish and toss with one tablespoon olive oil. Place the dish in the oven and cook for about 30 minutes - until the vegetables are soft.

2.Once the squash and sweet potatoes are cooked, add them to a pot together with the salt, black pepper and cayenne pepper and use a potato masher to crush them. Stir in the spring onions (scallions), cover the pot with a lid and keep the mash warm over a low heat.

3.Get some water boiling in another pot and then add the broccoli and simmer for 2 minutes. Add the samphire to the pot and continue to simmer for a further minute. Turn off the heat, drain the vegetables in a colander, return them to the pot and cover the pot with a lid to keep them warm.

4.Add 1 tablespoon each of butter and olive oil to a large frying pan over a medium-high heat. Use kitchen towel to pat each halibut fillet dry. Once the butter browns, place the fillets skin-side down in the frying pan and fry, without moving the fish, for 3 minutes. carefully turn over each fillet and fry for 1 minute. Remove the pan from the heat.

5.Divide the mash between four plates, place a halibut fillet on top of the mash and some samphire on top of the fish. Divide the broccoli between the plates and serve immediately.

Lemon Sole with Capers and Mushy Peas

Light, tasty and healthy - lemon sole with capers and mushy peas.

Lemon sole, native to Northern Europe, is a delicate type of flatfish. It's a favourite fish of mine and I often use it in my work as a chef.

You can use other types of sole or flounder fillets for this tasty and healthy dish.

I've chosen to serve the fish with non-starchy vegetables - tomatoes and green peas - which both contain low-GL carbohydrates and are thus kind to your waistline!

Tomatoes are healthier cooked and even more so with some added extra virgin olive oil.

Green peas are high in fibre, protein, vitamins, minerals and lutein. They are loaded with antioxidants and anti-inflammatory nutrients.

I always have peas in my freezer. When I don't feel like spending too much time cooking, I whip up a super-quick soup with a mix of green peas, ground ginger, black pepper, salt and either kale, spinach or broccoli.

It doesn't take that much longer to cook this lemon sole with capers and mushy peas to be honest. So it's winner in every sense to me.

Note: **Fish like sole fillets needs very little cooking.** To make sure that I don't over-cook the fish, I flash-fry the fillets two at a time and then place them on a baking tray covered with parchment (baking) paper. Once all the fish has been fried, I place the tray in a pre-heated oven for no more than 2 minutes.

For 4 people:

16-20 small ripe tomatoes

a drizzle of extra virgin olive oil

400g, 14oz, 2 1/2 cups, frozen peas

1 tablespoon butter

1 teaspoon sea salt

1/2 teaspoon black pepper

4 lemon sole fillets (or any other type of sole, or use flounder)

1 tablespoon Extra virgin olive oil

1 tablespoon butter

2 tablespoons capers

2 spring onions (scallions), chopped

juice of half a lemon

lemon slices to serve

1.Preheat the oven to 200C/fan180C/400F/gas mark 6. Place the tomatoes in an oven-proof dish, drizzle over a little olive oil and place the tomatoes in the oven for 10 minutes.

2.While the tomatoes are in the oven, place the peas in a pot over a high heat and pour over enough water (preferably hot from a kettle) to just cover the peas.

3.Cover the pot with a lid and soon as the water starts to boil, turn off the heat and drain the peas in a colander. Return the peas to the pot, add the butter, salt and pepper and use a potato masher to crush the peas. Cover the pot with a lid to keep warm.

4.Cover a baking tray with parchment (baking) paper. Add the butter and olive oil to a frying pan over a medium-high heat. When the butter starts to brown, add two fish fillets to the pan and fry for about half a minute before turning them over. Fry for another half a minute and then transfer the fish fillets to the baking tray. Repeat with the remaining fillets.

5.Season the fish with some salt and black pepper and place the baking tray and cook for in the oven for 2 minutes. Add the capers, spring onion and lemon juice to the frying pan and quickly heat it through.

Divide the mushy peas and tomatoes between four plates, add a sole fillet and top each fish with some of the caper mix. Serve with extra lemon slices.

Salmon, Sweet Potato and Chilli Fishcakes

Fishcakes with a twist - exotic salmon, sweet potato and chilli fishcakes which are super scrumptious. They are easy to prepare beforehand and can then be finished off just before you are ready to eat.

In most of my jobs as a cook, I am forever short of time and always looking for ways to get things done quicker – and never more so than when I was cooking lunch for 25-30 people at an office in London.

My aim was to serve them healthy food full of flavour; food that would keep them going when lunch was over. The lack of time to do it all in often resulted in healthier cooking methods, as with these salmon sweet potato and chilli fishcakes.

Instead of coating each fishcake with flour, eggs and breadcrumbs and then frying them in vegetable oil, I put the fishcakes on baking trays lined with baking parchment, scattered some breadcrumbs over the fishcakes and then cooked them en masse in the oven. I leave it up to you to choose what method you want to use.

Salmon sweet potato and chilli fishcakes for 4 people:

400g, 14oz, salmon

500g, 1lb 2oz, sweet potato, peeled and cut into chunks

½ red onion, peeled and finely chopped

3 spring onions (scallions), trimmed and finely chopped

1 red chilli, deseeded and finely chopped

¼ teaspoon freshly grated nutmeg

large handful of fresh coriander (cilantro), leaves and stalks finely chopped

Salt and pepper

Optional:

A little plain flour

2 eggs

200g, 7oz, 4 cups, fresh breadcrumbs

To serve:

Lime wedges

Sweet chilli sauce

1. Preheat the oven to 200C/400F/gas mark 6. Line a baking tray with baking parchment and arrange the salmon on top. Bake in the preheated oven for approximately 10 -12 minutes (it's OK if the fish is still a little bit rare in the middle). Set aside and cool.

2. Boil or steam the sweet potato chunks for around 20 minutes, until tender. Drain the sweet potatoes, transfer to a bowl and mash with a fork. Leave to cool.

3. Once the sweet potato is cold, flake the salmon and mix it into the sweet potato together with the chopped red onion, spring onion, chilli and coriander. Add the freshly grated nutmeg and season with salt and pepper. Taste the mixture to check the seasoning and then form the mixture into 4 patties. If you choose to cook the fishcakes in the oven - place them on a baking tray lined with baking parchment, cover with cling film and chill in the fridge until you are ready to cook them.

4. If you are going to coat them, then lightly beat the eggs in a shallow bowl. Put a little bit of plain flour on a plate and the breadcrumbs on another plate. Dip each fishcake in the flour, shake off any excess and then dip them in the eggs and finally roll them in the breadcrumbs. Cover and chill in the fridge until you are ready to cook them.

5. For the oven-cooked fishcakes, heat the oven to 220C/Fan 200C/425F/gas mark 7 and once the oven is hot, scatter some breadcrumbs over the fish cakes and place the baking tray with the fishcakes in the middle of the oven. Cook for approximately 10-15 minutes, until the fishcakes are piping hot and are starting to brown.

6. If frying - heat 3 tablespoons of vegetable oil in a large, deep-sided frying pan over a moderate heat and fry the fishcakes for about 5 minutes on each side until golden.

Apart from the lime wedges and the sweet chilli sauce, I like to serve these salmon sweet potato and chilli fish cakes with oven-baked tomatoes and steamed sugar snaps and broccoli.

Thai-Style Prawns

I've just bought a new pestle and mortar and have already used it to make a marinade for Thai-style prawns served with my personal favourite, cauliflower rice. Yummy!

Once you have made the marinade and grated the cauliflower, this dish comes together really quickly.

You could make this marinade a lot quicker by putting the ingredients in a food processor. It will still taste good when made this way – but not as good as it will be when made in a pestle and mortar.

When you pound your ingredients in a mortar, you are slowly teasing out the flavours of whatever you put in – it is more work but you get much more flavour from the ingredients. I personally like to do as much as I possibly can by hand.

I love Asian-style food. My only problem with it is the amount of sugar used in certain food – more so, it seems to me, in Korean, Japanese and Chinese food where they happily add several tablespoons of sugar to many a dish, including salads.

A mixture of the four basic tastes – salt, sweet, sour and bitter – makes for a well-balanced taste sensation. I just feel that the sweet part of the dish can be kept to a minimum.

For the marinade for these Thai-style prawns, I suggest you use either 1 heaped **teaspoon** of coconut palm sugar or honey. I have used both and found that they worked equally well (the honey I used was a delicious raw orange blossom honey).

Honey is a slightly healthier option but it is still sugar.

If you haven't tried cauliflower rice, please do. I was not a lover of cauliflower until I tried this but now I am hooked. Everybody that I've cooked it for have loved it, and no-one realized that it was made with cauliflower until I told them.

You can replace the lemongrass in the marinade with finely grated zest of either 1 un-waxed lemon or lime.

Thai-style prawns for 4 people:

Marinade:

1 lemongrass stalk - cut off the thinner top, leaving you with the "bulb" at the bottom, discard tough outer layer, cut off the bottom of the "bulb", halve it and slice very finely

2 garlic cloves, chopped

A thumb-size piece of ginger, peeled and finely chopped

2 shallots, chopped

2 large red chillies, de-seeded and chopped

8 small tomatoes – such as cherry or plum – halved

1½ tablespoon Thai fish sauce

1 heaped teaspoon of either coconut palm sugar or honey

2 tablespoons coconut oil

24 large, raw peeled prawns

2 tablespoons coconut oil

1 large cauliflower – trimmed and grated coarsely

Salt and pepper

A handful of fresh coriander (cilantro) – roughly chopped

10 mint leaves, chopped

1 tablespoon lime juice

1.Place the chopped lemongrass, garlic, shallots, ginger and chillies in a pestle and mortar (a reasonable deep one) and pound until you have a paste (keep scraping it down from the sides with a spoon). Add the tomatoes and continue to pound until they disintegrate as well.

2.In a bowl, mix the sugar or honey with the fish sauce and whisk until the sugar/honey has dissolved. Add this to the mortar and pound a bit more. If you are using a food processor, simply add all the ingredients for the marinade and pulse until you have a mushy paste – it won't take long.

3.Add 2 tablespoons of coconut oil to a large frying pan over a medium high heat. Once the oil is hot, add the prawns to the frying pan. Fry the prawns for about 1 ½ minute – turning them over half-way through - until they are pink on both sides. Add all of the marinade to the pan, increase the heat and let it all bubble away for a further minute. Add 1 tablespoon of lime juice to the pan and remove from the heat. Place the prawns and marinade in a bowl and cover it with foil to keep warm.

4.Wipe the frying pan clean with kitchen roll, add 2 tablespoons of coconut oil to the pan over a high heat and add the grated cauliflower to the pan together with some salt and black pepper. Keep stirring for about 2 minutes (the cauliflower rice should still be crunchy). Remove the pan from the heat and stir in 1 tablespoon of lime juice, the chopped coriander and mint leaves.

5.Divide the cauliflower rice between four plates and top with the Thai-style prawns and. Serve immediately.

Poached Salmon and Vegetables with New Potatoes

Summer time, and the food is easy – and light like this poached salmon and vegetables with new potatoes.

Once you've prepared the vegetables, it is also quick to make.

And it's healthy and kind to your waistline. What's not to like? I love it!

The broth that I poach the salmon in tastes amazing thanks to a simple trick. I add a splash of cider vinegar together with some lemon thyme, lemon zest and some salt and pepper to fish stock and let it simmer for a bit before adding the fish.

You can use a small glass of a tasty dry white wine instead of the vinegar but I think the vinegar adds more of a punch taste-wise. Save the wine for drinking!

I confess that as much as like to cook from scratch, the one thing I seldom make myself is stock. I also seldom mention a certain brand of food but – and I am not paid by this company, or any other – I do love Knorr fish stock.

I cook the potatoes and vegetables separately and add them to the broth once the fish is cooked. Doing it this way makes it much easier to control the cooking time of the different elements to this dish – I like my vegetables to be crunchy.

For 4 people:

500ml, 18floz, 2.2 cups fish stock

1 tablespoon cider or white wine vinegar

Finely grated zest from 1 un-waxed lemon

2 teaspoons fresh lemon thyme leaves (or you can use ordinary thyme if you can't get hold of lemon thyme)

½ teaspoon sea salt or Himalayan rock salt (it really is worth investing in a good salt – both for the taste and your health)

A pinch of white pepper (or you can use black pepper)

4 skin-less salmon fillets – alternatively you can use trout fillets

1 large carrot – cut into match stick thin batons

1 large red pepper (bell pepper) –I prefer the pointed variety - cut into thin strips

8-10 tenderstem broccoli (broccolini) spears – 1 cm (½ inch) pieces

12-16 small new potatoes (depending on size and how many you would like per person)

To serve: lemon or garlic mayonnaise (optional). An easy way to make this is by adding some lemon juice or crushed garlic to a nice mayonnaise

1.Start by making the broth. Place the fish stock in a large enough pot to hold the salmon. Add the vinegar, lemon zest, lemon thyme, salt and pepper to the stock and bring to a slow simmer.

2.Boil the potatoes in a separate pot. Unless the potatoes are very small, you could slice them to make them cook quicker. Once they are ready, sieve off the water and cover with kitchen roll first and then the lid - to keep them warm and to remove moisture from the potatoes.

3.Add water to another pot and get it boiling. Start by adding the carrot batons. Cover the pot with a lid and simmer for 2 minutes. Add the pepper and broccolini to the pot, cover with the lid and simmer for a further 3 minutes. Sieve off the water, cover the pot with the lid and leave to the side while you cook the salmon.

4.Add the salmon to the pot with the simmering broth and cover the pot with a lid. Poach the salmon fillets for about 10 minutes. Check with a knife to see that salmon is cooked.

Serve the poached salmon and vegetables in large soup bowls. Add a fillet of salmon to each bowl and divide the vegetable and potatoes between the bowls before pouring over the broth (use all of the broth as this is so tasty).

If using, let everyone help themselves to the mayonnaise.

Prawn and Mixed Fish

Light food full of flavour doesn't get much better than this prawn and mixed fish dish – a real favourite of mine. It's so incredibly fresh and light while also spicy and wonderfully flavoured.

As is the case with a lot of my food – it's easy to prepare beforehand and quick to finish off once you are ready to eat, so it's an excellent dish to serve when you have guests.

It is important to buy large raw prawn with shells as a lot of the flavour in this dish comes from cooking the shells for the broth.

I add shrimp paste to the broth as well - it really adds a lot of extra flavour. You can find it in well-stocked supermarkets or in shops specializing in Asian food.

For 4 people:

500g, 1lb 2oz, large raw prawns with shells - remove heads and shells, but save them

500g, 1lb 2oz, mixed fish, such as haddock, cod or lemon sole, cut into bite-sized pieces

1 tablespoon coconut oil - or use vegetable oil - for frying

1 teaspoon shrimp paste (see above

1 teaspoon coriander seeds, crushed

1/2 teaspoon ground cumin

Salt and pepper

400ml, 13½floz, 1¾ cups, coconut mil

200ml, 7floz, 0.9 cup, water

2 shallots, finely chopped

4 garlic cloves, finely chopped

A thumb-sized piece of ginger, finely chopped

2-3 large red chillies, de-seeded and finely chopped

Grated zest and juice of 1 lime

2 handfuls fresh coriander, stalks and leaves finely chopped

1.Heat the 1 tablespoon of coconut oil in a saucepan over a medium heat. Add the prawn heads and shells, shrimp paste, coriander seeds, cumin and season with some salt and pepper. Cook for about 4 minutes until the shells have turned orange. Add the coconut milk and 200ml of water and simmer for 15 minutes. Strain through a sieve into a clean pot and discard the prawn shells.

2.Meanwhile, heat the remaining tablespoon of coconut oil in a frying pan and fry the onion, garlic, ginger and chilli gently over a low heat for about 5 minutes. Stir every now and then to make sure it doesn't burn. Add this to the strained prawn-coconut milk together with the lime zest. Bring to a simmer and check the seasoning to see if you need any more salt. This can be prepared well in advance.

3.I cook the fish in the oven by simply covering an oven tray with baking parchment and then place the fish on the tray with nothing but a bit of salt and pepper on top and cook it in a 200C/400F/gas mark 6 hot oven for about 5 minutes. This is a healthier way to cook the fish, but you can of course also fry the seasoned fish in a lightly oiled frying pan.

4.Add the prawns to the coconut liquid and cook them for 2-3 minutes. Take the pan away from the heat and add the lime juice and the chopped coriander.

Divide the fish between 4 bowls and pour the sauce with the prawns over the fish.

I like to serve this dish with steamed sugar snaps. If you want a more substantial meal, serve this prawn and mixed fish dish with quinoa, or brown basmati rice, as well.

Miso Marinated Salmon

There's a lot of flavour in this miso marinated salmon dish –
and it is healthy as well.

It's all about the gut these days. There's a real buzz about
the importance of having good bacteria in our guts, and the
types of food that will increase the amount of those god
bacteria, like fermented food.

Miso is made from fermented soybeans and grains and
contains millions of beneficial bacteria.

I am using **sweet white miso** in this recipe. It is made from fermented soybeans and rice and is the mildest and least salty type of miso.

The darker the miso is, the longer it has been fermented and the saltier it is. Dark miso also has a very strong taste and is best used in small amounts as it can over-power a dish. Dark miso is not suitable for this marinade.

I am adding sesame oil to the marinade, a really mild unrefined, first cold pressing sesame oil though. The kind of sesame oil you mostly find in supermarkets, usually in a small bottle, has a very strong taste and, like dark miso, is best used in small amounts.

I have added a tablespoon of this mild sesame oil. **If you have got sesame oil with a very strong taste, add just one teaspoon of this and also add a tablespoon of olive oil to the marinade.**

Tip: Once opened, white miso can usually keep for up to a month if well sealed and kept in the fridge. It's great for adding to soups or other marinades. Just keep in mind that it is salty and that you need much less salt, or none, when adding some miso.

Miso marinated salmon for 2:

1 large, or 2 small sweet potatoes – peeled and diced

½ tablespoon olive oil

For the salmon marinade:

1 tablespoon sweet white miso

2 teaspoons finely grated ginger

1 tablespoon mild sesame oil

grated zest of 1 un-waxed lemon

¼ teaspoon ground black pepper

2 salmon fillets

Broccoli – cut into florets – and the more the merrier as they are super-healthy and very low in calories

1.Preheat the oven 200C/fan180C/400F/gas mark 6. Toss the diced sweet potato in a little bit of olive oil and spread them out in a roasting tray and sprinkle over some salt. Place the tray with the sweet potatoes in the oven and roast for around 25 minutes, until they are soft.

2.Once the sweet potatoes are in the oven, mix together all the ingredients for the marinade and divide the mixture over the 2 salmon fillets and place them in an oven-proof dish. When the sweet potatoes have been in the oven for 15 minutes, add the tray with the salmon to the oven and bake for 12-15 minutes, depending on how thick the fillets are.

3.Towards the end, steam or boil the broccoli florets for 1-2 minutes (I cook them as little as possible). Once the sweet potatoes are soft, take them out of the oven and mash them up with a fork.

4.Divide the mash between two plates and top with the miso marinated salmon and broccoli on the side.

Lightly Smoked Salmon with Mushy Peas

Looking for delicious fast food? Try this lightly smoked salmon dish. It takes very little time to make and is super tasty as well as healthy.

My problem with hunger is that when I've got time on my hands, I seem to go from not hungry to absolutely starving in seconds with nothing in between.

If I've got a recipe to test drive I know now to start preparing the food when I'm properly full, as being in starving mode makes me immensely impatient.

On the other hand, when I'm really busy on a job cooking food from the early hours of the morning until late at night, I lose my appetite almost completely.

I've done a lot of long weekends with marathon shifts without eating much at all - apart from tasting the food I've been cooking of course. But as soon as I've finished my last shift, my hunger comes back with a vengeance!

This recipe came about when I was at home writing one day and had some lightly smoked salmon fillets in the fridge and peas in the freezer.

As I was not paying attention to the clock ticking away, I suddenly found myself starving and not in the mood for any time-consuming cooking. I decided to quickly fry the salmon, make mushy peas and top it with a yogurt and fresh mint sauce. Oh boy, it was divine!

For 4 people:

400g, 14oz, 2½ cups frozen peas

25g, 1oz, 2 tablespoons, butter

5 mint sprigs, remove the stems and roughly chop the leaves

Salt and pepper

4 fillets lightly smoked salmon, skinned and each fillet cut into 3 pieces

1 tablespoon rapeseed or olive oil

100ml, 3½floz, ½ cup, natural (plain) yogurt

1.Place the peas in a pan with salted water. Bring to the boil, turn down the heat and simmer for 1 minute. Drain the peas in a colander, put them back in the pan, add the butter, half of the chopped mint and some salt and pepper and mash with a potato masher. Keep warm.

2.Add the oil to a frying pan and fry the salmon pieces over a moderate heat for 2-3 minutes on each side.

3.Mix the rest of chopped mint with the yogurt. Divide the mushy peas between 4 plates and top with the salmon and dollop over some mint yogurt.

Swedish Seafood Casserole

Saffron – used liberally in this Swedish seafood casserole - is a bit expensive but it is a vital ingredient in some Swedish types of food. I absolutely love the taste and smell of saffron and this dish is simply super-delicious and also light and really fresh.

We mostly buy it as ground saffron in Sweden and you actually have to ask for it when you get to the cashier in the food shops as it's not kept on the shelves in the store. Precious cargo, indeed!

This Swedish seafood casserole does require a bit of chopping and slicing but once you have prepared everything, you can cook the broth well in advance and then finish it off quite quickly when you are ready to eat.

I add some Madeira wine to the broth as well to give it a more intense flavour. You don't have to add it but I do recommend doing it.

For 4 people:

25g, 1oz, 2 tablespoons, butter

1 small fennel bulb - shoots and root cut off, tough outer layer removed, halved; tough bottom core cut out of each half and the two halves then chopped finely

2 small or one large shallot, chopped finely

2 fat garlic cloves, crushed

150ml, 5floz, slightly less than ¾ cup, white wine (you should be happy to drink the wine you use for cooking

50ml Madeira wine (optional)

1 heaped teaspoon of saffron threads

700ml, 1¼ pints, 3.1 cups, fish stock

100ml, 3½floz, ½ cup, light crème fraiche

Salt and white pepper

1 medium sized carrot, cut into matchstick-sized batons

Handful of sugar snaps, cut into thin strips

1 red pepper (bell pepper), deseeded and cut into thin strips

10 cherry tomatoes, halved

4 salmon fillets without the skin - each fillet cut in half

16 - 20 raw king prawns, shelled

12 scallops

1.Start by adding the saffron to the white wine. Melt the butter in a large pot over a low heat. Gently fry the fennel and shallot in the pot for 5 minutes, stirring from time to time to make sure it doesn't burn. Add the garlic to the pot and fry, stirring all the time, for a further minute

2.Add the white wine and saffron - plus the Madeira wine if using - to the pot and bring it to a boil, turn down the heat and let it simmer for 5 minutes until the wine has reduced by about half.

3.Add the fish stock and crème fraiche and bring it back to a simmer. **Season with salt and white pepper, and taste to make sure you are happy with the broth - the broth is the key to this Swedish seafood casserole!** Allow the broth to simmer for a further 5 minutes. (You can prepare this well in advance, cool it down and leave it covered in the fridge.)

4.Heat up the oven to 200C/Fan 180C/400F. Once the oven is hot, add the prawns and the all the julienned vegetables to the pot with the broth and bring it back to a simmer for about 3 minutes. Give it a good stir a couple of times. Take the pot off the heat and cover with a lid to keep it warm.

5.Cover a baking tray with baking parchment. Season the salmon and scallops with salt and pepper and quickly sear them, in batches, in a hot frying pan - 1 minute on each side for the salmon and 1/2 a minute on each side for the scallops. Place the seared salmon and scallops on the baking tray and place the tray in the oven for about 2 minutes. When the salmon and scallops are nearly done, quickly re-heat the broth with the prawns and vegetables.

Divide the fish and scallops between 4 soup bowls and top with the prawns, vegetables and broth.

Prawn and Mango Curry

I adore Asian-style food. And this incredibly tasty prawn and mango curry is an old favourite of mine.

While the supermarkets are full of many types of ready-made paste and sauces, I prefer to cook from scratch.

And really, it may be a bit more time-consuming to make this mango and prawn curry but it's not difficult to do – and the result is simply amazing

This prawn and mango curry does contain coconut milk but as long as you don't have too much, there is no need to worry about this type of fat.

Coconut milk is first of all really nutritious. It does contain saturated fat but coconut is rich in medium-chain fatty acids which the body processes differently than other saturated fats.

It is a great dish to prepare beforehand – you can finish it off after your guests have arrived. It will simply improve as the flavours intensify when left to stand.

Follow the recipe all the way until you have added the coconut milk and mango and simmered for 10 minutes. Let the sauce cool down, cover and place in the fridge. When you are ready to finish the mango and prawn curry, take out the sauce, get it simmering again and follow the recipe to the end.

For 4 people:

Goan masala paste

1/2 teaspoon cumin seeds

1 teaspoon coriander seeds

1 teaspoon black pepper corns

½ teaspoon cloves

3 large red chillies, deseeded and finely chopped

½ teaspoon salt

3 garlic cloves, finely chopped

1 tablespoon tamarind water (see below), or, if you can't get hold of tamarind, replace with 1 tablespoon of lime juice

thumb-sized piece of fresh root ginger, finely chopped

1 tablespoon red vinegar

½ teaspoon turmeric powder

Tamarind water: take a piece of tamarind pulp, about the size of a golf ball, and place it in a bowl with 100ml, 3½floz, ½ cup, of warm water. With your fingers, work the tamarind pulp into the water until it has broken down and the seeds have been released. Strain the syrupy liquid through a fine sieve – press down with a spoon - into another bowl. Discard the fibrous material left in the sieve.

Grind the cumin, coriander, black pepper and cloves to a fine powder in a pestle and mortar. Transfer to a food processor with all the other ingredients except for the turmeric powder and blend to a smooth paste. Transfer to a bowl and mix in the turmeric powder.

For the prawn and mango curry:

5 garlic cloves, roughly chopped

A thumb-sized piece of ginger, peeled and chopped

2 yellow onions, roughly chopped

2 tablespoons coconut oil, or use vegetable oil

6 cardamom pods, bruised

A small handful of curry leaves, fresh or dried (optional)

3 teaspoons garam masala

All of the Goan masala paste (see above)

400g, 14oz, 2¼ cups, chopped tomatoes

400ml, 13½floz, 1¾cups, can coconut milk

1 large ripe mango, peeled and cut into chunks

300g, 10½oz, tiger or other large prawns (you can replace the prawns with chunks of firm white fish)

1. Whizz the garlic, ginger and onion together with a splash of water to a paste in a food processor.

2. Heat the oil in a deep-sided frying pan, or in a casserole pot, and fry the cardamom for a minute over a medium heat. Throw in the curry leaves, if using, and fry for ½ a minute. Add the onion-garlic-ginger paste and 2 teaspoons of the garam masala and fry, stirring continuously, until the paste darkens, for about 5 minutes.

3. Add the Goan masala paste and continue to fry for another couple of minutes, still stirring so it doesn't burn. Stir in the chopped tomatoes and 100 ml of water and season with salt and pepper. Let everything simmer gently for 10 minutes.

4. Add the coconut milk and mango chunks and simmer for another 10 minutes.

5. Stir in the prawns (or chunks of fish) and cook for 3 minutes until they are just cooked. Stir in the remaining teaspoon of garam masala just before serving (if you are using fish, then stir very gently so you don't break up the fish too much).

6. Serve in bowls with quinoa (healthier) or rice (brown basmati rice is the best type of rice).

Ginger-Glazed Salmon with Citrus Couscous

A lovely ginger-glazed salmon dish.

It's light, it's fresh and the gorgeous flavours go so well together it's like having a beautiful symphony playing in your mouth.

I am big advocate for quinoa and often use it instead of couscous. Quinoa is healthier and contains a lot of protein so it is a good thing to serve with vegetarian food - it is also better for your waistline. When I do use couscous, like with this dish, I will only use wholemeal (whole-wheat) couscous.

This is about taste just as much as health. Wholemeal couscous taste so much more than refined couscous which, let's face it, has virtually no taste at all.

I have bought wholemeal couscous in supermarkets but the tastiest kind by far that I have ever bought is Infinity Foods Organic Wholemeal couscous. I found it in a health food shop.

I use the zest of lemons and lime quite a lot, like in this ginger-glazed salmon recipe. While it is easy to find un-waxed lemons, it's not always easy to find un-waxed limes. If you can only get hold of waxed lime fruits, make sure you scrub them really well with a clean scrubbing brush.

And when grating the zest, don't be too forceful. You only want the very outer layer of the fruit, not the bitter pith, the inner white part. I find that it's worth investing in some really good graters with different coarseness. You want a fine grater for citrus fruit.

I know it may seem extravagant, but I have two really sharp fine graters and use one of them solely for grating citrus zest.

For 4 people:

Marinade for the salmon:

2 teaspoons grated fresh ginger

2 garlic cloves, crushed

Juice of 1 lime (grate the zest first and leave to the side)

1 tablespoon coconut oil (melted if solid) - or use vegetable oil

1 teaspoon honey

4 salmon fillets

Salt and pepper

225g,8oz, 1¼ cup, wholemeal (whole wheat) couscous

400ml, 13½oz, 1¾ cup, hot vegetable stock

1 tablespoon olive oil

Grated zest of 1 lemon and 1 lime (use the zest from the lime used for the marinade)

150g, 5½oz, ¾ cup, sugar snaps

4 spring onions (scallions), chopped

3-4 tablespoons pomegranate seeds

1. Preheat the oven to 200C/fan180C/400F/gas mark 6. Mix together all the ingredients for the marinade. Cover a baking tray with baking parchment and place the salmon fillets on top. Divide the marinade over the salmon fillets. Leave to stand for 10 minutes.

2. Season the salmon with salt and pepper and place the baking tray in the oven. Cook in the oven for 10-12 minutes, or until cooked through.

3. While the salmon is cooking in the oven, heat the vegetable stock to boiling point. Mix the couscous with the lemon and lime zest and 1 tablespoon of olive oil in a bowl and pour over the hot stock. Cover the bowl with cling film and leave to the side.

4. Add the sugar snaps to a pan with boiling water and cook for 2-3 minutes. Drain and chop the sugar snaps in half. Take off the cling film and fluff up the couscous with a fork. Add the sugar snaps, chopped spring onions and pomegranate seeds to the couscous.

5. Divide the couscous between four plates and serve with the ginger-glazed salmon on top.

Egg and Crayfish Sandwich with Chilli and Garlic Aioli

My egg and crayfish sandwich with chilli and garlic aioli is a take on a Swedish variety – egg, prawn and mayonnaise open sandwich.

You will find this type of sandwich in most Swedish cafés - and at the airport in Stockholm where they charge an absolute fortune for them!

Crayfish (crawfish) is also very popular in Sweden. We have crayfish parties in the autumn where we wear silly hats, eat crayfish, drink schnapps and sing songs.

You can buy crayfish tails in most supermarkets here in Britain but you can of course swap them for cooked prawns.

I am using rye pumpernickel bread, which is the type of bread that will affect your weight the least. I think it makes this egg and crayfish sandwich taste so much more.

You could also use good sourdough bread, the second best choice for your weight.

I have had many an egg and prawn variety in Sweden where they put a mountain of mayonnaise on top of the bread. And the only type of lettuce most use is iceberg lettuce, a lettuce which is 99% water and almost 0% nutrients. Ah well, it's cheap to use I suppose.

Here's what I do. I butter the pumpernickel bread, cover it with watercress salad (or use rocket/arugula) add the sliced cooked egg and crayfish and serve the chilli and garlic aioli on the side.

To make the chilli and garlic aioli:

2 egg yolks – preferably organic or free-range

1 garlic clove, crushed

1 level teaspoon sambal oelek (a chilli paste) – or any other chilli paste

Grated zest from a lime (optional)

100ml, 3½floz, 0.45 cup sunflower or hemp oil

100ml, 3½floz, 0.45 cup olive oil

Salt and pepper

1.Add the egg yolks to a bowl and whisk together. Add the crushed garlic, chilli paste and lime zest, if using, and whisk again.

2.Continue to whisk and add a few drops of oil to start with, and then the rest of the oil very, very slowly while whisking vigorously (if you add the oil to quickly the mixture will split).

3.Once you have added all the oil, season with some sea salt and black pepper.

For the egg and crayfish sandwich:

4 slices of pumpernickel or sourdough bread, buttered

Watercress and/or rocket (arugula) leaves

4 hard-boiled eggs

350g, 12oz, 2 cups cooked crayfish (crawfish) tails – or use cooked prawns

Chilli and garlic aioli

Lime wedges

Top the buttered bread with leaves, sliced egg and crayfish and serve with the chilli-garlic aioli and some lime wedges on the side.

Cured Salmon Two Way

Cured salmon (gravad lax) was part of every big festivity in my family, like Christmas, Easter and Midsummer (which we celebrate in a big way in Sweden). But my mother didn't stop there – I more or less grew up on it.

And that might explain why it took me a while before I started making it myself. I still don't make it very often but every time I do, I cannot get over how much I do love the taste and the texture of it.

When I found a Gordon Ramsay recipe with a totally different way of curing, I fell in love with cured salmon all over again. Does it beat the Swedish way of curing? Nah, it's so different there is no comparison between the two. But like my mother, I would eat either of them at any time of the year even though Ramsay uses very wintry spices in this recipe.

Some Swedish people only cure the salmon for 24 hours but as far as my mother and I are concerned (and many more with us), it requires a curing period of 48 hours. The Ramsay recipe has a 24-hour curing time but I find that you can easily extend that with another 6 - 10 hours to get more flavour (it is very mild with only 24 hours curing).

No one in my family would cure their Swedish-style salmon (gravad lax) without a bit of alcohol, but you do not have to use it. My mother preferred to use either gin or cognac. Even though I'm not a whiskey drinker, I prefer to cure my Swedish-style salmon with a bit of whiskey.

Swedish cured salmon (gravad lax):

2 x 500g, 1lb 2oz, centre pieces (the thickest part) of salmon fillet, skin on, pin boned

4 tablespoons sugar

4 tablespoons sea salt

2 teaspoons white pepper corns, lightly crushed

100g, 3½oz, 1cup, fresh dill (including the stalks), roughly chopped

50ml, 2floz, ¼ cup, whiskey (or use either gin, cognac or vodka), optional

1. Place the two salmon sides, skin-side down, on a plate. Mix together the sugar, salt and white pepper and divide the mixture between the two salmon pieces, rubbing it into the salmon flesh with your hands.

2. Place all the chopped dill on top of one of the salmon pieces, and then the other salmon piece, now with the flesh-side down, on top of that and push it down a bit. Place the salmon, with one piece on top of the other, in a thick plastic bag. Add the whiskey to the bag, squeeze out as much air as possible and tie a knot on the bag as close as possible to the salmon.

3. Place the bag on a plate in the fridge, turning it over 3-4 times during 48 hours. Once it is ready, take the salmon out of the bag and using kitchen towel, thoroughly brush off all of the salt, sugar, pepper and dill mixture.

The cured salmon will easily keep for 6-7 days if well covered and kept in the fridge. You can also freeze it for up to 2 months.

I prefer to cut quite thin slices of the salmon. In Sweden it is often served on a rye bread of the pumpernickel type with some dill and mustard sauce.

Dill and mustard sauce:

1 tablespoon Dijon mustard

½ tablespoon sugar

1 tablespoon white wine vinegar

Salt and pepper

100ml, 3½floz, just under ½ cup oil, - I use rapeseed oil (canola oil) but you can use extra virgin olive oil

A handful of fresh dill, without the stalks, finely chopped

Whisk together the mustard, sugar and vinegar with a good pinch of salt and some pepper. Keep whisking while very slowly adding the oil - the sauce will split if you add the oil too quickly - until the sauce emulsifies and thickens. Once you have incorporated all the oil, stir in the chopped dill.

Gordon Ramsay's cinnamon and star anise cured salmon

150g, 5½oz, 0.9 cup, brown sugar

300g, 10½oz, 1 cup, rock salt

Zest of 3 oranges – if you can't find un-waxed oranges, use a vegetable brush to clean the oranges thoroughly

2 star-anise

1 cinnamon stick

500g, 1lb 2oz, centre piece of salmon fillet, skinned and pin boned

1. Whizz the sugar, salt, orange zest, star anise and cinnamon stick in a food processor. Tip over the salmon, cover with cling film and leave in the fridge for at least 24 hours.

2. Wash any remaining mixture off the salmon and leave to dry for 1 hour. Slice when needed.

This salmon is absolutely delicious on toasted sourdough bread with a bit of crème fraiche and some chopped chives.

Prawn and Fish Cakes – Thai-Style

Spicy and utterly delicious prawn and fish cakes which are perfect to serve as a starter or as part of a buffet!

They are quite easy and quick to make. I serve them with a chilli and fresh coriander (cilantro) sauce which is equally easy to make.

You can serve them on either a bed of rocket (arugula), which will add an extra peppery kick, or on a crunchy lettuce leave like cos lettuce.

Cooking-wise, either fry the Thai-style cakes in coconut oil first and then finish them off in the oven, or if you want to

185

save yourself the hassle of spluttering fat all over your cooker, only cook them in the oven. This is also a much healthier way of cooking.

Coconut fat is by far the healthiest fat to cook in and it will add a nice flavour to these little beauties. Here in Britain you can find coconut fat in health food stores and also in well-stocked supermarkets. It's not cheap but I think it is really worth investing in.

To make 16 small prawn and fish cakes with chilli sauce:

For the chilli sauce:

100ml, 3½floz, ½ cup, rice vinegar

2 teaspoons honey

1 red chilli, deseeded and finely chopped

A small handful of fresh coriander (cilantro), roughly chopped

For the cakes:

150g, 5½oz, raw salmon, chopped

300g, 10½oz raw peeled prawns

Half a small red onion, finely chopped

1 heaped teaspoon finely grated ginger

1 large red chilli, deseeded and finely chopped

Grated zest of an un-waxed lime, or use lemon

Handful of fresh coriander, stalk and leaves, chopped

1 tablespoon Thai fish sauce

¼ teaspoon black pepper

1.Preheat the oven to 200C/fan 180C/400F/gas mark 6.
Start by making the chilli sauce. Add the rice vinegar and
honey to a small pot, stir and bring to a boil. Let it boil quite
vigorously for about 4-5 minutes – until reduced by about
half. Take it off the heat and allow the vinegar to cool down
before adding the chopped chilli and coriander.

2.Place all the ingredients for the prawn and fish cakes in a
food processor and pulse for a short time until you have a
chunky mixture – it should not be too fine.

3.With your hands, form 16 small flat cakes. Cover a baking
tray with baking parchment. You can either brown the cakes
first by frying them quickly over a medium-high heat and
then place them on the baking tray, or put them directly on
the tray and brush them with a bit of coconut oil.

4.If you have browned them first they will need about 3-4
minutes in the oven, if not than leave them in the oven for
about 5-6 minutes.

Serve on lettuce leaves and drizzle over some of the sauce.

Pan-Fried Salmon with Anchovy and Walnut Vinaigrette

Yummy! If you are looking for a dish that is tasty, healthy and relatively quick to cook, try this pan-fried salmon dish.

Depending on your appetite, you could either serve this with some tomatoes, or with some toasted sourdough or other good bread with a tomato topping.

I dry-fry the walnuts over a medium high heat for 2-3 minutes before chopping them up, but you don't have to do that.

PS! I use tenderstem broccoli (broccolini) in this recipe. This type of broccoli is by far the richest source of glucosinolates - one of the most important anti-cancer and liver-friendly nutrients found in food. Glucosinolates are also found in broccoli, Brussels sprouts and other cruciferous vegetables.

For 4 people:

Vinaigrette:

4 anchovy fillets (I buy anchovy fillets in olive oil), finely chopped

1 garlic clove, finely chopped

2 tablespoons olive oil

Zest of 1 un-waxed lemon

Handful of parsley leaves, finely chopped

10 walnuts, chopped

Pepper

4 salmon fillets with skin

200g, 7oz, fine green beans

300g, 10½oz, tenderstem broccoli (broccolini)

Salt and pepper

Lemon juice

1.Start by making the vinaigrette. Bash the chopped anchovy and garlic in a pestle and mortar into a paste. Add the olive oil, lemon zest, parsley, chopped walnuts and season with a bit of black pepper. Stir it all together.

2.Put a pan with some salted water on to boil for the vegetables. Add a bit of oil to a frying pan over a medium-high heat. Season the salmon fillets with salt and pepper and place them - skin-side down - in the pan and cook for about

4 minutes - until the skin is crisp. Turn the fillets and cook for a further 2-3 minutes or until just cooked.

3.While the salmon is frying, add the green beans to the pan with simmering water. Boil for 2 ½ minutes, then add the tenderstem broccoli (broccolini) to the pan as well and simmer for a further 2 ½ minutes. Drain the beans and broccoli and return to the pan. Add the vinaigrette to the vegetables and toss until all the vegetables are coated with the vinaigrette.

4.Divide the beans and tenderstem broccoli (broccolini) between 4 plates and top with the pan-fried salmon fillets. Squeeze a bit of lemon juice over each portion.

Lime-Marinated Salmon with Mango Chutney Sauce

A sensationally tasty lime-marinated salmon dish which is perfect to serve as part of a buffet, or as a meal served with an avocado and tomato mixed salad. You can serve it warm or cold.

I have served this salmon - together with other dishes - on numerous buffets that I've made for different clients and there has a never been a scrap of salmon left, no matter how much I've made.

The mango chutney sauce that accompanies the salmon is a complete taste-sensation! Totally and utterly gorgeous!

As well as serving this lime-marinated salmon with a mixed salad, I often serve the salmon with a warm lemon and garlic infused potato salad (see recipe below).

You don't hear me mentioning potatoes often. This is not because I don't like them – Swedish people in general are crazy about potatoes - but because I believe it's better to swap potatoes for more nutritious root vegetables. And let's face it - it's not a good idea to indulge in things like potato salad if you are watching your weight.

My potato salad is a light-weight version though, with very little fat added. With a meal like this it is portion control that matters if you are watching your weight – less of the divine sauce and potato salad and more of the salmon and fresh salad.

Tip: To get more juice out a lime, press down on the lime with you hand and roll it back and forth on a chopping board for about a minute before cutting it in half

For 6 people as a meal, or for 10 people as part of a buffet:

Half a salmon, approximately 1½ kilo, 3-3½ pound, skin left on, pin-boned (you can ask the fishmonger to do this)

Marinade:

2 tablespoons sunflower oil

The juice from 1½ lime – grate the zest of 1 lime first and save this for the sauce

2 fat garlic cloves, crushed

2 tablespoons finely chopped parsley leaves

1 teaspoon fresh thyme leaves

Grated zest from 1 lemon

1/2 teaspoon pepper

1 teaspoon salt

1.Preheat the oven to 200C/fan 180C/400F/gas mark 6. Put the salmon - skin side down - in an oven-proof dish lined with baking parchment. Mix the ingredients for the marinade and brush it over the salmon. Leave to marinate at room temperature for 20 minutes.

2.Make the mango chutney sauce (see below) while the salmon is marinating.

3.Place the lime-marinated salmon in the oven and roast uncovered for about 18 minutes, a few minutes less if the salmon is quite thin. Check with a knife to see if the salmon is ready – it should still be slightly translucent in the middle.

Lime and mango chutney sauce:

500ml, 18floz, 2½ cups, crème fraîche, or use natural yogurt

Grated zest from 1 lime

2 spring onions (scallions), sliced

100ml, 3½floz, ½ cup, mango chutney

2 tablespoons finely chopped parsley leaves

A pinch of salt and pepper

Simply mix all the ingredients for the sauce and leave to the side.

For the potato salad:

500g, 1lb 2oz, 3¼ cups, small salad/new potatoes, cut in half

2 tablespoons chopped parsley leaves

1 garlic clove, crushed

Grated zest from 1 lemon

1 tablespoon light crème fraiche

Salt and pepper

Mix the chopped parsley, lemon zest, crushed garlic, light crème fraîche and some salt and pepper in a medium-sized bowl. Boil the potatoes and once cooked and drained, toss them in this mix while still warm.

Massaman Prawn Curry

I love using prawns in a curry. This is a Thai-style Massaman prawn curry.

It might seem like a lot of ingredients but it's not difficult to make this curry, and it doesn't take a long time either. Making your curries from scratch – rather than using ready-made pastes - is much tastier and healthier.

You can make the sauce well in advance. The last time I made this curry for friends, I made the sauce the day before. It only takes a few minutes to finish this dish once the sauce is done.

Tip: You can use firm white fish – cut into bite-size chunks - instead of prawns, or chicken. If you are using chicken, then choose chicken thighs as breast meat dries out quite easily. Add sliced skinless and boneless chicken thighs to the sauce first and simmer for 10 minutes before adding the sugar snaps. Once you've added the sugar snaps, simmer for a further couple of minutes.

Massaman Prawn Curry for 4 people:

Massaman curry paste:

2 teaspoons coriander (cilantro) seeds

1 teaspoon cumin seeds

2 star-anise

4 cardamom pods - left whole while roasting then split open and seeds removed for grinding once cooled down

3 cloves

¼ teaspoon black pepper corns

½ teaspoon ground cinnamon

3 teaspoons grated fresh ginger

4 garlic cloves, finely chopped

2 large red chillies, de-seeded and chopped

2 lemongrass stalks - cut off the thinner top, leaving you with the "bulb" at the bottom, discard the tough outer layer, cut the "bulb" in half and slice finely

The stalks from a handful of fresh coriander (cilantro) – remove the leaves and save them

1 heaped teaspoon shrimp paste (a lot of supermarkets sell it, or find it at Asian grocers)

Zest of 1 lime

1 teaspoon honey

2 tablespoons water

For the sauce:

2 tablespoons coconut oil

2 shallots, peeled and finely chopped

All the curry paste (see above)

4 ripe, medium-sized tomatoes (or use 12-14 cherry tomatoes) diced

400ml, 13½floz, 1¾ cups, coconut milk

150 ml, 5floz, ¾ cup, water

1 ½ tablespoon fish sauce

20 – 24 large peeled raw prawns

150g, 5½oz, ¾ cup, sugar snaps, slice

1 tablespoon lime juice

1.Start by dry-roasting the coriander and cumin seeds, star anise, cardamom pods, cloves and black pepper corns in a frying pan over a medium high heat for 1-2 minutes until the spices start to become aromatic and a few shades darker. Once cooled down, split open the cardamom pods and place the seeds together with the other roasted spices in a pestle and mortar. Grind to a fine powder. Once done, mix in the ground cinnamon.

2.Place the spice-mix and all the other ingredients for the Massaman paste in a small food processor and whiz to a paste. You can use a stick blender as well – place all the ingredients for the paste in a high, quite narrow bowl and use the stick blender to make a paste.

3.Heat the oil in a large frying pan or a wok over a medium heat. Add the chopped shallots to the pan and fry for about 5 minutes – stirring frequently - until soft but not browned. Add all of the paste to the pan and stir-fry for 2 minutes before adding the diced tomatoes. Continue to stir and cook for a further 10 minutes – until the tomatoes collapse – then add the coconut milk, water and fish sauce. Bring to a simmer and simmer for 10 minutes.

4.You can, as I've said, prepare this well in advance. Let the sauce cool down, cover and store in the fridge Once you're ready to finish off the Massaman prawn curry, get the sauce simmering again and add the prawns and sliced sugar snaps and simmer for about 3 minutes, until the prawns are pink and cooked through. Add the lime juice and coriander leaves to the curry before serving.

Prawn Noodle Stir-Fry

Easy to make and so delicious – this prawn noodle stir-fry is a pure delight!

The recipe that inspired me (I made some changes to it) comes from an article in a Telegraph magazine, where Rose Prince wrote about sustainable prawn farms in Sumatra.

"Mainstream tropical prawn farming is acknowledged as an environmental catastrophe, with the precarious eco system of the mangrove forests on the coast destroyed to make way for ponds. Prawns are densely packed in the water (up to 150 per cubic meter) and attract disease, so the water is routinely medicated."

I love prawns but I buy sustainably farmed ones – even though they are undoubtedly more expensive. I'd rather eat less of the good stuff than a truckload of adulterated cheaply produced food!

I use fewer chillies in my dishes than you'd find in original south-east Asian food. I don't want them to obliterate the taste of the other ingredients in whatever dish I'm cooking.

Regarding noodles: I am using thin wheat-free soba noodles in this stir-fry. They are the healthiest type of noodles but not usually used in stir-fries. Soba noodles are made from buckwheat flour and become very soft and quite fragile once cooked – they break up very easily when tossed in a stir-fry.

You can use rice or egg noodles instead of soba noodles.

For 4 people:

For the sauce:

5 medium-sized ripe tomatoes, chopped

4 cloves of garlic, finely chopped

3 shallots, finely chopped

2-3 large red chillies, deseeded and finely chopped

Thumb-sized piece of ginger, peeled and finely chopped

2 lemongrass stalks - cut off the thinner top, leaving you with the "bulb" at the bottom, discard tough outer layer, cut off the bottom of the "bulb", halve it and slice very finely

Grated zest of 1 lime

1 level teaspoon runny honey

½ tablespoon fish sauce

1 ½ tablespoon groundnut or vegetable oil

16 large prawns, peeled

200g, 7oz, egg or soba noodles, cooked according to pack instructions

To serve:

4 spring onions (scallions), sliced

Juice of a lime

1.Mix together the chopped tomatoes, garlic, shallots, chillies, ginger, lemongrass, lime zest, honey and fish sauce. Heat the oil in a wok or high-sided frying pan over quite a high heat. Add the sauce mixture to the wok or pan and fry until you have a thick puree, about 8-10 minutes.

2.Add the prawns and continue to fry for a further minute – until the prawns are pink - before adding the cooked noodles. Toss everything together and fry for a further 30 seconds, until everything is piping hot.

3.Add the lime juice and spring onions (scallions) to the prawn noodle stir-fry before serving.

Marinated Mackerel Fillets

While I love mackerel fried in nothing but a bit of butter, this fish can handle the heat of spices. This is a recipe for utterly tasty marinated mackerel fillets.

Mackerels are loaded with super-healthy Omega 3 fats, the type of fats that our brains and bodies depend upon.

Oily fish is the best source of omega 3 and mackerel is pretty much at the top of fish rich in Omega 3.

My only problem with mackerel is that unless I can manage to buy really fresh ones, I'm not that fond of them. This is not a type of fish that you should buy and leave in the fridge for a day or two.

My dream scenario is eating them more or less as soon as they are out of the sea – which luckily I've been able to do at times.

You can serve these marinated mackerel fillets with citrus-infused couscous.

Marinade:

1 teaspoon fennel seeds

1 teaspoon cumin seeds

1 teaspoon coriander seeds

Thumb-size piece of fresh ginger – finely grated

1 fat garlic clove, crushed

Grated zest and juice of 1 un-waxed lime

1½ tablespoon olive oil

A good pinch of cayenne pepper

Salt and pepper

4 -6 mackerel fillets (depending on size), with the skin left on and pin-boned

(To pin-bone filleted fish, run your fingers over the surface of the fillet to locate the ends of the bones. Use pliers or tweezers to pull out the bones.)

2 tablespoons rapeseed oil (canola oil) or vegetable oil

1.Dry-fry the fennel, cumin and coriander seeds in a frying pan over a medium heat for about a minute – stirring frequently – until fragrant. Place the roasted seeds in a pestle and mortar and grind to a coarse powder.

2.In a bowl, mix together the ground seeds with all the other ingredients for the marinade. Place the mackerel fillets flesh-side up on a plate and divide the marinade over the fillets. Leave to marinate for 10 minutes.

3.Add the oil to a large non-stick frying pan over a high heat. When the oil is really hot, place 2 mackerel fillets - skin-side down - in the pan. Fry the fillets for about 1 – 1½ minute, until the skin is nicely browned and crisp. Carefully turn the fillets over and fry for a further minute. Remove the fillets and keep them warm while frying the remaining fillets.

Asian-Style Trout

My kind of food, an Asian-style trout dish which is super-delicious, mega-healthy and - although rich in essential fats - kind to your waist-line.

Where do I begin? Well, trout is an oily fish which is rich in Omega 3 - an essential type of fat which in very good for your health.

I am also sprinkling sesame seeds over the finished dish. Sesame seeds are rich in Omega 6 – the other type of essential fat that we need to keep healthy.

I'm serving the fish with oven-roasted butternut squash and sweet potatoes. Both are full of healthy nutrients – including the powerful antioxidant beta-carotene – but for the sake of your waist-line, you are better off eating more of the butternut squash and less of the sweet potato.

As I want a part of any meal I serve to consist of raw as well as green vegetables, I also serve this Asian-style trout dish with spinach, watercress and rocket (arugula) leaves. It's a good idea to eat lots of these extremely healthy and very low-calorie leaves!

I sprinkle hemp oil infused with lemon zest – super-Yum - over the leaves and scatter chopped chives over the whole dish.

Hemp oil is also a rich source of Omega 3 – I buy a hemp seed oil called "Good Oil" which you can find in some of the supermarkets here in the UK. If you can't find it, you can use olive oil instead.

Asian-style trout for 4 people:

1 small butternut squash, cut into 8 wedges

2 medium-sized sweet potatoes, halved

A little bit of oil

Marinade for the trout:

2 heaped teaspoons finely grated ginger

2 garlic cloves, crushed

1 large red or green chilli, finely chopped

1 tablespoon light soya sauce

Juice of ½ orange

Juice of 1 lime

1 teaspoon honey

A little bit of salt and pepper

4 trout fillets – you can use salmon instead of trout

1 ½ tablespoon hemp oil (or use olive oil)

Grated zest of an un-waxed lemon

Spinach, watercress, rocket (arugula) leaves

2 tablespoons sesame seeds

3 tablespoons chopped chives

1.Pre-heat the oven to 220C/fan 200C/425F/gas mark 7. Place the butternut squash wedges and sweet potato halves on an oven tray lined with baking parchment. Brush the vegetables with a bit of oil and season with some salt and pepper. Place the tray in the oven and roast the vegetables for about 40 minutes.

2.In a small bowl, mix together the hemp oil and grated lemon zest and leave to the side.

3.Mix together all of the ingredients for the marinade. Place the trout fillets in an oven-proof dish lined with baking parchment. Divide the marinade over the fish and leave to marinate for 10 minutes before placing the dish in the oven. Bake the fish for about 10 minutes.

4.Serve the trout and roasted vegetables with lots of green leaves – divide any left-over marinade over the fish and roasted vegetables. Sprinkle the lemon infused oil over the green leaves and scatter sesame seeds and chopped chives over each portion.

Salmon and Noodles in an Asian-Style Broth

I was trying out new recipes the other day and came up with this salmon and noodles dish - it's a dish with lots of flavour.

And it's good for you, and light.

I am using thin wheat-free soba noodles in this dish. They are made from buckwheat flour (gluten and wheat free) and are the healthiest type of noodles – but you can use egg noodles instead if you prefer that.

I am also using an organic Japanese Tamari soya sauce (gluten and wheat free as well). If you can't get hold of tamari soya sauce, use a light soya sauce instead. And to continue this effort to use the best ingredients possible, I'm using raw organic honey for the marinade.

If you want more heat, you can sprinkle some chopped fresh chillies over each portion of this salmon and noodle dish.

For 4 people:

Marinade:

2 tablespoons mirin (sweetened rice wine – you'll find it among Asian food in most well-stocked supermarkets)

2 tablespoons Tamari soya sauce, or use light soya sauce

1 level teaspoon honey

3 teaspoons finely grated fresh ginger

Black pepper

4 salmon fillets

For the broth:

1litre, 1¾ pints, 4½ cups, fish stock

4 garlic cloves, finely chopped

2 lemongrass stalks (or use finely grated lemon zest from 1 lemon) - cut off the thinner top, leaving you with the "bulb" at the bottom, discard tough outer layer, cut off the bottom of the "bulb", halve it and slice very finely

2 tablespoons fish sauce

1 large carrot, cut into matchstick-sized batons

2 handfuls of green beans, trimmed and halved lengthways

12 tenderstem broccoli stalks (broccolini), sliced

200g, 7oz, soba or egg noodles

To serve:

2 tablespoons toasted sesame seeds

Fresh coriander, chopped

Optional: 1–2 red chillies, deseeded and chopped

1.Mix together the ingredients for the marinade. Place the salmon in a dish and pour over the marinade. Turn to coat several times. Leave to the side.

2.Toast the sesame seeds for about a minute in a dry frying pan over a medium heat – stirring frequently to make sure the seeds don't burn. Leave to the side.

3.Add water to a large pot and get it boiling for the noodles. Place the fish stock in another pot and add the chopped garlic, lemon grass and fish sauce. Bring to a simmer.

4.Cook the noodles according to the instructions on the packet, drain and refresh under fresh water.

5.Add the salmon fillets and all of the marinade to the pot with the stock - cover the pot with a lid and simmer for 3 minutes. Add the vegetables to the pot, cover with the lid and continue to simmer for a further 2-3 minutes, until the salmon is cooked.

6.Divide the noodles between four bowls. Carefully lift out the salmon and place one fillet on top of the noodles in each bowl. Give the vegetables a stir. Divide the vegetables and broth between the bowls and top each portion with toasted sesame seeds, chopped coriander and, if you are using it, chopped chilli.

Spanish-Style Prawns in a Tomato Sherry Sauce

It's both quite easy and quick to make these Spanish-style prawns (shrimps). The smoky-hot tomato-sherry sauce is so delicious and would go just as well with fried scallops.

This dish can be served as a starter – or as part of a tapas-style meal. It can also be served as a main meal with for example rice or quinoa and steamed or boiled green vegetables (sugar snaps/green beans/broccoli).

If you are using prawns you can either fry the prawns separately and serve with the sauce, or simply cook the prawns in the sauce once it is ready. Scallops though, are better fried.

You can use dry white wine instead of dry sherry for the tomato sauce.

Spanish-style prawns for 4 people:

1 tablespoon olive oil

½ medium-sized red onion, finely chopped

2 garlic cloves, crushed

1 large red chilli, deseeded and finely chopped

¼ - ½ teaspoon smoked sweet paprika (it is a dominant spice, but I like it and use ½ teaspoon in this recipe)

100ml, 3½floz, ½ cup, dry sherry (or use dry white wine)

400g, 14oz, 1¾ cups tin/can chopped/crushed tomatoes

1 tablespoon sun-dried tomato puree/paste, or use plain tomato purée

1 teaspoon fresh thyme – leaves only – or use ½ teaspoon dried thyme

50ml, 2floz, ¼ cup water

Salt and pepper

400g, 14oz, raw shelled prawns (shrimps), or scallops

1.Place the oil in a pot over a medium-high heat. Add the chopped onion and cook – stirring frequently – for about 5 minutes. Add the garlic, chilli and smoked sweet paprika to the pot and continue to cook for a further minute.

2.Add the sherry to the pot, increase the heat and bring to a vigorous boil for 3-4 minutes, until the sherry has been reduced by about half.

3.Add all the remaining ingredients, season with a bit of salt and pepper, stir and bring to a simmer. Leave the sauce to simmer – without a lid – for about 15 minutes, until it has thickened a bit. Taste to see if you need to add any more salt and/or pepper.

4.If you are using prawns, season the prawns with some salt and pepper and either fry them in 1 tablespoon of oil for about 1½ minute – turning them over half-way through – or add them to the sauce and simmer for about 2-3 minutes. If you are using scallops, season the scallops with some salt and pepper and fry them in 1 tablespoon of oil for about 1 minute on each side – taking care not to over-cook them.

Scallops with Spicy Mash and a Tomato Salsa

I think this dish is a showstopper – succulent large scallops with spicy mash (I use sweet potatoes for the mash) and a tomato salsa with attitude.

And hooray, it's good for you too! This is the way I like my food – massively tasty and healthy as well.

Scallops are low in calories and rich in vitamins and zinc, a very important mineral which is needed - among other things - to make insulin and to boost the immune system.

Apart from the tomato salsa, I serve these scallops with spicy mash with steamed tenderstem broccoli (broccolini) – which is super-healthy – and green beans.

You can swap the sweet potatoes for pumpkin or butternut squash, or use a mixture of them.

Talking about health and much vilified salt – I have started to use unrefined and mineral-rich Himalayan rose pink salt which according to many is the healthiest type of salt. It is a bit expensive, to be sure, but I find that I can use much less salt and still get the same result. It's a winner to me.

For 4 people:

800g, 1lb12oz, sweet potatoes, peeled and diced

1 tablespoon olive oil

½ teaspoon dried chilli flakes

Salt and pepper

Tomato salsa:

1 tablespoon olive oil

1 small red onion, finely chopped

2 garlic cloves, finely chopped

1 heaped teaspoon finely grated fresh ginger

½ tablespoon red wine vinegar

250g, 9oz, ripe small tomatoes (like cherry or plum), quartered

Salt and pepper

3 spring onion (scallions), chopped

A small handful of fresh coriander (cilantro) chopped

12-16 large scallops, dried on kitchen paper before frying

1.Pre-heat the oven to 200C/fan180C/400F/gas mark 6. Place the diced sweet potato, oil and chilli flakes in an oven-proof dish and toss together. Season with some salt and pepper. Place the dish in the oven and cook for about 30 minutes – giving the potatoes a stir mid-way through – until soft.

2.While the sweet potatoes are in the oven, add 1 tablespoon olive oil to a sauce pan over a low heat. Add the onion, garlic and ginger to the pan and stir and cook for 5 minutes. Add the red wine vinegar and the tomatoes, season with some salt and pepper and increase the heat a little. Simmer for about 10 minutes.

3.Use a potato masher to roughly mash the sweet potatoes. Mix in the chopped spring onions (scallions).

4.Add some olive oil to a frying pan over a medium high heat. When the oil is hot, place the dried scallops in the pan, season with a pinch of salt and pepper and fry for about 45 seconds–1 minute on each side. Remove from the heat.

5.Add the chopped coriander (cilantro) to the salsa. Divide the mash between 4 plates, top with the scallops and a big dollop of tomato salsa. Serve immediately.

Fish Tagine

Never mind the length of the ingredient list, this super-tasty fish tagine is relatively quick to make.

But if you have the time, make the sauce well in advance. This will intensify the flavours and you can finish off the dish – by adding the fish and peas to the re-heated sauce - really quickly once you are ready to eat.

Serve the tagine with couscous or quinoa – and make either of them more interesting by adding finely grated zest of lemon and/or lime, chopped spring onion (scallion) and thinly sliced celery.

I only use wholemeal (whole-wheat) couscous. This is about taste just as much as health. Wholemeal couscous taste so much more than refined couscous which, let's face it, has virtually no taste at all.

I have bought wholemeal couscous in supermarkets but the tastiest kind by far that I have ever bought is Infinity Foods Organic Wholemeal couscous. I found it in a health food shop.

Preserved lemons are sold in well-stocked supermarkets but if you can't find it there, look for it in shops where they sell Middle Eastern food.

Fish tagine for 4 people:

1½ tablespoon olive oil

3 shallots, finely chopped

2 fat garlic cloves, crushed/minced

2 heaped teaspoons finely grated fresh ginger

1 teaspoon ground coriander (cilantro)

1 teaspoon ground cumin

½ teaspoon ground paprika

¾ teaspoon fennel seeds, ground to a powder in a pestle and mortar

¼ teaspoon ground turmeric

A good pinch of saffron strands

1 heaped tablespoon tomato purée

600ml, 20floz, 2½ cups, fish stock

1 preserved lemon, halved, deseeded and finely chopped

Salt and pepper

600g, 1lb 5½oz, firm white fish – like haddock or cod – cut into large chunks

150g, 5½oz, 1 cup, frozen peas

Handful of fresh coriander (cilantro), chopped

1.Heat the olive oil in a casserole over a low heat. Add the shallots, garlic, ginger and all the spices – including the saffron – to the casserole. Stir and cook for about 7 minutes, until the chopped shallots are soft.

2.Add the tomato puree, fish stock, chopped preserved lemon and season with salt and pepper. Bring the sauce to a simmer. Let it simmer for 10 minutes. Taste and check the seasoning!

3.Add the fish to the sauce. Cover the casserole with a lid and simmer for 5 minutes. Remove the lid, add the peas and let it all come back to simmer for 1 minute. Scatter over the chopped coriander (cilantro) before serving.

Rolled Crepes Canapes

If you are looking for recipes for tasty canapes, try these rolled crepes canapes – they are delicious.

I make two types of rolled crepes – one with smoked salmon and one with smoked ham.

The way you make crepes, very thin pancakes, is the way we make pancakes in Sweden. Compared to pancake recipes from most other countries, Swedish pancakes contain much more eggs and none more so than the sublime pancakes my mother used to make.

I follow in her footsteps and use a lot of eggs when making pancakes, 3-4 eggs. And for these crepes that I use as savoury canapés, I add chopped spring onions (scallions) to the batter.

To make the rolled crepes canapes:

For the crepes:

3 large eggs - or 4 medium-sized eggs

120g, 4oz, 0.9 cup, plain flour

350ml, 12floz, 1½ cups full-fat milk

½ teaspoon salt

3 spring onions (scallions), finely chopped

1 tablespoon butter + some more for frying

For the smoked salmon filling:

100g, 3½oz, ½ cup, cream cheese

1 tablespoon horseradish sauce

150g, 5½oz, smoked salmon

For the smoked ham filling:

100g, 3½oz, ½ cup, cream cheese

½ tablespoon horseradish sauce

½ tablespoon grainy French mustard

200g, 7oz, smoked ham (I use German-style smoked ham)

1.Crack the eggs into a bowl and add the flour, salt and 1/3 of the milk. Whisk vigorously – best thing to use is an electric whisk – until you have a lump-free batter. Add the rest of the milk and whisk a bit more. Add the chopped spring onions (scallions) to the batter. Cover and leave to rest in the fridge for 30 minutes.

2.Melt 1 tablespoon butter in a large frying pan and add the melted butter to the pancake batter whilst whisking. You only need to use a small amount of butter, ¼ of a teaspoon, for frying each pancake.

3.The frying pan needs to be quite hot and the butter should be turning brown before adding a small ladle of pancake batter to the pan. Swirl the pan around to cover the entire base of the frying pan. Each pancake should be quite thin but not so thin that they fall apart.

4.Fry for about one minute, until you can see that it's nicely browned (just lift up a corner), before carefully flipping the pancake over. Fry for another minute. Transfer to a plate. I place a piece of baking parchment between each pancake so that they don't stick together. Leave the pancakes to cool down.

For the fillings, mix together cream cheese and horseradish sauce for the salmon filling, and the cream cheese, horseradish sauce and mustard for the ham filling.

Spread some of either filling across the lower part of one pancake and add slices of salmon or ham. Spread a little bit of the filling at the very top of the pancake and roll up the crepe tightly.

Cut of untidy ends and alternating between diagonal and straight cuts, cut the rolled up crepe into about 5-6 slices (depending on how large you made your pancakes).

Prawn and Fish Laksa

I have cooked many British types of comfort food at work. This prawn and fish laksa though, is what I would call Asian-style comfort food.

This is my cup of tea, the kind of comfort food that I prefer. I absolutely love it!

I am making my own type of laksa paste. It is not difficult to do and once it is done, the rest of the dish doesn't take very long to cook.

And as rich and creamy as it may look, this is quite a low-calorie recipe. The only fat I'm using here is coconut fat –

both a bit of coconut oil and coconut milk. Coconut fat is a very nutritious type of fat which can help to promote weight loss and which won't raise cholesterol levels.

I am serving my prawn and fish laksa without any noodles (fewer calories that way). I add a fair amount of chopped red peppers (bell peppers) and sliced sugar snaps or mange tout instead and top it all with sliced spring onions and coriander.

But you can of course add any noodles of your choice.

Tip: Coconut oil is by far the healthiest type of fat to cook your food in. It is sold in most health food shops. I use it every time I cook Asian-style food. Unless it's very warm, coconut oil is actually solid.

For 4 people:

Laksa paste:

3 shallots, chopped

3 garlic cloves, finely chopped

Thumb-size piece of ginger, finely chopped

2 lemongrass stalks - cut off the thinner top, leaving you with the "bulb" at the bottom, discard tough outer layer, cut off the bottom of the "bulb", halve it and slice very finely

2 large red chillies, deseeded and finely chopped

2 teaspoons shrimp paste (you can find it in well-stocked super markets or shops specialising in Asian food)

1 teaspoon each of ground coriander (cilantro), cumin, sweet paprika and turmeric

4 tablespoons coconut oil – or replace with 3 tablespoons vegetable or groundnut oil

For the broth:

500ml, 18floz, 2.2 cups, fish stock

400ml, 14½floz, 1¾ cups coconut milk

1 teaspoon honey (I use raw Manuka honey)

1 tablespoon fish sauce

500g, 1lb2oz, firm white fish, cut into bite-size pieces

200g, 7oz, peeled raw large prawns, de-veined

2-3 tablespoons fresh lime juice

To serve:

2 handfuls of sugar snaps/mange tout – add to a pan with some boiling water and cook for 2 minutes, sieve off the water and slice

1 red pepper (bell pepper), chopped

3 spring onions (scallions), sliced

Handful of fresh coriander (cilantro), chopped

1.Place all the ingredients for the paste in a food processor and blitz until you've got a smooth paste. Place the paste in a medium-sized pan over a moderate heat and stir and cook the paste for about 2 minutes.

2.Add the fish stock, coconut milk and fish sauce to the pot, bring to a simmer and simmer for 10 minutes.

3.Add the prawns and fish to the pot. Bring back to a simmer and cook for about 3 minutes, until the prawns are cooked through and the fish is cooked. Add the lime juice to the pot.

4.Divide the prawn and fish laksa between 4 bowls and top with the vegetables.

Salmon and Quinoa Kedgeree

My salmon and quinoa kedgeree is not only incredibly tasty, it is also healthier and less calorific than a more traditional kedgeree.

I am using lightly smoked salmon fillets, which are easy to find in the U.K. You can replace them with plain salmon if you can't get hold of the lightly smoked version, or use the more traditional undyed smoked haddock.

Fish in general is good for you, but oily fish like salmon and mackerel contain much more, super-healthy omega-3 essential fats. You could also use smoked mackerel for this kedgeree – which doesn't need any further cooking.

I poach the lightly smoked salmon in plain water as it is tasty enough on its own. If you are using plain salmon, poach it in fish stock.

Refined white rice has been stripped of most nutrients and has a similar effect on your blood sugar as plain sugar has.

Quinoa, on the other hand, is a proper super food. It is rich in vitamins, minerals and essential fats, contains protein of a better quality than that of meat and also contains slow-releasing carbohydrates – which is all good news for your waistline!

Salmon and quinoa kedgeree for 4 people:

4 eggs, organic or free-range

250g, 9oz, 1¼ cup, quinoa

600ml, 20floz, 2¾ cups, water

1½ tablespoon coconut oil, or use olive oil

2 shallots, or a small yellow onion, finely chopped

1 heaped teaspoon ground coriander

1 heaped teaspoon ground cumin

1 level teaspoon turmeric

¼ teaspoon chilli flakes

Salt and pepper

400g lightly smoked salmon fillets

A handful of watercress, or rocket (arugula) leaves, roughly chopped

1.Start by boiling the eggs – for about 6-7 minutes. Rinse under cold water to stop them cooking any further, peel and leave to the side.

2.Rinse the quinoa under plenty of cold water. Get the water boiling in a pot, add the quinoa and stir. Lower the heat and simmer for 15 minutes. Add some water to another pot (for the salmon) and bring to simmer.

3.Place the oil and the chopped onion in a frying pan over a low heat. Gently fry the onion for about 7 minutes, making sure the onion doesn't burn. Add the spices to the frying pan, season with salt and pepper and continue to cook for a further 3 minutes.

4.While the onion is cooking, place the salmon in the pot with the simmering water and poach for about 6 minutes. If you are using plain salmon, poach for 8-10 minutes. Remove the salmon from the water and place on a plate. Once it is cool enough to handle, break it up into flakes.

5.Once the quinoa has cooked, drain it in a colander and then tip it back into the pot. Stir in the spiced onions, the flaked salmon and chopped watercress (or rocket/arugula). Divide the salmon and quinoa kedgeree between 4 plates and top each portion with two egg halves.

Thai-Style Mussels

Had a bag of beautiful fresh local mussels – decided to use them to make Thai-style mussels. Yummy!

If you like mussels, you are in for a tasty and healthy treat. Mussels are rich in heart-healthy unsaturated omega-3 fats, the very important mineral zinc, vitamins and iron. It's health in shells!

And they are low in calories and yet filling.

The only type of fat I used when making these Thai-style mussels was coconut fat – coconut oil (for frying the vegetables) and coconut milk (for the broth). I am using full-fat coconut milk but you can swap this for a light version.

Coconut oil is the type of fat I mostly use for cooking all types of Asian-style food. The jury is still out on whether coconut fat can, as some claim, promote weight loss - and be good for your heart.

Going back to my gorgeous Scottish mussels – **the one Incredibly Important thing about mussels is to make sure that you are not using dead or damaged mussels as these can make you seriously sick.**

Go through each and every one. If a mussel is open, tap it lightly on the counter. It should close its' shell tightly, quite quickly. **Discard any that remain open plus any damaged ones.**

Pull off the beards of the mussels and using the back of a knife, scrape off any barnacles attached to the shells. Rinse under plenty of cold water.

Once the mussels are cooked, discard any mussel that has not opened its' shell.

Thai-style mussels for 4 people:

2 tablespoon coconut oil

2 shallots, finely chopped

2 garlic cloves, crushed

Thumb-size piece of fresh ginger – peeled and finely chopped

1-2 large red chillies, deseeded and finely chopped

1 kilo, 2¼lb, fresh mussels – cleaned as per above

1 teaspoon sesame oil

1 tablespoon Thai fish sauce

400ml, 13½floz, 1¾ cups coconut milk

Juice of a lime

2 spring onions (scallions), chopped – or use a good handful of fresh coriander (cilantro)

1.Add the coconut oil to a large pot over a low-medium heat. Place the chopped shallots in the pot and fry gently for about 5 minutes – making sure the onion doesn't burn.

2.Add the garlic, ginger and chilli to the pot and continue to fry for another couple of minutes. Place the mussels in the pot and cover the pot with a tight-fitting lid. Increase the heat a little bit and cook for 4-5 minutes – shaking the pot gently a couple of times – until the mussels have opened.

3.Remove the mussels from the pot – discarding any that have not opened – and leave to the side. Add the sesame oil, Thai fish sauce and coconut milk to the pot and bring to a simmer. Let the broth simmer for 3 minutes and then add the juice of a lime.

4.Turn of the heat and add the cooked mussels, spring onion (scallion) – or coriander (cilantro) – to the broth. Serve immediately.

Chicken Recipes

Marinated Chicken with Chilli, Coriander and Lime

It is easy to make this mega-tasty marinated chicken with chilli – and it becomes a really healthy, low-calorie meal if you combine it with oven-roasted sweet potatoes, tomatoes and either some steamed green vegetables or a salad.

I do use sweet potatoes a lot. Apart from that I love the taste of this vegetable, sweet potatoes are really nutritious. Just be aware though that sweet potatoes are rich in carbohydrates. They are best eaten in small amounts if you are watching your weight.

Tomatoes are healthier when cooked - a rare thing among vegetables – as cooking makes the super-nutrient lycopene in tomatoes more absorbable. I find that really tasty tomatoes baked in the oven replace the need for a sauce in many dishes.

When it comes to chicken, I prefer to use chicken thighs as the meat is so much more juicy and moist than chicken breast.

To make the marinade, I use my trusty, inexpensive stick blender and the beaker that came with it. I've got a fancy mini food processor/blender that doesn't work half as well for making something like this.

For 4 people:

Marinade:

1 large red chilli, deseeded and roughly chopped

2 garlic cloves, crushed

25g, 1oz, ¼ cup, coriander (cilantro) - leaves and stalks roughly chopped

3 teaspoons finely grated ginger

1 ½ teaspoon runny honey

2 tablespoons soy sauce

Juice of 1 lime

1 tablespoon groundnut or sunflower oil

Boneless and skinless chicken thighs – 1-2 per person depending on the size of the chicken thighs – trimmed and each thigh cut in half

4 medium-sized sweet potatoes, peeled and cut into bite-size pieces

20 small tomatoes

1. Preheat the oven 200C/fan180C/400F/gas mark 6. Place all the ingredients for the marinade in a blender and blend until everything is well combined. Cover an oven tray with baking parchment and place the chicken thighs flat on the tray. Smother the chicken with the marinade.

2. Toss the sweet potato chunks in a little bit of olive oil and spread them out in a roasting tray and sprinkle over some salt.

3. Place the tray with the sweet potatoes in the oven first and roast for 5 minutes. Add the tray with the marinated chicken to the oven and roast for a further 20 minutes – add the tomatoes for the last 10 minutes - until the chicken is completely cooked through and the sweet potato tender.

As I say in the beginning, to get as much nutritional value out of this meal as possible, serve this marinated chicken with chilli dish with some steamed/boiled green vegetables and/or a salad.

Chicken with Harissa and Squash Tagine

Bring on the flavours! This chicken with harissa dish is a full-flavoured stunner of a dish. And it's brimming with healthy, ingredients as well.

This is also a perfect dish to serve to meat-eaters and vegetarians at the same time. The chicken with harissa is cooked separately from the squash tagine, and there is left-over harissa for everyone to add to their portion of food.

You can buy ready-made harissa but I make my own. It's not difficult to make and it tastes so much better than supermarket varieties with their added preservatives and E-numbers.

If you want to go half-way, you can buy already roasted peppers in jars. The harissa can be made a day or two in advance.

For 4 people:

Roasted peppers (bell peppers) for the harissa:

2 large red peppers (bell peppers)

A dash of olive oil

Start by roasting 2 red peppers. Preheat the oven to 220C/ 425F/gas mark 7. Put the peppers into a roasting tray with a dash of olive oil and cook for 15 minutes, turning them from time to time, or until the skins blacken. Place the peppers into a bowl and cover with cling film. Set aside for 10-15 minutes, until the skin comes off easily. Break the peppers open, pull out and discard the stalks, pith and seed and peel off the skin. The roasted peppers will be used for the harissa. This can be made well in advance.

For the harissa:

2 roasted red peppers (bell peppers) (see above)

3 teaspoons tomato purée

2 teaspoons ground coriander (cilantro)

A good pinch of saffron strands

2-3 large red chillies (depending on how hot you like it to be - I use 2), deseeded and finely chopped

½ teaspoon salt

2 tablespoons olive oil

For the tagine:

2 tablespoons coconut oil - or use vegetable oil

1 red onion, finely chopped

2-3 teaspoons finely grated ginger

1 garlic clove, crushed/minced

1 large red chilli, deseeded and finely chopped

½ teaspoon ground cinnamon

1 level teaspoon turmeric

1 heaped teaspoon ground coriander (cilantro)

20 ripe small tomatoes – e.g. plum or cherry – halved

Salt and pepper

1 medium-sized butternut squash, peeled, deseeded and diced

1 large sweet potato, peeled and cut into bite-size chunks

500ml, 18floz, 2¼ cups, vegetable or chicken stock

A good pinch of saffron strands

2 large handfuls fresh spinach

400g, 14oz, 2½ cups, tin/can cooked chickpeas, rinsed

Boned and skinless chicken thighs, 1 - 2 thighs per person

1. If you are making your own harissa, start by roasting the peppers. Once they are ready, put all the ingredients into a food processor and process to a smooth paste. Unroll the chicken thighs and put them flat on a roasting tray covered with baking parchment. Spread about half of the harissa over the chicken thighs. Cover and leave the chicken with harissa

to marinate in the fridge. Turn on the oven to 200C/ 400F/ gas mark 6.

2. Add the saffron to the hot stock and leave to the side to infuse. Heat the oil in a large saucepan, add the onion, ginger, chilli and garlic to the pan and cook over a low heat for 5 minutes. Add the cinnamon, turmeric and ground coriander (cilantro), stir and cook for a further 2 minutes.

3. Add the chopped tomatoes, season with some salt and pepper, stir and cook for 5 minutes. Add the butternut squash and sweet potato and pour in the stock with saffron. Bring to the boil, then lower the heat, cover with a lid and gently simmer for about 20-25 minutes, until the butternut squash and sweet potato are soft.

4. While the tagine cooks, transfer the roasting tray with the harissa-covered chicken thighs to the oven and cook for 20-22 minutes, until the chicken is completely cooked through. If you are serving the chicken with harissa together with quinoa or couscous, get that cooking while the chicken is in the oven.

5. Just before serving, add the rinsed chickpeas and spinach to the squash tagine and heat through. Check the seasoning and serve with the extra harissa on the side.

Moroccan-Style Chicken

Out of all my chicken recipes, this Moroccan-style chicken dish is one of my favourites.

It's simply a winner in every way – bursting with near-intoxicating flavours yet light and low in calories.

On top of that, it's an excellent dish to prepare well in beforehand as the flavours simply intensify when resting.

I used to be a horrendous host when I was younger as I had prepared very little before my guests arrived. I would sit them down in the kitchen with a glass of wine and because I found it very hard to engage in conversation and cook at the same time - and I am a great talker - they sure had to wait before they got any food.

These days, if I've invited people over for a meal, I will serve something that I've cooked earlier and that only needs a few finishing touches once we're ready to eat.

And while I've done many a starter in my job as a cook, I do personally find it an outdated thing to have a sit-down three course dinner.

My advice to friends asking me for ideas is to simply have a platter with things to nibble on for your guests while you finish off a main course that has been prepared before.

I prefer to make the main course the main attraction, served with some side dishes, and most of the time will round of the meal with nothing but some really good chocolate. Champagne chocolate truffles, anyone?

Moroccan-style chicken casserole for 4 people:

A level teaspoon of saffron strands

400ml, 13½oz, 1¾ cup, chicken stock

2 tablespoons olive oil

1kg, 2¼lb, boneless and skinless chicken thighs

Salt and pepper

1 large onion, chopped

3 garlic cloves, crushed

Thumb-sized piece of fresh ginger, finely grated

1 teaspoon ground cumin

1 teaspoon ground coriander

1 teaspoon ground ginger

1 cinnamon stick

2-3 small preserved lemons, finely chopped

Small handful parsley or coriander (cilantro), chopped

1. Add the saffron to the stock and keep the stock warm in a small pan over a very low heat. Heat the olive oil in a casserole over a high heat and brown the chicken thighs in batches, seasoning each batch with salt and pepper and then setting each batch aside.

2. When you have browned all the chicken pieces, lower the heat and add the onion to the casserole, stirring every now and then, for 5 minutes. Add the garlic, fresh ginger and all the spices. Stir and cook for a further minute.

3. Return the chicken to the casserole together with the preserved lemon and pour over the saffron-infused stock. Bring to the boil then reduce the heat, cover with a lid and simmer for 25 minutes.

4. Check the seasoning and scatter over chopped parsley or coriander.

I serve this Moroccan-style chicken dish with either quinoa (best for your health and weight), or wholemeal (whole-wheat) couscous.

I start by marinating the chicken I use in this delicious chicken stir-fry – and I'm using kefir in the marinade.

Kefir is a fermented milk drink and like all fermented foods it can help to increase healthy bacteria in our bodies. If you can't find kefir though, you can use either buttermilk or full-fat Greek-style yogurt instead.

I'm also using another not so common ingredient in the marinade – sumac - which is a really lovely, citrusy spice derived from the red berries of the sumac shrub.

Again, if you can't get hold of it you can replace it with lemon juice.

I add roasted red peppers (bell peppers) to the marinade. You can buy roasted peppers in jars but I prefer to do it myself. Yes, it means more work but it's not difficult to do.

The chicken should preferably be marinated for a minimum of 3 hours – longer if you can.

Start by making the roasted peppers.

Pre-heat the oven to 220C/425F/gas mark 7. Cover a baking tray with baking parchment, place 2 large red peppers (I use pointed peppers) on the tray and place it in the oven. Roast for about 15 minutes – turning them over half-way through – until the skin blackens.

Once ready, place the roasted peppers in a bowl and cover with cling film. Set aside for 10-15 minutes, until the skin comes off easily. Break open the peppers, pull out and discard the stalk, pith and seeds and peel off the skin.

For the marinade:

2 roasted red peppers, chopped

2 red chillies, de-seeded and chopped

2 fat garlic cloves, crushed/minced

1 teaspoon ground cumin

1 teaspoon ground ginger

1 teaspoon sumac – or use 1 tablespoon lemon juice

1 teaspoon sea salt

½ teaspoon black pepper

1 teaspoon honey

2 tablespoons olive oil

150ml, 5floz, 0.7 cup Kefir (or use buttermilk or full-fat natural yogurt)

4 chicken breasts, each sliced into thin strips

Place all the ingredients for the marinade in a blender and whizz for about 30 seconds. Put the marinade in a non-metallic bowl and add the sliced chicken. Mix well, cover the bowl with cling film and place it in the fridge for a minimum of 3hours.

For the chicken stir-fry

1 tablespoon olive oil

1 red onion, halved and thinly sliced

2 medium carrots, cut into matchsticks

4 spring onions (scallions), thinly sliced

The marinated chicken + all the marinade

1.Add 1 tablespoon of olive oil to either a wok or large frying pan over a high heat. Once the oil is hot, add the sliced onion and carrots to the pan and keep stirring for a couple of minutes. Place the vegetables in a bowl and leave to the side.

2.Fry the marinated chicken, and all of the marinade, in batches for about 3-4 minutes until the chicken slices are cooked through (don't over-crowd the pan as this will make the chicken cook slower). Place each batch in the bowl with the vegetables until you have fried all the chicken slices.

3.Place everything back in the wok/frying pan and add the sliced spring onion (scallion). Stir for another minute until all the food is piping hot.

This chicken stir-fry goes really well with cauliflower rice, or simply add sliced broccoli as well as the onion and carrots to the stir-fry.

Tarragon Chicken with Vermouth Sauce

Chicken and tarragon – a match made in heaven! This tarragon chicken dish with a Vermouth sauce is a real crowd-pleaser.

I tend to mostly use chicken thighs when making this dish as the thigh meat is so much more tender and moist. But at times I've used the breast as well and if you do, you have just got to be more careful so the meat doesn't end up being dry.

To me, this is festive food and ultimately a bit more calorific than most things I cook. I like to serve it with rice and vegetables like oven-roasted tomatoes, sugar snaps, green beans and broccoli.

And the way I exercise calorie control with food like this is to load up on the vegetables and eat them before I even allow my cutlery near this gorgeous tarragon chicken dish.

For 4 people:

8 boneless and skinless chicken thighs, trimmed and each thigh cut in half, or 4 chicken breasts, each chicken breast cut into 5 even-sized pieces

1 tablespoon plain flour + some salt and pepper

1 ½ tablespoon olive oil + 1 teaspoon butter

A small handful of fresh tarragon leaves

100ml, 3½floz, ½ cup, Vermouth

250ml, 9floz, a little bit more than a cup, chicken stock

100ml, 3½floz, ½ cup, crème fraiche

1 tablespoon soy sauce

Salt and pepper

1. Heat the oven to 200C/400F/gas mark 6. Mix the flour with some salt and pepper on a plate. Roll the chicken pieces in the flour and shake off any excess flour.

2. Add the olive oil and butter to a large non-stick frying pan over a medium heat. When the butter and oil start to sizzle and brown a little, add half the tarragon leaves and the chicken pieces to the pan and brown the chicken all over. If you don't have a large enough frying pan, you might have to do this in two batches. Remove the chicken from the frying pan and place in an oven-proof dish.

3. Lower the heat a little and add the Vermouth and the rest of the tarragon leaves to the frying pan. Bring to a simmer while stirring and scraping up the sediments from the bottom of the frying pan. Let it simmer for 2-3 minutes. Add the stock, crème fraiche and soy sauce and season with salt and pepper. Stir, bring the sauce back to a simmer and let it simmer for 5 minutes.

4. Check the seasoning of the sauce before pouring it over the chicken and place the dish in the oven. Cook for 15 minutes until the chicken is properly cooked through.

If you are using chicken breast cut into chunks for this tarragon chicken dish, check after 10 minutes in the oven to see if the pieces are cooked through.

Chicken Curry with Lemongrass and Tomatoes

One word – YUMMY! I love this chicken curry with lemongrass and tomatoes.

Apart from all the lovely flavours, it is also healthy. Tomatoes are healthier when cooked – a rarity among vegetables – and I also add finely shredded Brussels sprouts to this curry.

Brussels sprouts may be an unusual vegetable to add to a curry but I think they are a perfect addition as they have a strong, somewhat peppery taste. I managed to get hold of purple-sprouting Brussels sprouts this time, but I also use the green ones.

They are super-healthy. Brussels sprouts are part of the family of cruciferous vegetables – which also include broccoli, cabbage, kale, cauliflower and cress – and contain anti-cancer and liver-friendly nutrients.

Cruciferous vegetables are best eaten raw or just lightly cooked. I only add the shredded Brussels sprouts during the last two minutes of cooking – leaving them still crunchy and with a fair amount of their nutrients still intact.

You can swap the sprouts for some spinach or some sliced sugar snaps – again only adding them at the last couple of minutes of cooking.

I am using boneless and skinless chicken thighs. If you want to use chicken breast instead, be careful not to dry out the meat.

If you can't get hold of lemongrass, use finely grated zest of an un-waxed lime or lemon instead.

Chicken curry with lemongrass and tomatoes for 4 people:

For the paste:

3 tablespoons coconut oil (melted if solid) – or use vegetable oil

2 shallots, chopped

2 garlic cloves, chopped

Thumb-sized piece of ginger, chopped

2 lemongrass stalks - cut off the thinner top, leaving you with the "bulb" at the bottom, discard tough outer layer, cut off the bottom of the "bulb", halve it and slice very finely

2 red chillies, deseeded (or leave the seeds in for a spicier curry) and chopped

A small handful of coriander (cilantro) - stalks only, chopped – keep the leaves for garnish

For the rest of the curry:

1 teaspoon turmeric

¼ teaspoon black pepper

20 cherry tomatoes, quartered

400ml, 14½floz, 1¾ cups coconut milk

1 teaspoon honey

1½ tablespoon Thai fish sauce

8 boneless and skinless chicken thighs (preferably organic or free-range) - cut into bite-size pieces

10-12 Brussels sprouts, trimmed, halved and finely sliced (optional)

1 tablespoon fresh lime juice

1.Place the coconut oil, shallots, garlic, ginger, lemongrass, chopped chilli, and coriander stalks in a food processor and pulse to a rough paste.

2.Place all of the paste in a pan over a medium-high heat. Add the turmeric and black pepper to the pan and fry - stirring continuously - for 5 minutes. Add the tomatoes and continue to fry for a further 5 minutes.

3.Add the coconut milk, honey and fish sauce to the pot, stir and bring to a simmer. Add the chicken pieces, stir and allow the curry to simmer for about 20 minutes – give the curry a stir every now and then - until the chicken is cooked through. If using, add the shredded Brussels sprouts during the two last minutes of cooking.

4.Once ready, take the pan off the heat and stir in the lime juice and coriander (cilantro) leaves.

I serve this chicken curry with lemongrass with either quinoa or brown basmati rice.

Chicken and Broad beans in a Sherry, Mustard and Tarragon Sauce

I love chicken, and I love broad beans (fava beans). I use both in this scrumptious chicken and broad beans dish.

This is a casserole which is bursting with flavour, and yet it is low in fat.

The big flavours come from fresh tarragon, French mustard and dry sherry. I don't like to drink sherry but I love the taste of it in cooked food.

If you haven't got a bottle of dry sherry at home, I recommend buying a bottle for cooking. It is quite inexpensive and it will keep for a long time. The alcohol in the sherry will of course evaporate when cooked but the taste is sensational.

You can swap the sherry for dry white wine.

Broad beans (fava beans) require a bit of work as you need to remove the tough outer skin of each bean once they are cooked. It is easy to do though - I find the process of removing the skins therapeutic.

I used chicken thighs on the bone last time I cooked this (I personally remove the skin which is the fatty part of the chicken). You can use bone and skinless thighs instead but if you do that, reduce the cooking time to 30 minutes.

Chicken and broad beans in a sherry, mustard and tarragon sauce

For 4 people:

2 tablespoons olive oil

8 chicken thighs on the bone

2 shallots, finely chopped

2 garlic cloves, crushed/minced

A handful of fresh tarragon leaves – roughly chopped – or use 1 heaped teaspoon of dried tarragon leaves

800ml, 1.4 pints, 3.5 cups chicken stock

225ml, 8floz, 1 cup dry sherry

1 tablespoon Dijon mustard

2 tablespoons half-fat crème fraiche

500g frozen broad (fava) beans

1.Add the olive oil to a large and deep frying pan over a medium high heat. Once the oil is hot, add 4 of the chicken thighs to the pan and brown for about 1 minute on each side. Remove to a plate and then do the same with the rest of the chicken thighs.

2.When all of the chicken thighs have been removed from the pan, reduce the heat and add the chopped shallots, crushed garlic and half of the tarragon leaves to the pan. Keep stirring for about 3 minutes until the onion softens but doesn't brown.

3.Return the chicken thighs to the pan and add the sherry. Turn up the heat to medium high and simmer for about 5 minutes until the sherry has been reduced to about half. Pour in the chicken stock and season with some salt and more generously with black pepper. Bring it back to a simmer, turn down the heat a little and cook without a lid for 50 minutes.

4.While the chicken is cooking, place the broad (fava) beans in a pan with boiling water. Once the water comes back to a boil, simmer the beans for 4 minutes. Drain and the cool the beans under running cold water to stop them for cooking any further. Once the broad beans are cool, peel of the thin skin of each bean (the skin slips off easily when you pinch the ends).

5.Once the chicken is cooked, remove the chicken thighs to a dish, cover and keep warm. Turn up the heat and let the sauce simmer for a further 3-4 minutes, then stir in the mustard, crème fraiche and broad beans and continue to cook for another minute. Check the seasoning to see if you need any more salt or pepper.

Pour the sauce over the chicken thighs and scatter the remaining tarragon over the chicken.

Poached Chicken in an Asian-Style Broth

It takes some time to make this poached chicken dish but it is really worth it. It is super-tasty and also really light, despite the coconut milk that I add to the broth.

Coconut milk is, along with other coconut products, quite nutritious. It does contain saturated fat but coconut is rich in medium-chain fatty acids which the body processes differently than other saturated fats. These medium-chain fatty acids promote weight maintenance without raising cholesterol levels

Time-wise...Well, you have to poach a whole chicken for about 1 hour and 20 minutes (you need a big pot for this).

But it's not difficult to make this dish. There is plenty of time to prepare the vegetables for the stir-fry while the chicken is simmering – and probably enough time to read half the weekend newspaper as well.

Any left-over poached chicken could be used for a salad the next day, or be added to a soup.

For 4 people:

1 whole good quality organic or at least free-range chicken

1 onion, peeled and halved

thumb-size piece of fresh ginger, peeled and sliced

3 lemon grass, bashed

A bunch fresh coriander (cilantro), stalks and leaves separated (save the leaves for garnish)

3 garlic cloves, peeled and roughly chopped

2 whole cloves

1 teaspoon sea salt

1/2 teaspoon whole peppercorns

For the broth:

800ml, 1½ pint, 3½ cups, chicken stock from the water you've been poaching the chicken in

400ml, 3½floz, 1¾ cups, coconut milk

Salt and pepper

For the stir-fried vegetables:

2 tablespoons coconut oil - or use vegetable oil

Thumb-size piece of fresh ginger, peeled and finely chopped

2 red chillies, de-seeded and finely chopped

1 fat garlic clove, peeled and finely chopped

1 small head of broccoli, cut into small florets, stem sliced

1 medium-sized carrot, peeled and cut into matchstick batons

1 red pepper (bell pepper), de-seeded and roughly chopped

2 spring onions (scallions), sliced

2 tablespoons light soy sauce

To serve:

Juice of 2 limes

Coriander (cilantro) leaves

1.Place the chicken in a large pot and cover with water. Add the onion, ginger, lemongrass, coriander (cilantro) stalks, garlic, cloves, salt and peppercorns to the pot. Bring to a boil, then lower the heat and simmer for about 1 hour 20 minutes. Skim off any scum, white froth, that forms.

2.Take the poached chicken out of the pot, discard the skin and use a fork to shred as much meat as possible off the bones. Strain the stock into a large bowl and throw away the solids.

3.Add 800ml/3½ cup of the stock and the coconut milk to a pot (you can freeze the rest of the stock). Bring to a simmer, taste and add a bit of salt and pepper if needed.

4.For the stir-fried vegetables, add the oil to a wok or large frying pan over quite a high heat. Once the wok or pan is hot, add the garlic, chilli and ginger and stir-fry for 30 seconds, then add the broccoli, carrots and red pepper (bell pepper) and keep everything moving, stirring frequently for 3 minutes. Add the spring onion (scallion) and the soy sauce and stir-fry for a further 30 seconds. Remove the wok or frying pan from the heat

5.Add the juice of 2 limes to the simmering broth. Divide the chicken meat between 4 bowls, ladle the broth over the chicken, top with the stir-fried vegetables and scatter some coriander (cilantro) leaves over each portion.

Parmesan Breaded Chicken and Tomato Basil Sauce

"Is it fish?" A lot of people ask this when they see my Parmesan breaded chicken escalopes (scallops/cutlets). I can only assume this is because of how thin they are.

Why do I make them so thin? Well, apart from the fact they are quicker to cook this way, these thin chicken escalopes becomes super-moist and utterly delicious. We're talking a proper crowd-pleaser.

To make my Parmesan breaded chicken as tasty and healthy as possible, I make my breadcrumbs from sourdough bread. I know I go on and on about this but if you care about properly made healthy food, sourdough bread, or bread made with very little yeast and a long fermentation, is the way to go when it comes to bread.

I usually serve my breaded chicken with a tomato sauce of some kind and then either with different oven-roasted vegetables and some green vegetables, or with pasta and green vegetables.

If I'm using pasta then I prefer to use either spelt wholemeal (whole-wheat) pasta or pasta made of pulses, a much healthier alternative to white pasta and really tasty.

For 4 people:

3 organic or free-range chicken breast

80g, 3oz, 0.6 cup, plain white flour (preferably organic stone-ground flour)

2 organic or free-range eggs

100g, 3½oz, 2 cups, fresh breadcrumbs

5 tablespoons grated Parmesan or Grana Pandano cheese

¼ teaspoon cayenne pepper, optional

Salt and pepper

Olive oil for frying

For the tomato sauce:

1 tablespoon olive or rapeseed oil

½ red onion, peeled and finely chopped

1 garlic clove, crushed

400g, 14oz, 2 cups, chopped tomatoes

3 tablespoons sun-dried tomato paste (or use plain tomato paste if you can't get hold of it)

3 tablespoons balsamic vinegar

100ml, 3½floz, ½ cup, water

Salt and pepper

Handful of fresh basil leaves, roughly torn

1.Pre-heat the oven to 220C/fan 200C/425F/gas mark 7. If you are going to serve the breaded parmesan chicken with oven-roasted vegetables, place them in the oven before continuing with the rest.

2.Start by making the tomato sauce. Place the oil and chopped onion in a pot over a medium heat. Gently cook the onion, stirring every now and then, until it starts to soften but not brown, approximately 5 minutes. Add the crushed garlic and cook for a further minute, stirring and making sure the garlic doesn't burn.

3.Add the chopped tomatoes, tomato paste, balsamic vinegar, water and season with salt and pepper. Stir and bring to a simmer. Let it simmer for about 10 minutes, adding the basil leaves at the end. Taste and check the seasoning.

4.While the tomato sauce is simmering, cut each chicken breast into thin (3mm - 1/8in) escalopes (scallops/cutlets). My way of doing it is to place my hand on the chicken breast and while pressing down on it slightly, cutting thin slices out of the chicken breast with a sharp knife. Don't rush it so that you end up cutting yourself. If the escalopes become too thick, place them on a cutting board lined with baking parchment and cover with another piece of baking parchment. Use a meat hammer or rolling pin and bash the escalopes until they are thin enough.

5.Scatter the flour over a plate and season with salt and pepper. Place the eggs in a bowl and lightly beat. Place the breadcrumbs, Parmesan cheese and cayenne pepper if using it in another bowl and mix well. Dust each escalope - on both sides - in the flour, then dip the escalope in the beaten egg and finally coat each side with the breadcrumb and Parmesan mixture. Place the breaded chicken escalope on a plate as you continue with the rest.

6.Add some oil to a large frying pan over quite a high heat and quickly brown the Parmesan breaded chicken escalopes in batches. Transfer the escalopes to a roasting tray lined with baking parchment and place the tray in the oven for about 5 minutes, until the chicken is cooked through.

Serve the parmesan breaded chicken escalopes with the tomato sauce and either oven-roasted vegetables or pasta and green vegetables like broccoli and/or green beans.

Saffron Chicken Casserole

My kind of food - a full-flavoured low-calorie saffron chicken casserole which is quite quick to make and mega-delicious.

It is a fantastic dish to make in advance. Just quickly re-heat it when you are ready to eat. The flavours will intensify when the casserole is left to stand.

I've chosen to make it with boneless and skinless chicken thighs, which shortens the cooking time.

You can obviously use chicken thighs on the bone if you wish, and also add chicken drumsticks. **You will need to**

increase the cooking time if you do by about 25 minutes, until no pink meat remains.

I serve this saffron chicken casserole with boiled/steamed green beans and either quinoa, wholemeal (whole wheat) couscous or oven-roasted vegetables.

For 4 people:

8 boneless, skinless chicken thighs

2 tablespoons coconut oil - or use vegetable oil

1 red onion, finely diced

3 garlic cloves, finely chopped

Thumb-size piece of ginger, peeled and finely chopped

2 red chillies, de-seeded and finely chopped

1 teaspoon saffron threads

½ teaspoon ground turmeric

2 cinnamon sticks

400g, 14oz, 2¼ cups, tin of chopped tomatoes

2 tablespoons tamarind water (see below), or, if you can't get hold of tamarind, replace with 1 tablespoon of lemon juice

1 teaspoon runny honey

200ml, 7floz, 0.9 cup, water

1 bay leaf

Salt and pepper

Tamarind water: take a piece of tamarind pulp, about the size of a golf ball, and place it in a bowl with 100ml, 3½, ½ cup, of warm water. With your fingers, work the tamarind pulp into the water until it has broken down and the seeds have been released. Strain the syrupy liquid through a fine sieve – press down with a spoon - into another bowl. Discard the fibrous material left in the sieve.

1.Pre-heat the oven to 180C/Fan 160C/350F/gas mark 4. Heat the coconut oil in a casserole over a medium high heat and brown the chicken thighs in batches, seasoning each batch with salt and pepper and then setting each batch aside.

2.Lower the heat and add the onion, garlic, ginger, chilli, saffron, turmeric and cinnamon sticks to the casserole. Stir and cook for about 10 minutes, until the onion is soft. Add the chopped tomatoes, tamarind water, runny honey, water and a bay leaf. Season with salt and pepper, stir and bring to a simmer. TASTE, to make sure you are happy with the seasoning.

3.Return the chicken to the casserole and cover with a tight-fitting lid. Place the casserole in the oven and cook for about 25 minutes, until the chicken thighs are cooked through.

This saffron chicken casserole tastes wonderful when straight out of the oven, but like a lot of food it tastes even better when left to stand. If you are not going to eat it straight away, you need to place it in the fridge once cooled down.

Chicken Pasanda

Chicken pasanda is a super-delicious chicken curry made with "warm" spices rather than fiery ones.

But you do add fresh chilli as well. You are meant to use green chillies in this curry but as I don't really like the green ones – just as I'm not very fond of green peppers (bell peppers) – I use red chillies. The choice is yours.

The sauce for the chicken pasanda is creamy but light and made with yogurt and stock to which you add flaked almonds.

I have started to use whole spices that I grind myself more often. Ground spices deteriorate so much quicker than whole spices and you do get more flavour from grinding whole spices.

And rather than using a ready-made spice mix – like curry powder or garam masala – I've started to make my own.

This way you are in control of what goes into your dishes and can experiment more. I used to grind my spices in a pestle and mortar but then I found a used coffee grinder in a charity shop (£2.50!). This excellent piece of equipment is great for grinding spices.

You need to marinate the chicken for at least 1-2 hours. If you've got a bit of time, marinate the chicken for the curry in the morning. It doesn't take that long to cook this curry once the chicken has been marinated.

To make this a healthier and more of a low-calorie meal, eat this chicken pasanda curry with vegetables rather than with rice. I serve this with a gloriously fresh-tasting tomato salsa (see recipe below) and green beans.

You can also serve it with oven-roasted butternut squash wedges. Brush the wedges with olive-oil and sprinkle with a bit of salt and dried chilli pepper flakes and place in the oven - 200C/400F/gas mark 6 - for around 35-40 minutes.

For 4 people:

For the marinade:

1 heaped tablespoon coriander (cilantro) seeds

2 teaspoons cumin seeds

8 cardamom pods – left whole while roasting then split open and seeds removed for grinding once cooled down

5 whole cloves

½ teaspoon black pepper corns

1/3 of a cinnamon stick

½ teaspoon ground ginger

1 level teaspoon turmeric

5 heaped tablespoons full-fat, Greek-style natural yogurt

8 skinless and boneless chicken thighs – each chicken thigh quartered

1½ tablespoon coconut oil

1 onion, finely chopped

3 teaspoons grated ginger

2 garlic cloves, crushed

2 green or red chillies, deseeded and finely chopped

200ml, 7floz, 0.9cup, chicken stock

100g, 3½oz, 1 cup, flaked almonds

Fresh coriander, roughly chopped

For the tomato salsa:

250g, 9oz, 1½ cup, ripe small tomatoes, quartered

2 spring onions (scallions), chopped

1 small handful of fresh coriander - leaves only – chopped

1 small handful of mint leaves, chopped

Juice of 1 lime

Pinch of salt

1.Start by dry-roasting the coriander and cumin seeds, cardamom pods, cloves, black pepper corns and piece of cinnamon stick in a frying pan over a medium high heat for 1-2 minutes until the spices start to become aromatic and a few shades darker. Once cooled down, split open the cardamom pods and place the seeds together with the other roasted spices in a pestle and mortar. Grind to a fine powder. Once this is done, mix in the ground ginger and turmeric.

2.Mix together the spices and yogurt in a bowl. Add the chicken pieces to the yogurt and toss until all the pieces are well coated. Cover the bowl and place it in the fridge for at least 1-2 hours.

3.Heat the oil in a large heavy-based pan (that has a lid) over a low heat and add the chopped onion. Cook for about 10 minutes – stirring frequently – until the onion is really soft but not browned. Add the ginger, garlic and chilli to the pan and continue to cook for a further couple of minutes.

4.Add the chicken pieces and all of the marinade to the pan. Turn up the heat and keep stirring until the chicken starts to colour. Add the stock, season with a bit of salt, stir and bring to a boil. Reduce the heat, cover the pan with a lid and simmer for 30 minutes.

5.While the chicken pasanda curry is simmering, make the salsa. Mix together all the ingredients in a bowl (glass or porcelain) and leave to stand.

6.Remove the lid from the pan, stir in the flaked almonds and continue to simmer – without the lid now - for another 5 minutes. Check the seasoning and sprinkle over some chopped coriander before serving.

Mexican Chicken, Guacamole and Tomato Salsa on Sourdough Bread

Food doesn't have to be complicated and yet taste fantastic.

This light and mega-tasty Mexican chicken and guacamole dish is quick and easy to make. There's a bit of chopping to do but very little cooking involved.

It's a perfect dish to make when you want to eat flavoursome healthy food but haven't got the time, or energy, to spend a lot of time cooking.

I serve the Mexican chicken and guacamole with tomato salsa on a bed of rocket leaves, spinach and watercress which sits on top of toasted sourdough bread. You can skip the bread altogether if you want an even lighter meal. And vegetarians can use slices of halloumi cheese instead of chicken, using the same marinade for the cheese.

For 4 people:

Marinade:

1 teaspoon smoked paprika (or use ordinary paprika if you can't get hold of the smoked variety)

½ -1 teaspoon dried chilli flakes (depending how spicy you like it to be)

2 garlic cloves, crushed

2 tablespoons olive oil

Salt and pepper

3-4 skinless organic or free-range chicken breasts

Guacamole:

2 ripe avocados

Juice of 1 lime

½ small red onion, peeled and finely chopped

1 red chilli, deseeded and finely chopped

1 small handful of fresh coriander - leaves only – chopped

Salt and pepper

For the tomato salsa:

250g, 6oz, 1½ cup, ripe small tomatoes, quartered

2 spring onions (scallions), chopped

1 small handful of fresh coriander - leaves only – chopped

1 small handful of mint leaves, chopped

Juice of 1 lime

A good pinch of salt

Rocket leaves/watercress/baby spinach

4 large slices of sourdough bread

1.In a bowl, mix together the ingredients for the marinade. Cut the chicken breasts into thin slices and add these to the bowl. Mix thoroughly and leave to the side.

2.Halve, peel and de-stone the avocados. Place the avocados in a bowl and roughly mash them up with a fork. Add the lime juice, chopped red onion, chilli and coriander, season with salt and pepper and mix together.

3.For the tomato salsa, place all the ingredients in another bowl and mix together.

4.Fry the chicken slices in batches over quite a high heat until nicely browned and cooked through – I find that by using a non-stick frying pan I don't need to add any more oil than what is in the marinade.

Toast the sourdough bread and divide between four plates. Top each piece of bread with rocket leaves and if you have any, also watercress and/or baby spinach. Then divide the tomato salsa, guacamole and chicken over each piece of bread.

Lemon and Garlic Chicken with Quinoa and Mint Pesto

Lemon and garlic are great to use for marinades. I've used it for this lemon and garlic chicken dish, together with lemon thyme. You can use ordinary thyme if you can't find lemon thyme.

I'm serving the chicken with quinoa mixed with a super-fresh and utterly tasty mint and parsley pesto.

I love experimenting with different ingredients for pesto. As I aim to make my food healthy as well as tasty, I've added crunchy pumpkin and sunflower seeds - along with a lot of other tasty and healthy ingredients - to this one.

These seeds are rich in essential fats and full of other super-healthy nutrients. I eat a fair amount of seeds and nuts every day.

To make this lemon and garlic chicken dish ultra-good for you, I also serve it with oven-roasted tomatoes and steamed tenderstem broccoli (broccolini) – a cross between kale and broccoli.

This type of broccoli is apparently the richest source by far of glucosinolates - which are one of the most important anti-cancer and liver-friendly nutrients found in food. ("The optimum nutrition bible" by Patrick Holford)

For 4 people:

Finely grated zest of 1 un-waxed lemon

2 garlic cloves, crushed

1 heaped tablespoon fresh lemon thyme leaves

3 tablespoons olive oil

4 -8 (depending on size) boneless and skinless chicken thighs

250g, 9oz, 1½ cups, quinoa

800ml, 1½ pints, 3½ cups, vegetable stock

Mint and parsley pesto:

10 fresh mint leaves

2 large handfuls fresh parsley – leaves only

1 garlic clove, crushed

3 spring onions (scallions), chopped

1 tablespoon chopped chives

1 tablespoon sunflower seeds

1 tablespoon pumpkin seeds

1 tablespoon lemon juice

1 tablespoon oil – I use Omega 3-rich hemp oil but you can use olive oil

A good pinch of salt and pepper

Ripe and fragrant small tomatoes

Tenderstem broccoli (broccolini)

1.Start by mixing together the lemon zest, garlic, lemon thyme and oil. Cover an oven-safe dish with baking parchment and place the chicken thighs flat on the tray. Smother the chicken with the marinade. Cover the dish and place it in the fridge for at least 30 minutes - longer if you've got the time.

2.Pre-heat the oven to 200C/fan180C/400F/gas mark 6. Put the vegetable stock in a pot and heat to boiling. Season the lemon and garlic chicken with salt and pepper and place the dish in the oven. Cook for about 18 - 20 minutes - until the chicken is completely cooked through. Add tomatoes to the dish for the last 8 minutes.

3.While the chicken is cooking, add the quinoa to the boiling stock, stir and then lower the heat to a simmer. Cook for 15 minutes, drain in a colander before tipping the quinoa back into the pot.

4.Make the pesto while the quinoa is cooking. Place all the ingredients in a food processor and pulse for about 10 -15 seconds. Add the pesto to the cooked and drained quinoa and mix together.

5.Steam or boil the tenderstem broccoli for about 3 minutes.

Divide the quinoa with pesto between four plates and place the chicken on top and divide the broccoli and tomatoes between the plates. Serve immediately.

Chicken Burger with Wasabi Mayo

I admit that this is not an ordinary burger - it is my take on a chicken burger. I serve marinated chicken with wasabi mayo and butternut squash and chilli mash instead of a burger bun. It is sensationally delicious!

It is really a take on a chicken burger as I don't mince the chicken meat and shape the mashed chilli-squash into the bottom of a burger bun. And instead of ordinary mayo, I serve my burger with a dollop of wasabi-mayo.

You can of course serve the chicken in a bun of some sort.

I use moist and juicy chicken thighs and marinate them for a couple of hours before cooking them. If you've got the time, you can leave the chicken to marinate overnight, or in the morning if you are cooking them in the evening.

I serve theses chicken burgers together with a large salad on the side.

For 4 people:

Marinade for the chicken:

2 garlic cloves, crushed

2 teaspoons finely grated fresh ginger

2 tablespoons light soya sauce

2 tablespoons coconut oil - or use vegetable oil

½ teaspoon black pepper

8 boneless and skinless chicken thighs - each thigh cut in half

1 small butternut squash, peeled, halved, deseeded and diced

1 large red chilli, deseeded and finely chopped (leave the seeds in if you want more heat)

1 tablespoon coconut oil - or use vegetable oil

Salt and pepper

2 tablespoons sesame seeds

2 large handfuls fresh coriander, chopped

1 teaspoon wasabi paste

1 tablespoon mayo

1.Mix together the ingredients for the marinade in a non-metallic bowl. Add the halved chicken thighs to the bowl and mix well. Cover the bowl and leave in the fridge for at least 1 hour – longer if you have the time.

2.Pre-heat the oven to 220C/fan200C/425F/gas mark 7. Place the diced butternut squash and chopped chilli in a roasting pan, add the oil, season with a bit of salt and pepper and toss everything together. Bake in the oven for about 30 minutes – giving the squash a stir mid-way through – until the butternut squash is soft and golden.

3.Take out the chicken from the fridge and place the chicken thighs flat in an oven dish. Pour over all the marinade. When the butternut squash has been in the oven for 15 minutes, place the dish with chicken in the oven as well and cook for about 15-17 minutes, until the chicken is completely cooked through.

4.Mix together the wasabi paste and mayo and leave to the side

5.Use a potato masher to mash the butternut squash and chilli. Add the sesame seeds and chopped fresh coriander to the mash and divide the mash between 4 plates. Place the chicken on top of the mash and add a dollop of wasabi mayo on top of the chicken.

Vietnamese Chicken Meatballs

You can serve these utterly moreish Vietnamese chicken meatballs as a starter, as part of a buffet or as canapés - on a spoon or on little gem salad leaves.

You can also top them with a little bit of sweet chilli sauce – but don't drown them in it as they are so tasty on their own.

I serve them with a cucumber, tomato and chilli salsa which has a sharp, fresh taste and add zing to the chicken meatballs. It's a really light and tasty combination!

I cook them in some raw coconut oil/butter – in an oven-proof dish in the oven. Coconut oil/butter is the healthiest type of fat to cook your food in. The fat in coconut oil is what's called short-chain saturated fat, unlike butter which is a long-chain saturated fat.

I buy it at a health-food shop and use it when I'm cooking Asian-style food.

If you haven't got any coconut oil, simply place the chicken balls on an oven-tray lined with baking parchment and cook in the oven.

To make approximately 30 Vietnamese chicken meatballs:

500g, 1lb2oz, skin and bone-less chicken thighs – organic or free-range

2 shallots, finely chopped

2 garlic cloves, crushed/minced

2 teaspoons finely grated fresh ginger

3 lemon grass stalks, cut off the thinner top of each stalk - leaving you with the "bulb" at the bottom - discard tough outer layer, cut off the bottom of the "bulb", cut it in half and slice **very finely** - if you can't get hold of lemon grass, swap for finely grated zest of 2 un-waxed lemons

1 teaspoon honey

3 tablespoons Thai fish sauce

Handful of fresh coriander (cilantro), chopped

Black pepper

1 tablespoon coconut/oil butter (optional)

Cucumber-tomato-chilli salsa:

Dressing:

1 tablespoon rice vinegar

1 tablespoon Thai fish sauce

1 tablespoon lime juice

1 tablespoon sunflower oil

½ teaspoon honey

Black pepper

1/3 of a cucumber, diced

200g, 7oz, ripe tomatoes, diced

1 small red onion, finely chopped

1 red chilli, deseeded and finely chopped

Handful of fresh coriander (cilantro), chopped

1.Preheat the oven to 200C/fan 180C/400F/gas mark 6. Pulse the chicken thighs in a food processor until minced. Transfer the mince to a bowl and add the chopped shallots, crushed garlic, grated ginger, chopped lemon grass, honey, fish sauce and chopped coriander. Season with black pepper and mix thoroughly.

2.With your hands, shape the mix into little balls – you should be able to make 28- 30. Add the coconut oil/butter to an oven-proof dish (if it's solid, place the dish in the oven until it has melted). Add the chicken meatballs and cook in the oven for 15-17 minutes – turning them over mid-way through.

3.While they are cooking, mix together the ingredients for the salad dressing. Place the cucumber, tomatoes, onion, chilli and coriander in a bowl. Add all of the dressing and mix together.

Chicken Curry with Miso

A different curry, a delicious Japanese-style chicken curry with miso which is full of flavour but milder than some other curries.

I am using whole spices which I dry-roast and grind in a pestle and mortar. This is not difficult to do – and the taste of your food is vastly improved when you are grinding your own spices instead of using shop-bought ready-made curry powder.

I sometimes use an old coffee grinder to grind my spices but as the cumin seeds are too small for the one I have, I use a pestle and mortar for this curry spice mix.

The miso I am using in this recipe is a sweet white fermented rice and soybean puree/paste. Eating fermented food is a good way to promote a healthy intestinal flora and to boost your immune system.

Miso is also very tasty and will help to thicken up the sauce. It is great to use in soups. Just remember that miso is quite salty (the darker the miso the saltier it is).

I bought mine in a health food shop but you can find it among Asian food in well-stocked supermarkets, or in an Asian supermarket.

Not only is this chicken curry with miso utterly delicious, it is also very low in calories. The only fat I am using is the healthy coconut oil that I cook the ingredients in.

Coconut oil/butter is the healthiest fat to cook your food in. The fat in coconut oil is what's called short-chain saturated fat, unlike butter which is a long-chain saturated fat.

I always use it now when I'm cooking Asian-style food and here in the U.K. it is sold in most supermarkets, as well as in health food shops.

If you want to keep this a low-calorie-meal, don't eat it with refined white rice as this will make your blood sugar level shoot up. Quinoa or brown rice is the best alternative.

For 4 people:

Spice mix:

2 heaped teaspoons coriander (cilantro) seeds

2 heaped teaspoons cumin seeds

½ teaspoon yellow mustard seeds

¼ teaspoon fenugreek seeds

¼ teaspoon dried chilli flakes

½ teaspoon ground turmeric

1 tablespoon coconut oil/butter (or use vegetable oil)

3 shallots (or use 1 yellow onion) finely chopped

2 garlic cloves, crushed/minced

1 thumb-size piece of ginger, finely grated

14 small ripe tomatoes (like cherry or plum), quartered

8 skinless and boneless chicken thighs, each cut into 3 pieces

1 heaped tablespoon sweet white miso paste/puree

300ml, 10floz, 1.3 cups, water

Salt and freshly ground black pepper

1.Start by dry-roasting the coriander, cumin, mustard, fenugreek seeds and chilli flakes in a frying pan over a medium-high heat for 1-2 minutes – until they become fragrant. Place the spices in a pestle and mortar and grind to a fine powder. Mix in the ground turmeric.

2.Place the coconut oil/butter in a large non-stick frying pan over a low heat. Add the onion, garlic and ginger and stir and cook for 5 minutes. Add the spice mix and continue to stir and cook for a further 30 seconds before adding the tomatoes to the pan. Continue to cook for a further 10 minutes, stirring every now and then.

3.Add the chicken pieces, increase the heat and keep turning the chicken pieces over until they start to colour. Add the miso paste and water and season with some salt and freshly ground black pepper. Stir and bring to a simmer. Allow the curry to simmer over a medium-high heat for about 20 minutes. Taste and check the seasoning to see if you need any more salt and/or pepper.

This chicken curry with miso is great dish to make beforehand as the flavours will intensify when left to stand. Serve the curry with rice (preferably brown rice) or quinoa and steamed green vegetable – such as tenderstem broccoli (broccolini) sugar-snaps, green beans.

Spicy Pomegranate-Marinated Chicken

I am using pomegranate molasses for this very tasty spicy pomegranate-marinated chicken dish.

You can often find the molasses in well-stocked supermarkets these days. If you can't find it there, try health food shops or shops specialising in Middle-Eastern food.

I serve the chicken with quinoa and stir-fried vegetables. You can use couscous instead of quinoa (quinoa is healthier and less calorific), but try using wholegrain couscous if you do. If you are trying to lose weight, it's a good idea to give up – or at least reduce - all types of refined carbohydrates.

I've used chicken thighs on the bone at times but as it's a fair bit quicker to cook boneless ones, that's what I recommend for this recipe. To make the chicken as tasty as possible though, you need to marinate the chicken for a couple of hours before cooking it.

For 4 people:

For the spicy pomegranate-marinated chicken thighs:

2 tablespoons pomegranate molasses

2 teaspoons ground coriander (cilantro)

2 teaspoons ground cumin

¼ teaspoon dried chilli flakes

½ teaspoon ground black pepper

1½ tablespoon olive oil

8 boneless and skinless chicken thighs

For the quinoa:

200g, 8oz, 1cup, quinoa

400ml, 13½floz, 1¾ cup water

1 vegetable stock cube

For the stir-fried vegetables:

1½ tablespoon coconut or vegetable oil - coconut is best

1 small head of broccoli, cut into small florets, stem sliced

Thumb-size piece of fresh ginger, peeled and finely chopped

2 garlic cloves, peeled and finely chopped

2 spring onions (scallions), sliced

2 tablespoons light soy sauce

1.Mix together the ingredients for the marinade. Cover an oven-safe dish with baking parchment and place the chicken thighs flat in the dish. Smother the chicken with the marinade. Cover the dish with cling film and place it in the fridge for 2 hours. Remove the chicken from the fridge 30 minutes before you are going to cook it.

2.Preheat the oven 200C/fan180C/400F/gas mark 6. Rinse the quinoa under plenty of cold water. Leave to drain in a sieve. Sprinkle a bit of salt over the chicken thighs, place them in the oven and cook for 20 minutes.

3.Bring the water for the quinoa to a simmer in a pot and dissolve the stock cube in the water. Add the rinsed quinoa to the water, bring back to a simmer and cover the pot with a lid. Simmer over a low heat for 15 minutes, until the quinoa has absorbed most of the water.

4.When the chicken and quinoa are nearly ready, add the oil to a wok or large frying pan over quite a high heat. Once the wok or pan is hot, add the broccoli and stir-fry for 1minute minute. Add the ginger and garlic to the pan and fry for a further 30 seconds. Add the spring onion (scallion) and the soy sauce and stir-fry for a further 30 seconds. Remove from the heat.

5.Add the stir-fried vegetables to the cooked quinoa and divide between four plates. Top each plate with two chicken thighs and drizzle with any juices left in the dish you cooked the chicken in.

Ginger and Soy Chicken

This is a very tasty ginger and soy chicken dish.

In an effort to make it as healthy as possible I am frying the chicken for as short time as possible before adding stock.

I don't want to be a spoilsport but, frying is one of the un-healthiest ways of cooking food as this produces free oxidising radicals which can destroy cells and increase the risk of cancer, heart disease and premature ageing.

The longer you fry the food at a high temperature, and the more burnt the food is, the higher the risk is.

The healthiest fat to use for frying is coconut oil, olive oil and butter – in that order. I use coconut oil for all types of Asian-style dishes as I think that the taste of coconut enhances this type of food. For other types of food, I tend to mostly use olive or rapeseed oil.

I'm either serving this ginger and soy chicken with herb and citrus quinoa, roasted tomatoes and some kind of green vegetables, or I skip the quinoa and simply add sliced sugar snaps and spring onions (scallions) to the broth during the last minute of cooking.

I cook the quinoa in vegetable stock to which I add the juice of a lemon or lime – 2 parts stock to 1part quinoa – for 15 minutes. Once the quinoa is cooked, I add sliced spring onion (scallion) and herbs such as lemon thyme, mint and parsley.

You could serve the broth with cooked noodles as well. Gluten-free soba noodles are both tasty and healthy.

Whichever way you choose to serve it, hand out a spoon as well as the broth is simply divine.

For 4 people:

Marinade:

1 tablespoon finely grated fresh ginger

2 garlic cloves, crushed

Finely grated zest from 1 un-waxed lemon

1 teaspoon sesame oil

4 tablespoons Tamari soy sauce – or use light soya sauce

2 tablespoons coconut oil - or use vegetable oil

½ teaspoon black pepper

8 skinless and boneless chicken thighs – organic or free-range – cut into bite-size pieces

Coconut oil - for frying

Salt

500 ml, 18floz, 2.2 cups chicken stock

1.In a glass or ceramic bowl, mix together all the ingredients for the marinade. Add the chicken pieces and mix well. Cover the bowl and leave the chicken to marinate in the fridge for at least 30 minutes – preferably longer.

2.Add some coconut oil to a large frying pan and fry the chicken pieces in batches - sprinkling some salt over each batch - over a medium-high heat for about a minute (don't over-crowd the pan). Remove each batch and leave to the side.

3.Once you have fried all the chicken, add some of the stock to the frying pan to de-glaze the pan and add this to a medium-sized pot or casserole dish. Add the rest of the stock, all the chicken and any marinade left in the bowl that you marinated the chicken in. Bring to a boil, then reduce the heat and simmer for about 10-12 minutes. Check the seasoning.

This can easily be done well in advance – the flavours of this ginger and soy chicken dish will intensify when left to stand – leaving you plenty of time to prepare whatever else you'd like to serve this dish with.

Piri-Piri Chicken with Roasted Squash

Choc-full of flavour and light! Oh yes, this piri-piri chicken with roasted squash is not only full-on flavour-wise, it is also low in calories.

And by serving it with a mixture of vegetables it becomes a healthy meal as well. I add tasty small tomatoes at the end of roasting and steamed or boiled vegetables such as the tenderstem broccoli (broccolini) in the photo.

Tomatoes and carrots are better for you when cooked – a rarity among vegetables. Cooked carrots release more beta carotene than raw. Cooked tomatoes have less vitamin C than fresh but the cooking makes the health-boasting lycopene in tomatoes more absorbable. Cook tomatoes in a little olive oil to boost the absorption of lycopene.

Tenderstem broccoli is by far the richest source of a phytochemical called "glucosinolates" – a very important anti-cancer and liver-friendly nutrient found in food.

You can of course add many more vegetables to this piri-piri chicken dish than I have done here – like roasted carrots, beetroots and parsnips and green vegetables such as beans and peas.

And it is always a good idea to also serve a salad with raw vegetables, topped with a tasty mustard-vinegar-olive oil dressing. A bit of mustard is good for you as it is rich in curcumin – a powerful antioxidant also found in turmeric.

For 4 people:

Piri-piri marinade:

3 garlic cloves – finely chopped

3 large red chillies – deseeded and finely chopped

3 teaspoons smoked paprika

3 tablespoons lemon juice

1 tablespoon red wine vinegar

2 tablespoons olive oil

¾ teaspoon sea/rock salt

¼ teaspoon black pepper

8 skin and boneless chicken thighs

1 small butternut squash, halved, deseeded and each half cut into 4-6 wedges

16-20 small tomatoes

Tenderstem broccoli (broccolini) and/or beans, peas

1.Preheat the oven to 200C/Fan 180C/400F/gas mark 6.
Place the butternut squash wedges in an oven-proof dish
and toss with a bit of olive oil. Place the dish in the oven and
roast for 35 minutes.

2.Add all the ingredients for the piri-piri marinade to a small
food processor and process until smooth. Place the chicken
thighs flat in another oven-proof dish and smother the
chicken with the marinade.

3.When the squash wedges have been in the oven for 15
minutes, place the dish with the chicken in the oven as well.
Cook the chicken for about 20-22 minutes – until the chicken
is cooked through.

4.Add the tomatoes to the squash during the last five
minutes. Stem or boil whatever green vegetables you are
serving as well.

Divide the piri-piri chicken and vegetables between four
plates and spoon over the marinade from the chicken dish.
Enjoy!

Dukkah-Marinated Chicken with Lentils and Roasted Vegetables

The inspiration for this dish, dukkah-marinated chicken with lentils and roasted vegetables, comes from the Middle East.

Dukkah is an Egyptian seed, nut and spice mix. I am using sesame seeds, pistachio nuts, coriander seeds, cumin seeds and chilli flakes in my take on this mix.

Like with all spice mixes, the ingredients vary from one recipe to another. You can buy ready-made dukkah dips but it is so easy to make yourself – and I feel it is so much more satisfactory, and fun, when you have made it yourself.

Seeds and nuts are full of essential fats, vitamins and minerals. The best way to absorb all these healthy nutrients in seeds and nuts is to eat them crushed up – and this seed, nut and spice mix is pounded in a pestle and mortar until you have a dry, finely ground mixture.

I am using Puy lentils – they are my favourite type of lentils. If you can't get hold of these lentils, you can swap them for green lentils.

To top off this dish, I add some delicious crumbled feta cheese before serving. I was on a dairy-free diet for quite some time but I now eat feta cheese made from goat and sheep milk every now and then.

This will make a bit more dukkah than you need for the marinade but it will keep for a month if you store it in an air-tight container. The way this mix is often eaten is by dipping flatbread first in olive oil and then in dukkah mix.

For 4 people:

Dukkah mix:

2 tablespoons sesame seeds

1 tablespoon pistachio nuts

1 tablespoon coriander (cilantro) seeds

½ tablespoon cumin seeds

A good pinch of chilli flakes

Marinade:

3 heaped tablespoons dukkah mix

A thumb-sized piece of ginger, peeled and finely grated

Finely grated zest from 1 lemon

2½ tablespoon olive oil

1 teaspoon sea salt

A good pinch of black pepper

8 bone and skinless chicken thighs

1 small butternut squash, diced

3 large red peppers (bell peppers) - cut into large chunks

Olive oil

250g, 9oz, slightly more than 1 cup, Puy lentils

To serve:

Feta cheese crumbled

Watercress and/or rocket (arugula), spinach leaves

1.Pre-heat the oven to 200C/fan 180C/400F/gas mark 6. Start by dry-roasting all the ingredients for the dukkah in a frying pan for about 2 minutes – stirring continuously - until they start to colour and release an aroma. Place the ingredients in a pestle and mortar and grind until you have a fine mixture.

2.Mix together all the ingredients for the marinade. Cover an oven tray with baking parchment and place the chicken thighs flat on the tray. Smother the chicken with the marinade.

3.Toss the diced squash and pepper chucks with 1 tablespoon of olive oil and a good pinch of sea salt in a roasting tin and roast in the oven for 25-30 minutes.

4.As soon as the vegetables are in the oven, cook the Puy lentils according to pack instructions. I cook the lentils in vegetable stock for approximately 22 minutes before draining them.

5.While the lentils are cooking, place the tray with chicken thighs in the oven as well and cook for about 20 minutes - until the chicken is cooked through.

Once everything is cooked, mix the roasted vegetables with the Puy lentils and divide between four plates. Top each plate with two dukkah-marinated chicken thighs and crumble over some feta cheese. Serve together with green leaves.

Chilli, Ginger and Garlic Beef

Red meat can be quite fatty but I'm using lean minced beef (5% fat) for this chilli, ginger and garlic beef dish.

This beef dish is great to freeze as well so it can be a good idea to double up on all the ingredients.

You can use the spicy beef mix in different ways.

For a healthier and leaner meal, eat it together with a raw salad made with grated carrots and beetroots and dark green leaves with an olive oil, balsamic vinegar and mustard dressing.

You can also eat it with roasted vegetables such as carrots, pumpkin and sweet potatoes and cooked/steamed broccoli or green beans.

Or you can toast wholemeal pitta bread and let everyone fill their pitta bread with the beef and things like lettuce, avocado, red peppers and some natural yogurt mixed with feta cheese.

And you can eat it with baked potatoes, sweet potatoes or any other potato, and a side salad.

For 4 people

1 small red onion - finely chopped

3 teaspoons grated ginger

2-3 garlic cloves - crushed/minced

2 red chillies - deseeded and chopped finely

1 tablespoon Extra virgin olive oil

12 small tomatoes (cherry or plum) - quartered

500g, 1lb 2oz, lean beef mince

1 tablespoon Extra virgin olive oil

2 tablespoons balsamic vinegar

2 tablespoons soy sauce

1 heaped tablespoon sun-dried tomato paste

1 1/2 teaspoon sea salt

1/2 teaspoon black pepper

100ml, 3 1/2floz, 1/2 cup, water

2 spring onions (scallions) - finely chopped

Add 1 tablespoon of olive oil, the onion, ginger, garlic and chillies to a large frying pan over a medium heat. Keep stirring for a couple of minutes and then add the tomatoes to the pan and stir.

Leave to fry, stirring every now and then, for a further 5 minutes - until the tomatoes start to collapse. Place this mixture in a bowl and leave it to the side.

Add another tablespoon of olive oil to the frying pan and increase the heat to medium-high. Add the mince to the pan and fry, breaking up the mince with a spoon. Keep stirring until browned.

Add the red onion and tomato mix to the frying pan together with the balsamic vinegar, soy sauce, tomato paste and water. Season with the salt and pepper and stir everything together. Lower the heat and leave to simmer for about 15 minutes, until all the liquid has evaporated.

Just before serving, stir in the chopped spring onions (scallions).

Slow-Cooked Lamb Casserole

I love using the cheaper cuts of lamb for a slow-cooked lamb casserole. The meat becomes gloriously tender and the taste is sensational.

Autumn is my favourite season – a season suited for food like casseroles. And lamb is my favourite type of red meat.

In this slow-cooked lamb casserole, I use the neck fillet and trickle some honey over the meat and cook it in red wine. It obviously needs a bit of time in the oven, but it's easy to make. Casseroles are great to make well in advance as the flavours intensify when left to stand.

Lamb meat is undoubtedly rich in fat - to make this an as low-calorie meal as possible, avoid serving this casserole with things like white rice or mashed potatoes. Go for of lots of vegetables instead.

Apart from the carrots in the casserole, I like to serve this slow-cooked lamb casserole with lots of green vegetables - like beans, peas and broccoli - and oven-roasted sweet potato wedges and tomatoes.

For 4 people:

1.2 kilo, 2lb 10½oz, lamb neck fillets, each fillet cut into 3-4 pieces

1 tablespoon plain flour (I use white spelt flour)

Salt and pepper

2 tablespoons olive oil

1 small red onion, finely chopped

3 medium-sized carrots, each carrot cut into 4 pieces

4 fat garlic cloves, finely chopped

1 tablespoon fresh thyme

1 tablespoon honey

350ml, 1½ cups, full-flavoured red wine (always use wine that you are happy to drink as well)

4 small sweet potatoes - cut into wedges

Small tomatoes

Green beans and/or other green vegetables, such as broccoli, peas

1. Preheat the oven to 170C/ Fan 150C/350F/Gas Mark 3. Season the flour with salt and pepper. Roll the lamb neck pieces in the seasoned flour. Shake off any excess flour.

2. Heat the olive oil in a casserole dish and fry the pieces of meat over a medium high heat until browned on all sides – depending on the size of your casserole dish, you might have to do this in batches. Remove the meat from the casserole dish and leave it to the side.

3. Lower the heat a bit and add the chopped onion to the casserole dish, stir and cook for 3-4 minutes (if needed, add a little bit more oil). Add the garlic and cook for a further minute – keep stirring to make sure the garlic doesn't burn.

4. Return the meat to the casserole dish together with the carrots and thyme. Trickle over the honey and pour in the wine. Cover the casserole dish with a lid and bring to a simmer. Transfer the casserole dish to the preheated oven and cook for about 2 hours – until the meat is really tender. Check the seasoning to see if you need more salt and/or pepper.

I cook the rest of the vegetables once the meat is ready – leaving the slow-cooked lamb casserole to rest with the lid on.

1.Turn up the heat of the oven to 200C/Fan 180C/400F/Gas Mark 6. Toss the sweet potato wedges in a little bit of olive oil and sprinkle some salt over the wedges. Place them in a roasting tray and roast in the oven for around 25 minutes, until tender. Add the tomatoes during the last 10 minutes.

2. Boil or steam the beans - and/or other green vegetables - when the oven-roasted vegetables are nearly ready.

Spanish-Style Meatballs in a Red Wine Tomato Sauce

Meat doesn't necessarily have to turn food into a heavy meal. This Spanish-style meatball recipe is such a deeply satisfying dish, full of lovely flavours yet quite light.

To me the most important thing with any type of meatball is that the meat mixture needs to be quite moist before shaping into balls. Far too many recipes I've come across produce near rock-hard meatballs once cooked.

I like to serve these Spanish-style meatballs with oven-roasted carrots - or any other root vegetables - and steamed green beans tossed in a little olive oil, a squeeze of lemon juice and some grated Parmesan cheese.

Tip! Once you have mixed together all the ingredients for the meatballs - and before you shape the mixture into meatballs - fry a teaspoon of the mixture to check if you are happy with the seasoning. This way you can add some more if need be.

For 4 people

500g, 1lb 2oz, 2¼ cups, lean beef mince

1 large red onion

4 tablespoons water

1 large egg

1 garlic clove, crushed

30g, 1oz, 1/3 cup, grated Parmesan cheese

2 tablespoons olive oil

1 teaspoon sea salt

Pepper

100ml, 3½floz, ½ cup, full-flavoured red wine (always use wine that you are happy to drink as well)

400g, 14oz, 2¼ cup, tin chopped tomatoes

Parsley, to serve

1. Start by finely grating the red onion (you want a moist mush) into a bowl. Add the water, egg, crushed garlic clove, grated Parmesan, 1 teaspoon of salt and some pepper to the onion and mix it all together. Add the mince and mix thoroughly. Wet your hands and form the mixture into around 24 small balls. Heat the olive oil in a large frying pan and

quickly fry the meatballs until they are brown all over. You will have to turn them quite carefully to not break them up. Depending on the size of your frying pan, you may have to do this in two batches.

2. Transfer the meatballs to a large saucepan. Deglaze the frying pan with a little of the red wine, making sure you stir and scrape up all the sediment, and pour this and the rest of the red wine over the meatballs. Let it bubble away over a medium heat until syrupy, about 5 minutes. Stir in the chopped tomatoes, 50ml, 2floz, 0.2 cup, water, some salt and pepper. Bring to a boil then lower the heat and cover with a lid.

3. Leave to simmer for 10 minutes then take off the lid, increase the heat and cook for a further couple of minutes to thicken the sauce a little. **Check the seasoning of the sauce.** Serve the Spanish-style meatballs sprinkled with the chopped parsley.

Beetroot Burgers with a Feta Cheese and Garlic Sauce

It is an incredibly tasty combination - juicy lamb and beetroot burgers with a feta cheese and garlic sauce. These are a few of my favourite things – lamb, beetroot and above all, feta cheese.

I won't go as far as calling it an addiction but I do love this type of cheese and I use it quite a lot both in hot and cold dishes. This love of feta blossomed unhindered the winter I lived in Greece, on the island of Crete.

I lived in a small village up in the hills and in the little village shop, behind the counter, stood two massive tins each containing a huge block of feta cheese. The owners would happily allow you to try each one to see which one you preferred and once you had chosen one, they'd cut as big a piece as you wanted out of the block.

Those were my feta days! I loved eating nothing but some bread and a piece of feta with some local olive oil drizzled over it and scattered with some dried herbs like thyme, oregano and rosemary (which all grow on the island). Or I cooked large white beans in a tomato, garlic and herb sauce to go with my feta, or... I'll stop there.

There is a fair few recipes on my website where feta cheese plays a part.

Tip! When buying feta cheese, make sure it says that it's made from sheep and goat's milk – there are some bad imitations out there made from cow's milk.

I serve these lamb and beetroot burgers on toasted sourdough bread, topped with the feta cheese and garlic sauce and with oven-roasted, tasty-healthy-low-calorie sweet potatoes on the side.

Yep, sweet potatoes are another great love of mine, and I use them quite often.

Add a salad with different green leaves and juicy tomatoes sprinkled with a little olive oil and balsamic vinegar and you've got a super-tasty and very healthy meal in front of you.

For 4 people:

4 small sweet potatoes cut into wedges

Olive oil

Burgers:

500g,1lb 2oz, 2¼ cups (firmly packed), lamb mince

1 medium-sized red onion, finely grated

1 large raw beetroot, finely grated

1½ teaspoon ground coriander

1½ teaspoon ground cumin

Salt and pepper

4 slices of sourdough bread, or some other good bread

Feta and garlic sauce:

100ml, 3½floz, ½ cup, natural or Greek yogurt

1 large garlic clove, crushed

100g, 3½oz, ¾ cup feta cheese, crumbled

Salt and pepper

1.Heat the oven to 200C/fan 180C/400F/gas mark 6. Toss the sweet potato wedges with 1 tablespoon olive oil. Place the wedges on a baking tray, sprinkle some salt over them and cook in the oven for 20-25 minutes until tender.

2.Mix together all the ingredients for the feta and garlic sauce and leave it to mature.

3.Mix together all the ingredients for the lamb burgers in a bowl, season the mixture with salt and pepper. With your hands, mould the mixture into 4 patties. Brush the patties with oil and heat a frying pan. Cook for about 4 minutes on each side until browned and cooked through.

Toast the bread, and top each slice with one of the lamb and beetroot burgers and add some feta cheese and garlic sauce to each burger. Serve with the sweet potato wedges on the side.

Lebanese-Style Lamb in Pitta Bread

To me, this Lebanese-style lamb dish is comfort food. Unlike Western-style comfort food - which usually contains a lot of butter and cream – this is lighter and healthier food.

I find the aromas and taste of the spices used in Middle Eastern food irresistible - so warm and inviting. And with such seductive spices, it's easy to cook food full of flavour.

There is no denying that the lamb meat has quite a high fat content – I use lean lamb mince for this recipe. A good way to reduce the calories of any meal is to up the intake of the vegetables served.

This makes for a relaxed meal where everyone adds as many things as they want to their own pitta bread. For the lettuce, choose watercress and/or rocket leaves – both are properly peppery but the most nutritious one is the watercress, a nutritional goldmine.

At the opposite end is iceberg lettuce, found in so many ready-made salads, which contain about 99%water and near 0% nutrients. It is the darker green lettuce leaves which are the most nutritious.

For 4 people:

1 tablespoon olive or rapeseed oil

1 red onion finely chopped

1 garlic clove, crushed

500g, 1lb 2oz, 2¼ cups, lean lamb mince

1 red chilli (or more if you want an even spicier kick to the meat) - deseeded and finely chopped

1 teaspoon ground allspice

1 teaspoon ground cumin

¾ teaspoon ground cinnamon

2 tablespoons tomato purée

200ml, 7floz, 0.9 cup, water

Salt and pepper

To serve:

Wholemeal (whole-wheat) pitta bread

Watercress and/or rocket leaves

1-2 red chillies, finely sliced

Red peppers (bell peppers), halved, deseeded and sliced

Pomegranate seeds

Natural yogurt (I use Greek-style yogurt)

1. Heat the oil in a heavy based pan and cook the onion over a medium heat for 5 minutes. Add the garlic and cook for a further minute, then add the lamb mince. Stir to break up the mince and continue to cook until the mince is brown all over.

2. Add the spices, chilli, tomato purée and water to the pan. Season the mince mixture with salt and pepper and stir. Cook over a low-medium heat for 20 minutes – stirring every now and then – until all the liquid has evaporated. Check the seasoning.

Toast the pitta bread and place all the extra things to add to the pitta bread in separate bowls along with the hot Lebanese-style lamb mix.

Lamb Kofta in a Tomato Sauce

One word – sublime! There are such breath-taking flavours in this lamb kofta dish that I find it hard to do justice to it with words alone.

The spices do the talking in this dish. I'm sometimes lazy and use ground spices when cooking. Ground spices deteriorate much quicker than whole spices – you do get more flavour from grinding whole spices.

For this dish, I use mostly whole spices that I dry-roast first and then grind to a powder using a pestle and mortar. The correct way would probably be to dry-roast each spice separately but there are limits to my patience.

There was a time when I was considering starting a food outlet serving nothing but different types of meatballs. These lamb kofta would have been my Indian version.

For 4 people:

For the kofta:

1 medium-sized red onion

500g, 1lb 2oz, 2¼ cups (firmly packed), lean lamb mince

1 heaped teaspoon grated fresh ginger

2 garlic cloves, crushed

1 large red or green chilli, deseeded and finely chopped

1 egg

Salt and pepper

For the tomato sauce:

2 teaspoon coriander (cilantro) seeds

2 teaspoons cumin seeds

2 whole cloves

4 cardamom pods, crack open the pods and use only the seeds inside

1 teaspoon ground cinnamon

2 tablespoon oil, groundnut, sunflower or vegetable oil

1 red onion, finely chopped

200g, 7oz, 1¼ cups, ripe tomatoes, chopped into small pieces

200ml, 7floz, 0.9 cup, water

100ml, 3½floz, ½ cup, natural Greek-style yogurt

2 large handfuls fresh spinach

1. To make the kofta, start by finely grating the red onion (you want a moist mush) into a bowl. Add the grated fresh ginger, the crushed garlic, chopped chilli, the egg and season well with salt and pepper. Give it all a stir, add the lamb mince and mix thoroughly.

2. Have a tray that will fit in your fridge ready. Wet your hands with cold water and form the mixture into 20 meatballs. Place the meatballs on the tray, cover with cling film and place the tray in the fridge.

3. For the tomato sauce, start by dry-frying the coriander (cilantro) seeds, the cumin seeds, the cloves and cardamom seeds in a frying pan over a medium heat, stirring, for 1-2 minutes until the spices start to become aromatic and a few shades darker. Place the roasted spices in a pestle and mortar and grind to a reasonably fine powder. Mix in the ground cinnamon.

4. Heat the oil in a large sauce pan or casserole dish, add the chopped onion and fry over a medium heat, stirring every now and then, for 5 minutes. Add the spices and continue to stir and fry for 30 seconds before adding the chopped tomatoes. Continue to stir and fry for another 5-7 minutes until the tomatoes have collapsed. Add the water, then the yogurt and stir. Season with salt and pepper and bring the sauce to a simmer. Taste and check the seasoning.

5. Carefully slide in the chilled meatballs into the sauce. Bring it all back to a simmer, cover with a lid and simmer gently for 20 minutes. Take off the lid, carefully turn the meatballs over, and continue to simmer without the lid for a further 10 minutes. At the end, add the spinach and carefully stir it in until it has wilted.

I like to serve this lamb kofta dish with steamed green beans and my Asian-style carrot salad. For an even more substantial meal, serve it with roasted butternut squash and/or sweet potato.

Venison Casserole

I don't use game meat very often but when I do, like when cooking this venison casserole, I am reminded of how much I love it.

This is the type of meat I grew up on, especially moose meat. I adore the somewhat strong taste you get from these animals that roam the forests – a taste that you will not get from deer or moose that are farmed like cattle in fields.

If I'm buying venison from a butcher in Britain, I make sure it's from wild deer. When I'm visiting family in Sweden I mostly use moose meat. One of my brothers will give me meat from his freezer.

Game meat is very lean meat and while this is good news for the waistline, it's easy to over-cook and end up with very dry meat.

Unless I'm cooking the fillet of venison or moose – which I prefer to cook whole like fillet of beef – I often freeze the meat first and then cut the meat into thin slices when it's only slightly thawed. These thin slices of meat need very little cooking and is the last thing I fry and add to this venison casserole.

Start by soaking the dried mushrooms in water – they need at least 45 minutes soaking time.

For 4 people:

500g, 1lb 2oz, venison or moose meat (frozen first and then cut very finely when only slightly thawed, you can do this well in advance)

150g, 3½oz, dried porcini or chanterelle mushrooms, soaked for a minimum of 45 minutes and then rinsed under cold water.

½ tablespoon butter

500ml, 18floz, 2¼ cups, vegetable stock

1 small red onion, peeled, halved and finely slice

1 tablespoon rapeseed or olive oil

10 juniper berries, grind the berries in a pestle and mortar

250ml, 9floz, slightly less than 2¼ cups, full-flavoured red wine (always use wine that you are happy to drink as well)

1 ½ tablespoon soy sauce

2 tablespoons balsamic vinegar

1 tablespoon tomato paste

½ tablespoon redcurrant jelly

Salt and pepper

2 medium sized carrots cut into batons

2 large sweet potatoes cut into thick wedges

12-16 small tomatoes

Broccoli and/or other green vegetables

1.Pre-heat the oven to 200C/Fan 180C/400F/gas mark 6. Toss the carrot batons and sweet potato wedges in a little bit of olive oil. Place them on a baking tray, scatter a bit of salt over the vegetables and roast in the oven for 45 minutes, turning the vegetables half-way through. Add the tomatoes during the last 10 minutes.

2.Melt the butter in a casserole dish. Add the porcini mushrooms and fry gently for 3-4 minutes, stirring every now and then. Add the vegetable stock, bring to a boil and then lower the heat. Simmer for about 20 minutes, until the stock has reduced by half.

3.While the mushrooms are simmering, place 1 tablespoon oil in a frying pan over a moderate heat and add the sliced onion and the ground juniper berries. Fry the onion for 5 minutes until it starts to soften. Add the red wine, bring to a boil, lower the heat and simmer for 5 minutes. Add the soy sauce, balsamic vinegar, tomato paste and redcurrant jelly, stir and simmer for a further 5 minutes. Season with salt and pepper.

4.Add the onion and red wine mix to the casserole dish with the mushrooms. Stir and check the seasoning. Add a bit of oil (I use rapeseed oil for frying) to a large frying pan over quite a high heat and quickly brown the meat in batches –

seasoning each batch with a bit of salt and pepper. Add the browned meat to the casserole dish. Stir, check the seasoning and let it simmer for five minutes.

5.Boil or steam broccoli and/or other green vegetables.

Serve the venison casserole with the roasted vegetables and boiled/steamed green vegetables.

Slow-Cooked Lamb Shanks

I either serve these slow-cooked lamb shanks whole with all the vegetables that I add to the casserole, or I use the meat and vegetables to make a delicious shepherd's pie.

It does take a bit of time to make a shepherd's pie like this – mostly because of the slow-cooking - but you end up with a sensationally tasty dish.

I have made this type of shepherd's pie for up to 30 people in one go. You can slow-cook the lamb shanks and vegetables and prepare it all, once cooked, well in advance. It tastes even better the next day. All you have to do to finish it off is to add some mash and bake it in the oven.

As I like full flavoured food without too much calories, I don't cover the gorgeous slow-cooked meat and vegetables with heaps of buttery potato mash. I usually make my mash with a mixture of parsnips, celeriac and potato and only add a thin layer of this on top.

If you really want to hold back on the calories, toss the vegetables for the mash in a bit of olive oil, season with salt and pepper and oven-roast them. When they are done, mash them up without adding any butter. You will get a lot of super-tasty stock from the casserole and you can just add more of this to the meat mixture.

A quicker, much more slim-line and still mega-tasty way to eat these slow-cooked lamb shanks is to serve them straight out of the casserole with an assortment of vegetables that has cooked alongside the meat.

Just add some steamed or boiled green vegetables and you will serve up a tasty and healthy feast.

Whichever way you choose to eat these slow-cooked lamb shanks, an important part is to reduce the stock once the meat is starting to fall off the bone. Remove the meat and vegetables from the casserole dish. Bring the remaining stock to a rapid boil to reduce the stock and to intensify the flavours.

Slow-Cooked Lamb Shanks

For 4 people:

First of all, you need a large casserole dish with a tight-fitting lid - something that I personally think it's worth investing in if you haven't already got one. If you are using a casserole dish that is not flame-proof, you can brown the meat in a frying pan and then transfer the meat to the casserole dish.

4 lamb shanks

4 garlic cloves, finely chopped

1 large onion, peeled and quartered

Vegetables for the casserole: I add as many vegetables as I can fit in with the lamb shanks in the casserole – like carrots, butternut squash and sweet potato. Once peeled, and the butternut deseeded, I cut the carrots and sweet potatoes in two and the butternut in large chunks.

5 sprigs of fresh thyme

1 tablespoon Worcestershire sauce

Lamb or chicken stock – you'll need enough to almost cover the lamb shanks and vegetables, around 1 ½ – 2 litres, 1 ¾ - 2 ½ pints, 6 ½ - 8 ½ cups

Salt and pepper

If you are making a shepherd's pie, make the mash with potatoes alone or a mixture of potatoes, parsnips and celeriac - about 800g, 1lb 12oz, altogether.

1.Pre-heat the oven to 170C/Fan 150C/325F/gas mark 3. Season the lamb shanks with salt and fair bit of pepper. Add a bit of oil to the casserole dish (or a large frying pan if your casserole dish is not flame-proof) over a medium high heat. When the oil is hot, add two lamb shanks at a time and brown the shanks on all sides. Remove the ones that are done and do the same with the other lamb shanks.

2.Return all the lamb shanks to the casserole dish. If you have browned the meat in a frying pan, deglaze the frying pan by adding a bit of water to the pan and pour this into the casserole dish. Add the chopped garlic, onion, vegetables of your choice and thyme to the casserole dish (I add as many vegetables as possible). Add the Worcestershire sauce and then the stock – your meat and vegetables should be almost covered.

3.Bring everything to a simmer, cover the casserole dish with a tight-fitting lid and place the casserole dish in the oven for 1 ½ - 2 hours, until the meat starts to fall of the bone.

4.Once it's ready carefully remove the meat and vegetables from the casserole dish. If you are going to eat the slow-cooked lamb shanks and vegetables as they are, keep them warm while reducing the stock. Place the casserole dish on the stove-top or pour the remaining stock into a sauce pan and bring to a rapid boil. Cook until the liquid is reduced by about half. If you are making a shepherd's pie, you might want to reduce it a bit more.

5.Taste and check the seasoning of the reduced stock to see if you need to add any more salt and/or pepper. If you are serving the lamb shanks whole with the cooked vegetables, pour some of the reduced stock over each portion.

6.To make a shepherd's pie, once the slow-cooked lamb shanks have cooled down enough to handle, remove all the meat from the bones and shred it with your hands. Roughly mash all the vegetables from the casserole dish. Place the meat and mashed vegetables in a lightly greased oven-proof dish. Add as much of the stock as you like – if your mash that will go on top is very soft you don't want the meat and vegetables to be too wet. Any left-over stock is great to freeze and will make a mean gravy for another meal.

7.Once you have added your mash on top, place the dish in the oven, 220C/fan 200C/425F/gas mark 7, and cook until the shepherd's pie is bubbling hot and the mash on top is nicely browned.

Herb-Crusted Lamb Chops on a Bed of Vegetables

A tasty way to cook lamb chops - herb-crusted lamb chops on a bed of roasted and steamed vegetables.

There is of course a bit of fat in the meat. I choose to cook the herb-crusted lamb chops in the oven – which requires no extra fat as I place the chops on baking parchment. It is a healthier way to cook the meat.

The herb crust is divine and would be great to use on firm white fish as well.

I serve the lamb with lots of vegetables. I'm not going to deny that it can be expensive to buy organic food but when it comes to vegetables, I choose to buy organic varieties as often as possible.

For this dish, I oven-roast the carrots and the red peppers (bell pepper) – and I prefer the pointed varieties of peppers that tend to taste SO much better – steam the beans and broccoli and boil the peas very quickly. (I add frozen peas to boiling water and as soon as the water comes back to boiling, I drain the peas in a sieve.)

Once cooked, I toss the green vegetables in a bit of lemon juice, olive oil, some shredded fresh mint leaves and a bit of salt and pepper. I then crumble some really nice feta cheese (made of sheep's and goat's milk – NOT cow's milk) over all the vegetables. Super-Yum!

For 4 people:

For the herb crust:

1 tablespoon fresh thyme leaves

A handful of fresh rosemary leaves

A handful of parsley

A handful of fresh mint leaves

3 tablespoons breadcrumbs – I make mine from sourdough bread

2 level tablespoons pine nuts

4 anchovy fillets (I buy anchovy fillets in olive oil)

2 tablespoons olive oil

¼ teaspoon black pepper

3-4 lamb chops per person

Rapeseed (canola) or olive oil

4 large carrots, peeled and cut into batons

2 red peppers (bell peppers), deseeded and cut into chunks

1 small head of broccoli, cut into small florets, stem sliced

250g, 9oz, 1¼ cup green beans

250g, 9oz, 1¾ cup, peas, fresh or frozen

1 tablespoon lemon juice

½ tablespoon olive oil

Small handful of fresh mint leaves, shredded

Salt and pepper

Feta cheese (get a nice one - made with sheep's and goat's milk – it makes all the difference)

1.Pre-heat the oven to 200C/fan 180C/400F/gas mark 6. Place the carrot batons in a roasting tin, drizzle over a bit of oil and toss together. Season with a bit of salt and place the carrots in the oven. The carrots will need about 35 minutes of roasting – give them a stir half-way through and add the peppers (bell peppers) at the same time, coating them in the oil as well.

2.Place all the ingredients for the herb crust in a small food processor and blend together. Place the lamb chops on a baking tray covered with baking parchment. Divide the herb crust over the lamb chops. Cooking time in the oven depends on the thickness of the chops but around 15-18 minutes (I like mine to be pink). Once cooked to your liking – cover the herb-crusted lamb chops and leave them to rest for 5 minutes before serving.

3.Boil or steam the beans, broccoli and peas. Once drained, put them back into the pan and toss with the lemon juice, olive oil, shredded mint leaves and a bit of salt and pepper.

I mix all of the vegetables on a large serving plate and add crumbled feta cheese on top of the vegetables, followed by the lamb chops.

Moroccan Lamb Meatballs

I do like lamb meat, and that includes lamb mince.

These Moroccan lamb meatballs are simply divine, as is the sauce you cook them in. I also add sweet green peas to the sauce towards the end. I love this dish!

I do use quite a few different spices in this recipe, but these spices are good to have at home if you are a fan of Middle-Eastern food – as well as Asian-style food.

I serve this dish with oven-roasted carrots and steamed broccoli and green beans – making it into a healthy and easy-digestible meal.

You can add quinoa or couscous to the meal as well – protein-rich and super-nutritious quinoa being the best choice.

Following "food combining" rules as much as possible means not eating concentrated protein foods (meat, poultry, fish, whole eggs) together with concentrated starch foods (potatoes, wheat, rice, oats, pasta and bread).

Both of these food groups go well together with vegetables though (apart from potatoes) – including beans, lentils and chickpeas.

The reason behind food combining is that concentrated protein and concentrated starch are digested totally different. So to be able to digest all of what you eat in the best possible way and thus get the as much nutrients out of your food as possible, you are better off not eating these two food groups together.

For 4 people:

For the sauce:

1 tablespoon olive oil

½ large red onion (the other half is used for the meatballs), finely chopped

1 teaspoon ground allspice

½ teaspoon ground cloves

½ teaspoon ground cinnamon

¼ teaspoon ground nutmeg

½ teaspoon chilli flakes

500ml, 18floz, 2¼ cups, chicken stock

2 heaped tablespoons tomato puree/paste

Salt and black pepper

200g, 7oz, 1¼ cups frozen peas

For the Moroccan lamb meatballs:

½ large red onion, finely grated

2 garlic cloves, crushed

Handful of fresh mint leaves, finely chopped

1 egg

2 teaspoons ground cumin

1 level teaspoon salt

½ teaspoon black pepper

500g, 1lb 2oz, 2¼ cups (firmly packed), lean lamb mince

1.Start by making the sauce. Place the oil in a spacious pan or pot that has a lid over a medium high heat. Add the chopped onion and cook - stirring frequently - for about 5 minutes, until the onion has softened.

2.Add all of the spices and continue to stir and cook for a further minute before adding the stock and tomato puree/paste. Stir and bring to a simmer. Season with some salt and pepper and leave the sauce to simmer and thicken for about 15minutes.

3.While the sauce is cooking, make the meatballs. Mix together the grated onion, crushed garlic, chopped mint, egg, cumin, salt and pepper in a bowl. Add the mince to the bowl and mix everything together thoroughly. With your hands, form the mixture into little balls – slightly smaller than a walnut.

4.Check the seasoning of the sauce before adding the meatballs. Bring back the sauce to a simmer and keep rolling the balls around so that they cook evenly, for about 15 minutes. Add the frozen peas to the pan/pot, stir, cover with the lid and increase the heat. As soon as it comes back to a boil, turn off the heat. Leave for a couple of minutes before serving.

Japanese-Style Beef with Marinated Carrots and Cucumber

The idea for this Japanese-style beef came after I had been to a couple of Japanese restaurants. I felt an urge to cook Japanese food afterwards. Everything I'd eaten – from sushi to salads and hot main courses - had been so incredibly tasty.

So I started to look at recipes for Japanese food and goodness me, what an amazing amount of sugar they use in a lot of dishes!

It seems counter-productive to me when you add 3 tablespoons of sugar to a marinade and then pour it over otherwise healthy vegetables. I can't see the need for the sugar when there are so many other tasty ingredients in the marinade.

I used a recipe I had for Japanese-style beef with marinated cucumber and carrots and swapped the sugar in the vegetable marinade and stock for the beef for a bit of honey, and cut down on the amount of soya in the stock. It tasted amazing!

For 4 people:

Vegetable marinade

3 tablespoons rice vinegar

1 teaspoon soy sauce

1 heaped teaspoon honey (I use raw Manuka honey)

A good pinch of salt and pepper

½ cucumber, sliced really thinly

1 medium-sized carrot, cut into thin ribbons (use a potato peeler)

Stock: ½ green pepper (bell pepper), diced

½ green apple, diced

½ yellow onion, diced

1 fat garlic clove, sliced

Thumb-sized piece of fresh ginger, sliced

200ml, 7floz, 0.9 cup water

4 tablespoons soya sauce (I use organic gluten-free Tamari soy sauce)

1 tablespoon mirin (you can find this in most well-stocked supermarkets)

3 tablespoons rice vinegar

1 teaspoon honey

1 teaspoon sesame oil

1-2 tablespoons vegetable or groundnut oil

500g, 1lb2oz, sirloin or fillet of beef, sliced very thinly

Salt and pepper

Basmati rice - or use quinoa (healthier and better for your weight)

1.Using a whisk, mix together the ingredients for the marinade in a bowl. Add the thinly sliced cucumber and carrot ribbons to the bowl, mix well, cover the bowl and place it in the fridge. Leave to marinate for 1 hour (give the vegetables a stir half-way through).

2.Once the vegetables have been marinating for 30 minutes, place all the ingredients for the stock in a pot and bring to a simmer. Simmer for 30 minutes before straining the stock through a sieve into a clean pot.

3.While the stock is simmering, cook the rice or quinoa according to pack instructions.

4.Heat the oil in a large frying pan or wok over quite a high heat. Once the oil is sizzling, quickly stir-fry the sliced beef - until browned - and season with salt and pepper. Transfer the beef to the pot with the stock and bring to a simmer for 1 minute.

5.Place a portion of rice/quinoa in 4 bowls or deep plates, divide the Japanese-style beef and stock between the bowls and top with the marinated vegetables.

Lamb Biryani with Saffron Rice

In a traditional lamb biryani you cook the meat and rice together in a sealed pot. But I prefer to cook my marinated lamb and saffron rice separately.

This is a dish that takes a bit of time to make – mostly because you marinate the meat overnight – but it is really worth it!

If you've got the time, cook the lamb in the morning and leave it to "mature" until serving it in the evening. Not only will the taste have improved but you've only got the rice and some vegetables to cook before serving it, making it a great dish to cook when you are having guests.

I am using mostly whole spices that I grind to a powder myself but you can swap most of whole spices for ground spices.

Even though there are a fair number of ingredients in this recipe, it is not difficult to make.

Lamb biryani for 6 people:

For the marinade:

6 cardamom pods - open the pods and take out the seeds inside, discard the outer shell

5 cloves (or ½ teaspoon ground cloves)

3 teaspoons coriander seeds

2 teaspoons cumin seeds

½ teaspoon fennel seeds

½ teaspoon black pepper corns

1 teaspoon ground cinnamon

1 teaspoon ground turmeric

1 teaspoon ground ginger

5cm, 2inch, piece of ginger – peeled and finely grated

3 garlic cloves, crushed

3 large red chillies, deseeded and finely chopped

A handful each of fresh mint (leaves only) and coriander (leaves and stalks), finely chopped

2 tablespoons water

1kilo, 2 1/4lb, boneless lamb leg or shoulder, cubed

2 tablespoons coconut or vegetable oil

1 large red onion, finely chopped

4 medium-sized ripe tomatoes, chopped

250ml, 8 ¾floz, 1.2 cups, natural yogurt

50ml, 2floz, ¼ cup, water

Salt

250g, 9oz, 2 ¼ cups, basmati rice

600ml, 20floz, 2.7 cups, water

½ teaspoon salt

2 whole cloves

3 cardamom pods, bruised

A good pinch of saffron strands

1.Grind the cardamom seeds, cloves, coriander, cumin, fennel seeds and black pepper corns to a fine powder in a pestle and mortar or spice grinder. Place in a non-metallic bowl and add the ground cinnamon, turmeric and ginger. Add the grated fresh ginger, crushed garlic, chopped chillies, mint, coriander and the water and mix together. Add the cubed lamb to the bowl and toss together. Cover and leave to marinate in the fridge overnight.

2.Heat the oil in a large heavy-based saucepan or casserole over a low heat. Place the chopped onion in the pan and stir and cook for 5 minutes. Add the chopped tomatoes and continue to cook for a further 5 minutes.

3.Increase the heat to medium-high. Add the lamb, all the marinade and the water to the pan. Season with some salt and stir. Bring to a simmer and cook over a low heat for about 1 ½ hour, or until the meat is really tender. Taste and check the seasoning.

4.Place the rice, water, salt, cloves, cardamom pods, and saffron in pot with a lid. Stir and bring to a simmer. Cover with a lid and simmer over a low heat for 10 minutes. Remove the pan from the heat and leave to stand for a couple of minutes before fluffing up the rice with a fork. Remove the cloves and cardamom pods before serving.

I serve the lamb biryani with steamed green beans and sugar snaps. And I sometimes cook a large, diced sweet potato together with the lamb – it's a great combination.

Slow-Cooked Beef Tagine

You need a bit of patience to cook this slow-cooked beef tagine - but the end result is really worth the wait.

It doesn't take that long to prepare though, before it goes into the oven. You need to cook the tagine for about 2 hours but once it is in the oven, it pretty much takes care of itself.

To make this an as low-calorie meal as possible, serve it with nothing but vegetables - such as oven roasted carrots, squash, beetroots (beets) and tomatoes and steamed or boiled green beans and/or broccoli.

The inspiration for this slow-cooked beef tagine comes from a "Moro cook book" by Sam & Sam Clark. I have changed it somewhat and added more things.

You add prunes to this casserole and I got hold of some really tasty Agen prunes soaked in a bit of brandy that I used for this casserole. I'm not sure how much of a difference the brandy did to the taste of the tagine though!

For 4 people:

A good pinch of saffron strands soaked in 2 tablespoons of hot water

1 tablespoon butter

2 tablespoons olive oil

2 medium-sized red onions, peeled and finely grated

2 garlic cloves, crushed

1½ teaspoon ground ginger

1½ teaspoon ground cinnamon

½ teaspoon ground black pepper

1 kilo, 2¼lb, stewing steak (stew meat), diced

150g, 5½oz, ready to eat prunes

1 large sweet potato, peeled and cut into chunks

Salt

Water

150g, 5½oz, 1 cup, frozen peas

1.Pre-heat the oven to 150C/300F/gas mark 2. Place the butter and oil in a casserole dish over a medium high heat. Add the grated onion, garlic, ground ginger, cinnamon and pepper to the casserole dish and fry for a minute.

2.Increase the heat and add the diced meat to the casserole dish. Stir and fry for a further 2 minutes. Add the soaked saffron, prunes and sweet potato, season with some salt and add enough water to cover the meat. Stir and bring to the boil. Cover the casserole dish with a tight-fitting lid and place it in the pre-heated oven.

3.Cook the beef tagine for about 2 hours (it might take a bit longer), until the meat is really tender and falls apart. Once it is ready, take it out of the oven, check the seasoning and add the frozen peas. Place it back in the oven for a further 5 minutes.

Indian Lamb Mince Pie

I have definitely got a soft spot for Asian-style food – a spot about as big as Asia itself.

This utterly delicious Indian lamb mince pie is just one of so many Asian-style dishes that I love.

I add a garam masala spice mix to this dish. You can use a ready-made mix if you want to, but I will also give you the recipe for a spice mix that I make myself.

It requires a bit of elbow grease to make yourself – unless you've got an electric grinder, of course – but I think it is fun and rewarding to make. This will make more garam masala than you need for this recipe - it will keep for months though, if you store it in an air-tight container in the fridge.

Apart from being super-tasty, this Indian lamb mince pie is quite healthy and relatively low in calories. The fat mainly comes from the meat. The only other fat I use myself is coconut fat, a healthy type of fat which can help to promote weight loss.

I use butternut squash and sweet potatoes for the mash – more squash than sweet potatoes though. While both vegetables contain slow-releasing carbohydrates, squash contains fewer carbohydrates and for that reason, it is better for your weight.

Garam Masala Spice Mix:

1 heaped tablespoon coriander seeds

2 teaspoons cumin seeds

8 cardamom pods – left whole while roasting then split open and seeds removed for grinding once cooled down

5 whole cloves

½ teaspoon black pepper corns

1/3 of a cinnamon stick

1 level teaspoon turmeric

1.Dry-roast the coriander and cumin seeds, cardamom pods, cloves, black pepper corns and piece of cinnamon stick in a frying pan over a medium high heat for 1-2 minutes until the spices start to become aromatic and a few shades darker. Remove from the heat.

2.Once cooled down, split open the cardamom pods and place the seeds together with the other roasted spices in a pestle and mortar or a spice grinder. Grind to a fine powder. Once done, mix in the ground turmeric.

Indian Lamb Mince Pie for 4 people:

2 tablespoons coconut oil – or use vegetable oil

1 red onion, finely chopped

2 garlic cloves, crushed/minced

1 large red chilli, deseeded and finely chopped

2 heaped teaspoons garam masala spice mix

1 level teaspoon ground ginger

500g, 1lb2oz, 2¼ cups (firmly packed), lean lamb mince

1 heaped tablespoon tomato purée

Salt

200ml, 7floz, 0.9 cup, water

1 tablespoon coconut oil – or use vegetable oil

1 medium-sized butternut squash – peeled, halved, deseeded and diced

2 medium-sized sweet potatoes – peeled and diced

3 spring onions (scallions), chopped

Handful of fresh coriander (cilantro), chopped – optional

Salt and pepper

1.Preheat the oven to 200C/fan 180C/400F/gas mark 6. Place 1 tablespoon of oil and the diced squash and sweet potatoes in a roasting pan/tray and mix together. Cook in the oven for about 30-35 minutes – until the vegetables are soft.

2.While the vegetables are cooking, place 2 tablespoons of coconut oil in a large frying pan over a low heat. Add the chopped onion to the pan and cook for 5 minutes, stirring every now and then.

3.Add the garlic, chilli and all the spices to the frying pan, stir and cook for a further minute. Turn up the heat to medium and add the mince. Stir to break up the mince and brown all over. Once the mince is browned, add the tomato puree and water. Season with some salt, stir and bring to a simmer. Lower the heat and continue to simmer for about 25 minutes.

4.Once ready, take out the diced squash and sweet potatoes from the oven. Use a potato masher or fork to mash the vegetables. Add the chopped spring onions (scallions) and coriander (cilantro) to the mash, season with some salt and pepper and mix it all together.

5.Place the cooked mince in an oven-proof dish and top with the mashed vegetables. Cook in the oven for 10-15 minutes – until piping hot.

I like to serve this Indian lamb mince pie together with a large salad full of peppery leaves – such as water cress and rocket (arugula) – and different coloured peppers (bell peppers).

Soup Recipes

Watercress and Spinach Soup

Tasty and healthy - a watercress and spinach soup which looks stunningly green thanks to very little cooking.

The less you have to cook most vegetables, the better it obviously is nutrition-wise but it also makes the vegetables retain their vibrant colour.

If you haven't tried watercress before, you should know that it has a strong taste - it's properly peppery like rocket, but it is also a nutritional goldmine.

I add watercress to a lot of salads as well to increase the nutritional value, but if the watercress is "older" with thick stalks, then I remove the thickest part of the stalks before adding to the salad. But not so for this soup where I use all of the watercress.

You need to use quite a large pot when making this watercress and spinach soup as the spinach takes up a lot of room until it has wilted down

For 4 people:

1 large yellow onion, roughly chopped

25g, 1oz, 2 tablespoons butter + 1 tablespoon olive oil

100g, 3½oz, 3½ cups, watercress

250g, 9oz, 7½ cups, spinach

300ml, 10floz, 1.3 cups, hot water + the same amount of ice-cold water

Salt and pepper

Feta cheese or natural yogurt

1. Start with the watercress by separating the leaves from the stalks. Put the leaves to one side and chop the stalks roughly.

2. In a large pan, gently fry the onion and the stalks from the watercress in the butter and olive oil until the onion is soft, around 5 minutes. Be careful it doesn't burn. Heat up 300ml, 10floz, 1.3 cups, of water to boiling point.

3. Add the watercress leaves, the spinach and the hot water to the pan, increase the heat and stir until the leaves have wilted and the water comes back to a simmer. This should only take 1-2 minutes. Take the pan off the heat and add the

ice-cold water to the pan to stop the vegetables from continuing to cook.

4. Either blend the soup with a stick blender in the pan or use an ordinary blender (depending on the size of your blender, you might have to do this in batches) and then return the soup to the pan. Reheat the soup and serve in soup bowls and either crumble over some feta cheese or add a dollop of natural yogurt to each bowl.

Chicken and Noodle Soup

If it's true that chicken soup can help when you've got a cold, then this full-flavoured chicken and noodle soup should definitely do the trick.

This soup is a veritable natural pharmacy. Apart from the chicken - which is apparently good to eat to help cure a cold – there is healthy and tasty ginger, garlic, chilli and turmeric in my soup.

Colds aside, this is a good soup to warm you up on a cold weather's day. And while it is filling, it is still a light soup and perfect for anyone watching their weight.

I am using gluten-free soba noodles (made with buckwheat flour) in my soup but you can use other noodles – rice noodles or egg noodles, for example. Soba noodles are the healthiest type of noodles but the most filling type is probably egg noodles.

I add the sliced carrots and sugar snaps at the very end of cooking as I want them to still be crunchy.

If you have the time, then this soup really benefits from being cooked in advance (minus the noodles) as the broth infuses the chicken pieces when left to stand. Just be careful if you leave it for a long time - make sure you cover up the soup and place it in the fridge once it has cooled down.

For 4 people:

1 tablespoon coconut oil

2 garlic cloves, finely chopped

1 large red chilli, de-seeded and finely chopped

Thumb-size piece of fresh ginger, finely chopped

½ teaspoon ground turmeric

1.1 litre, 1.9 pints, 5 cups chicken stock

Finely grated zest of 1 un-waxed lime or lemon

1 teaspoon sesame oil

1½ tablespoon Thai fish sauce

Black pepper

4 chicken breasts, diced

1 medium-sized carrot, cut into thin matchstick-sized strips

150g, 5½oz sugar snaps, sliced

Juice of half a lime or lemon

200g, 7oz, noodles

1.Place the coconut oil in a heavy-bottomed pot over a low heat. Add the chopped garlic, chilli, and ginger to the pot and fry for a couple of minutes - stirring continuously to make sure the garlic doesn't burn. Add the turmeric and continue to fry for a further minute.

2.Add the chicken stock, grated lime or lemon zest, sesame oil, Thai fish sauce, diced chicken breast to the pot and season with some black pepper. Stir, increase the heat and bring to a simmer.

3.Allow the soup to simmer for about 7 - 10 minutes – you want the cubed chicken to be cooked through but not dried out. Add the sliced carrots and sugar snaps during the last two minutes of cooking.

4.While the soup is simmering, cook the noodles according to pack instructions. Divide the noodles between 4 large bowls, add the lime or lemon juice to the soup and ladle chicken soup into each bowl.

You can add extra garnish to the chicken and noodle soup – such as fresh coriander (cilantro) or sliced spring onions (scallions).

Traditional Spanish Gazpacho

A very kind Spanish man once gave me his families' secret recipe for a traditional Spanish gazpacho.

I was on a walk through the mountainous interior of Spain – it took me four weeks to walk inland from Malaga to the French border – looking for authentic Spanish food.

He told me that this recipe has been passed on from one generation to another in his family. I felt humbled that he was willing to share it with me.

The one thing that I think is absolutely essential for a good gazpacho is the quality of the tomatoes. The tomatoes I ate in sunny Spain were as sweet as candy.

You can buy really tasty tomatoes here in the U.K. where I live. It doesn't matter what type of tomatoes you use – just make sure they are really ripe and fragrant tomatoes.

When it comes to vinegar, I suggest you use sherry vinegar or cider vinegar for the traditional Spanish Gazpacho. I use a mixture of cider and balsamic vinegar for my version though.

Apart from being sensationally tasty, this is also a really healthy soup. In the traditional recipe they add a slice of bread, I don't. And while they add a green pepper (bell pepper) to their soup, I add a red one. I buy the pointed, sweet variety of peppers as they are usually so much tastier than the ordinary ones.

If you are adding bread, try using really good bread – like sourdough.

Traditional Spanish Gazpacho:

2kilo, 4½lb, ripe tomatoes – roughly chopped

1 green pepper (bell pepper) - roughly chopped

1/3 of a cucumber – roughly chopped

1 garlic clove – crushed/minced

1 slice of bread

12 tablespoons olive oil

6 tablespoons vinegar

175ml, 5.9floz, ¾ cup, water

Salt and black pepper – about 2 level teaspoons of a good sea salt and a good pinch of black pepper

Place the slice of bread in a bowl and pour over enough water to cover the bread. Take out the bread and use your hands to squeeze out the water. Add the bread and all the other ingredients to a blender or food processor and pulse until you have a relatively smooth soup.

I like it to be slightly chunky. Check the seasoning before serving.

For my version of Gazpacho:

1 kilo, 2¼lb, 6 cups, ripe tomatoes – roughly chopped

1 red pepper (bell pepper) – roughly chopped

¼ cucumber – roughly chopped

1 fat garlic clove – crushed/minced

6 tablespoons olive oil

2 tablespoons cider vinegar

1 tablespoon balsamic vinegar

100ml, 3½floz, 0.4 cup, water

1 level teaspoon sea salt

A good pinch of black pepper

Place all the ingredients in a blender or food processor and pulse until you have a relatively smooth soup. Check the seasoning before serving.

French Fish Soup

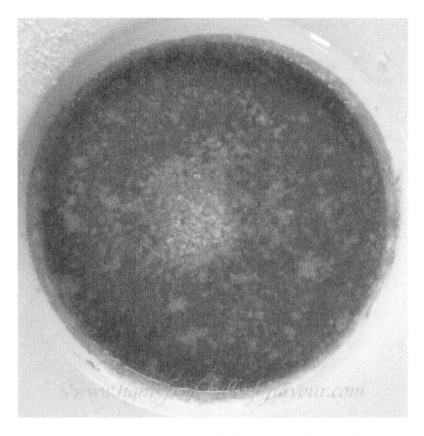

If you love French food but don't like how fattening it can be, try this French fish soup. It is loaded with flavour and has real pizzazz – without the calories.

I have spent a fair amount of time in France – half a year in Paris, a winter in rural Provence, a summer high up in the French mountains and a couple of autumns picking grapes in Alsace.

I've always said that I will believe there is a heaven if, when I die, I find that my afterlife will be spent in a French bakery.

What I'm not so fond of is the cream- and butter-rich part of the French cuisine. This soup though, is a perfect example of how it's possible to cook something that is both filling and bursting with flavour, yet low in calories.

French fish soup is often served with "rouille", a yummy but calorie-laden kind of mayonnaise, grated cheese and toasted pieces of bread. Take away these toppings and you've got a healthy and - if you follow my recipe below - still mega-tasty soup.

Serves 4 as a main course:

1 red onion, finely chopped

1 small fennel bulb - shoots and root cut off, tough outer layer removed, halved; tough bottom core cut out from each half and then sliced finely

1 medium-sized carrot, finely chopped

3 garlic cloves finely chopped

2 tablespoons olive oil

¼ teaspoon cayenne pepper

300ml, 10floz, 1.3 cup, white wine (use a decent wine that you would be happy to drink as well)

1 sachet, 4g, 1 heaped teaspoon, of saffron threads

4 tablespoons tomato purée

1 litre, 1¾ pints, 4½ cups, fish stock

Salt and pepper

500g, 1lb 2oz, white fish, such as haddock, plaice, cod - but any white fish will do, cut into large pieces

Optional – grated Parmesan cheese

1. Start by soaking the saffron in the white wine. Fry the onion, fennel and carrot in the olive oil in a large pot over a medium heat for 5 minutes, until the vegetables start to soften. Keep stirring to make sure the vegetables don't burn.

2. Add the garlic and cayenne pepper, stir and fry for another minute. Add the white wine and saffron to the pot and bring to the boil, reduce the heat and simmer for 4-5 minutes, until the wine has reduced by half.

3. Add the tomato purée, the stock and season with salt and pepper, stir and bring to the boil. Reduce the heat and simmer for a 5 minutes. Add the fish, bring back to a simmer and simmer for a further 5 minutes.

4. Let the soup cool down to room temperature before whizzing the soup in a blender – or use a stick blender in the pot. Reheat and check the seasoning.

This French fish soup is very tasty on its own but sprinkling over a bit of grated Parmesan cheese is not going to add many calories and will enhance the flavour even more.

I like to serve it with toasted sourdough bread topped with tomatoes, garlic and parsley and a salad consisting of mixed lettuce leaves and avocado. I'll sprinkle a bit of olive oil and some really decent balsamic vinegar over the salad and – voilà! - you've got a meal so massively super-tasty it's hard to believe that it's also incredibly nutritious and low in calories.

Asian-Style Salmon Soup

Let's get one thing straight from the start - this Asian-style salmon soup is a very light dish indeed. But the flavours are simply amazing, so fresh. I absolutely love it.

I have a huge appetite. Sitting still makes me hungrier – not to mention sitting still and writing about food. I'm less hungry when on the go and never more so than when in the kitchen cooking up a storm.

Cooking stills my hunger. I have personally never known a better way to lose weight than to cook a lot. I still taste all the food I cook, of course, but being in the middle of cooking one dish after the other reduces my hunger immensely.

I'm not going to deny it though - to properly still my hunger on a very hungry day, I'd have to add more than one fillet of salmon to my own bowl of this Asian-Style salmon soup.

For 4 people:

1 litre, 1¾ pints, 4½ cups, fish stock

1 teaspoon honey

2 garlic cloves, finely chopped

3cm piece ginger, finely sliced

1 lemongrass stalk - cut off the thinner top, leaving you with the "bulb" at the bottom, discard tough outer layer, cut the "bulb" in half and slice very finely

1 large red chilli, finely chopped

1 lime, zest and juice

2 tablespoons Thai fish sauce (nam pla)1 spring onion (scallion), sliced

Handful of coriander (cilantro) leaves

4 salmon fillets, skinned and each fillet cut into 3 pieces

1. Start by heating up the oven to 200C/fan 180C/400F/gas mark 6. Pour the stock into a sauce pan, add the honey and bring to a simmer. Add the garlic, ginger, lemongrass, chilli and lime zest to the pan and simmer for 10 minutes.

2. While the soup is simmering, cover a baking tray with baking parchment. Place the salmon pieces on the tray, season with a bit of salt and cook in the oven for 5-6 minutes.

3. Add the fish sauce and the lime juice to the soup. Place 3 pieces of salmon in each bowl, divide the soup between the bowls and scatter over the spring onion (scallion) and coriander (cilantro).

Spicy Sweet Potato Soup

I am a big fan of soup and this is one of my favourites – a spicy sweet potato soup with chilli and butter beans. It is spectacularly tasty, very filling and highly nutritious.

Sweet potatoes and butter beans are low GI food – and while all beans have a low GI, butter beans have one of the lowest calorie content of them all. Beans provide good amounts of both protein and fibre and these two nutrients help to keep you full for longer.

This spicy sweet potato soup is the kind of food I like to have in my freezer for times when I'm in a hurry or simply too tired to cook.

PS! Sweet potatoes are very nutritious but they contain a lot of carbohydrates. While the carbohydrates in sweet potatoes are slow-releasing, it is best to only eat small amount of them if you are trying to lose weight. You could use half sweet potatoes and half butternut squash (or pumpkin of some sort).

For 4 People:

1 red onion, chopped

1 red chilli, finely chopped

1 tablespoon ground coriander

1 tablespoon ground cumin

½ teaspoon ground cinnamon

1 tablespoon vegetable or groundnut oil

600g, 1lb 5oz, 4 cups, peeled and diced sweet potatoes

1 tablespoon tomato purée

1000ml, 1¾ 4½ cups, vegetable stock

400g, 14oz, 2 cups, tin of cooked butter beans, drained and rinsed

Salt and pepper

Natural yogurt

Chopped parsley

1. In a large pan, gently fry the onion, chilli and spices in the oil until the onion is soft – about 5 minutes.

2. Add the sweet potatoes, tomato puree and stock. Stir and bring to a boil, then reduce the heat and simmer covered for 15 minutes.

3. Add the butter beans and simmer for a further couple of minutes.

4. Let the soup cool down to room temperature. Either blend the soup with a stick blender in the pan or use an ordinary blender (depending on the size of your blender, you might have to do this in batches) and then return the soup to the pan. If you find that it is too thick, simply add some water. Season with salt and pepper.

5. Reheat the soup before serving and check the seasoning. Top each bowl of soup with a swirl of yogurt and some chopped parsley.

Lentil and Carrot Soup

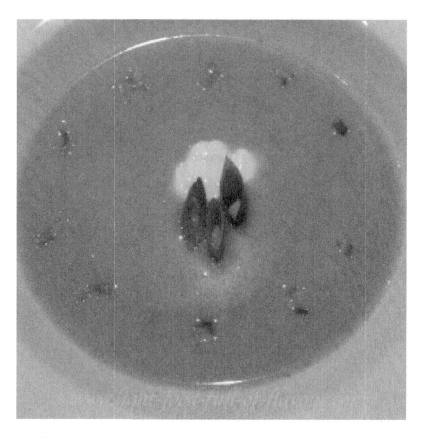

Yum! This tasty, spiced lentil and carrot soup is the perfect soup for a cold autumn's day.

It's easy to make, filling, low in calories and healthy. What more can you ask for!

Lentils are low in fat, packed with nutrients and have the third highest protein content of all plant-based food. And carrots benefit from being cooked – a rare thing among vegetables – as cooked carrots release more beta-carotene than raw carrots.

You do need to soak the lentils beforehand. All lentils and beans contain phytic acid. Phytic acid interferes with the absorption of nutrients in food and also makes the food harder to digest.

But if you soak and then rinse the lentils or beans, you reduce the amount of phytic acid in the food. I leave any lentils or beans to soak for a couple of hours and then rinse them before I'm going to cook them.

If you want more heat, add some chopped chilli before serving the soup.

I sometimes add thinly sliced chicken breast that I marinate in a little bit of oil and the spice-mix Ras-el-hanout before stir-frying over a high heat. It does make the soup into more of a meal.

Or, for a vegetarian version, toss cooked chickpeas in warm olive-oil infused with plenty of ground cumin and add it to the soup.

For 4 people:

1½ tablespoon olive oil

1 large red onion, chopped

2 large carrots, peeled and chopped

1 garlic clove, finely chopped

1½ teaspoon ground cumin

1 teaspoon ground ginger

150g, 5½oz, ¾ cup pre-soaked (see above) red lentils

1 litre, 1¾ pints, 4½ cups, vegetable or chicken stock

Salt and pepper

1 tablespoon lemon juice

To serve:

2 spring onions (scallions), chopped

Greek yogurt

1. Heat the oil in a large pan and fry the onion and carrot for five minutes over a medium heat, stirring every now and then. Add the garlic and spices and fry for another minute while continuing to stir.

2. Add the lentils and stock to the pan and season with salt and pepper. Bring to the boil, then lower the heat, cover the pan with a lid and simmer for 25 minutes. Lift the lid a couple of times and give the soup a good stir.

3. Remove the soup from the heat and let it cool down a bit. Either blend the soup until smooth with a stick blender in the pan or use an ordinary blender (depending on the size of your blender, you might have to do this in batches) and then return the soup to the pan. If you find that it is too thick, simply add some water.

4. Add the lemon juice to the lentil and carrot soup, reheat and check the seasoning. Serve with a dollop of yogurt and a scattering of chopped spring onion (scallion).

Pea Soup Two Ways

I love pea soup. Apart from being easy-peasy (sorry, couldn't resist) to make, I think it's also ultra-delicious in all its simplicity. And for those who find this kind of soup a bit sweet, adding fresh coriander (cilantro) and ground ginger changes the soup dramatically and delivers a soup with real oomph.

The humble green pea packs a punch nutrition-wise – it's loaded with vitamins and minerals among other things. Green peas are also a really low-fat food.

People on extreme calorie-watch think I've added cream to my soups when they see them. I find it hard to convince them that although the soups are creamy in texture, there isn't a drop of cream in them.

Pea soup the traditional way for 4 people:

1 tablespoon olive oil

1 tablespoon butter

2 shallots, chopped

450g, 1lb, 3 cups, fresh or frozen peas

350ml, 12floz, 1½ cups water or vegetable/chicken stock

Salt and pepper

Optional extras:

Parsley, Feta cheese, smoked salmon or dry-fried Parma ham

1.Place the oil, butter and chopped onion in a pot. Gently fry the onion, stirring, over a low to medium heat until the onion is soft but not brown, 5-7 minutes.

2.Add the peas and the water or stock to the pot. Bring to a simmer. If you are using frozen peas, simmer for about 30 seconds before removing the pot from the heat. If you are using fresh peas, simmer for 5 minutes before removing the pot from the heat.

3.Either use a stick blender to liquidize the soup straight in the pot, or let the soup cool down to room temperature and use a liquidizer. If you think the soup is too thick, just add some more water.

4.Reheat the soup in the pot and season with salt and pepper (I like mine a bit peppery to reduce the sweetness of the peas) - taste to make sure you are happy with the seasoning. Serve the soup with either some chopped parsley, Feta cheese, pieces of smoked salmon or shredded, dry-fried Parma ham (quickly fry slices of Parma ham in a dry frying pan over a high heat until crisp).

Pea soup with coriander (cilantro) and ginger

Same ingredients as above +

I heaped teaspoon ground ginger

2 handfuls fresh coriander (cilantro) - leaves and stalks separate

Fry the ground ginger and coriander stalks together with the onion. Before liquidizing the soup, add the coriander leaves as well.

Thai-Style Chicken Soup

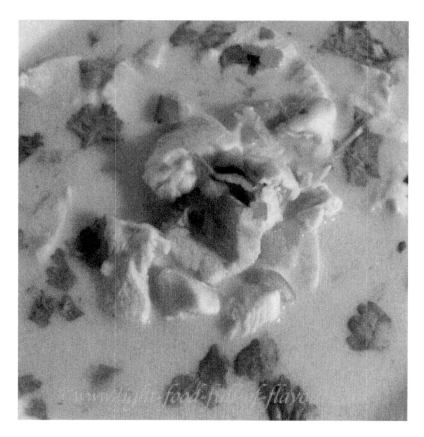

Even though my Thai-style chicken soup may not be as light as my Asian-style salmon soup - this one has coconut milk in it - it's still as gloriously fresh tasting.

This is Thai food. There is chilli involved. I don't overdo the amount of chilli that I add to my food though as I do not want it to be the only thing you can taste.

Asian-style food contains so many wonderful spices and ingredients and I want to experience the taste of all of them in my mouth.

And then there is coconut milk, which is not the big bad wolf after all. It is first of all really nutritious. It does contain saturated fat but coconut is rich in medium-chain fatty acids which the body processes differently than other saturated fats. These medium-chain fatty acids promote weight maintenance without raising cholesterol levels (Wikipedia).

I have decided to stop using "light" versions of food as they often have added sugar, salt and additives that are simply not good for you.

It's a bit pointless - isn't it - to replace what is taken away with something far worse!

As a lot of nutritionists will tell you, it's better to eat smaller portions of full-fat food.

For 4 people:

600ml, 20floz, just over 2½ cup, chicken stock

A thumb-size piece of fresh ginger, peeled and finely chopped

2 red chillies, deseeded and finely chopped

2 lemongrass stalks - cut off the thin top, leaving you with the thicker "bulb" at the bottom, discard tough outer layer and cut off the root, cut the "bulb" in half and slice very finely

Two handfuls of fresh coriander, stalks and leaves separated, stalks finely chopped

1 tablespoon tomato purée

Zest and juice of 1 lime

1 teaspoon runny honey

3 tablespoons fish sauce

3 chicken breast, thinly sliced

400ml, 13½floz, 1¾ cups, coconut milk

1.Place the stock, ginger, chilli, lemon grass, chopped coriander stalks (save the leaves for garnish), tomato puree, lime zest, honey and fish sauce in a pot. Bring to a boil.

2.Add the thinly sliced chicken breast to the pot, reduce the heat and simmer for a couple of minutes. Add the coconut milk and simmer for a further five minutes.

3.Add the lime juice to the soup and garnish each portion with coriander leaves.

Avocado and Spinach Soup

A cold avocado and spinach soup to cool you down on a hot day!

I love food too much – both raw and cooked – to sign up to the raw food-movement full time. I'm happy though, to incorporate raw food as part of my diet – especially in the summer when it is hot outside.

Whether you are on a raw food diet or not, this cold avocado and spinach soup is a really fresh, light and immensely healthy soup – and it's surprisingly filling.

To make it more of a meal you can combine the soup with a salad and/or some good bread. If you want to make the meal a complete raw food meal, you can combine it with salad like my super delicious Orange and Tomato Salad.

I am a HUGE lover of avocados and eat half an avocado on most days of the week – if not in a salad or in a soup like this one, then sliced on top of rye sourdough bread.

Avocados are rich in heart-healthy unsaturated fat and vitamin E. Spinach is simply a nutritional goldmine (see Nutritional Information). The combination of the two - together with all the other ingredients – makes for a super-healthy soup.

I serve this avocado and spinach soup with a dollop of natural yogurt and dry-roasted pumpkin and sunflower seeds. If you are a raw-food follower, you'd obviously have to use un-roasted seeds.

Topping the soup with pumpkin and sunflower seeds will add a lot of healthy nutrients to the soup. Between them these two seeds are rich in essential Omega 3 and Omega 6 fats plus several vitamins and minerals. Pumpkin seeds are also protein-rich and will help to make you feel fuller on less food.

Alternatively, you could serve the soup with some crumbled feta cheese (use a good one made from sheep and goat's milk), chopped chives and pumpkin and sunflower seeds.

For 2-4 people (depending on what else you are serving)

2 large, ripe avocados

100g, 3½oz, 3½ cup, fresh spinach

4 spring onions (scallions), chopped

3 tablespoons chopped fresh chives

2 tablespoons chopped fresh parsley

12 almonds, chopped

2 tablespoons lemon juice

500ml, 18floz, 2 1/5 cups, water

Salt and pepper to taste

Place all the ingredients in a food processor or blender and blend until smooth. Check the seasoning and serve with yogurt and seeds, or feta cheese, chopped chives and seeds.

Minestrone Soup

Minestrone soup needs a bit of love and attention – but once everything is in the pot, it pretty much takes care of itself. It definitely improves when left alone for a while before you tuck in. In fact, it tastes even better the following day.

There are many different recipes for minestrone soup. Some recipes are quicker to make but I follow the lead of an Italian recipe that advice a long simmering time. The result is a filling and stunningly tasty soup.

It can be eaten as a vegetarian version or with meat. I add the rind of a Parmesan cheese when cooking it, and love to eat it with either crumbled feta cheese or grated Parmesan cheese and cooked chicken.

I also add nutritious beans – a much better choice than adding refined white pasta or rice as both of these are lacking a lot vitamins and minerals.

And if you want to lose weight, you are much better off adding beans to the soup and avoiding white rice and pasta.

For 4-6 people:

3 tablespoons olive oil

1 large red onion, finely chopped

2 garlic cloves, finely chopped

2 medium-sized carrots, diced

2 celery sticks, sliced

5 mini zucchinis, or 1 medium-sized, diced

100g, 3½oz, 2 cups, shredded red or white cabbage

400g, 14oz tin/can of plum tomatoes with juice, or use chopped tomatoes - buy the best quality you can find of either (add 1 tablespoon tomato paste/puree if you are using chopped tomatoes)

600ml, 20floz, slightly more than 2½ cups, vegetable stock

Rind of a parmesan cheese (optional)

1 sprig of rosemary and 1 sprig of thyme – or add a little bit of dried herbs

¾ teaspoon sea salt

½ teaspoon black pepper

400g, 14oz, tin/can of cannellini beans, drained and rinsed

150g, 5½oz, 1½ cups, green beans, sliced, or peas

1.Place the oil a large pot over a low - medium heat and add the onion and garlic to the pot. Cook for about 10 minutes – stirring frequently to avoid burning the vegetables – until the onion is soft.

2.Add the carrots, celery, cabbage and zucchinis to the pot. Stir and cook for a minute. Add the tomatoes with their juice - breaking up the tomatoes if using whole plum tomatoes – stock, herbs, salt and pepper. Stir and bring to a simmer.

3.Cover the pot with a lid, turn down the heat and allow the soup to simmer over a low heat for about 1 hour and 45 minutes – give the soup a stir a couple of times during this time.

4.Add the cannellini beans and green beans to the pot. Stir and re-cover the pot with the lid. Cook for a further 15 minutes. If you are using frozen peas, add them a couple of minutes before the soup is ready.

5.Remove the Parmesan rind from the soup and check the seasoning. Serve it with grated Parmesan cheese or crumbled feta cheese.

Carrot and Watercress Soup

I am not using many ingredients in this super-tasty carrot and watercress soup but this is still a fiery soup.

Both the ginger and watercress (you can use rocket/arugula as well) that I add to this soup adds plenty of heat and both are super-nutritious.

Ginger also has many powerful medicinal properties - it aids digestion, can reduce pain and fever and is an anti-inflammatory. It can give pain relief and increased movement in people with osteoarthritis and rheumatoid arthritis.

To save the nutrients in the watercress from being lost through cooking, I don't add it until I'm about to blend the soup.

It is also low in calories and relatively quick and easy to make – a real winner! I serve it with a dollop of yogurt and my red pepper salsa You can use a tomato chilli jam instead of the salsa.

For 4 people:

2 tablespoons coconut oil (healthiest), or olive oil

2 garlic cloves, finely chopped

1 teaspoon found ginger

800g, 1lb12oz carrots, peeled and diced

600ml, 20floz, 2.7 cups water

Salt and pepper

75g, 2¾oz watercress (or use rocket/arugula)

To serve:

Natural Greek-style yogurt

Red pepper (bell pepper) salsa (or use a tomato chilli jam) – optional

1.Place the oil in a large pot over a low heat. Add the chopped garlic and ground ginger to the pot and stir and cook for 1 minute – making sure the mixture doesn't burn.

2.Add the diced carrots and continue to cook for a further 5 minutes. Add the water and season with salt and pepper. Bring to a simmer, cover the pot with a lid and simmer for 20 minutes.

3.Remove the soup from the heat and let it cool down a bit before adding the watercress (or rocket/arugula). You can either blend the soup until smooth with a stick blender in the pan, or you can use an ordinary blender, and then return the soup to the pan.

4.Check the seasoning and gently re-heat the carrot and watercress soup (without letting it boil) before serving.

I like the consistency of my soups to be quite thick but if you find that it is too thick, simply add some water.

Asian-Style Beetroot Soup

I love this super-delicious Asian-style beetroot soup (beet soup). It is absolutely full on when it comes to flavour. And it is healthy and low in calories – what's not to love!

It is also quite quick to make. I use organic, cooked beetroots (beets) in natural juices - they are available in a lot of supermarkets in the UK - but you can of course use raw beetroots that you cook yourself.

I cook my vegetables for this soup in coconut oil, which is the healthiest fat to use for cooking (it is sold in most health food shops). It will also give this soup an extra flavour kick and if you can't get hold of coconut oil, I suggest you add a couple of tablespoons of creamed coconut or coconut milk to the soup.

I serve my Asian-style beetroot soup with a dollop of natural yogurt and also scatter some chopped spring onions (scallions) on top.

For 4 people:

2 tablespoons of coconut fat (or use vegetable oil)

4 spring onions (scallions), chopped

A large thumb-sized piece of fresh ginger, finely grated

2 fat garlic cloves, crushed

2 large red chillies, deseeded and finely chopped

2 lemon grass stalks, cut off the thinner top of each stalk - leaving you with the "bulb" at the bottom - discard tough outer layer, cut off the bottom of the "bulb", cut it in half and slice very finely

A large handful of fresh coriander - leaves and stalks separated, stalks chopped

500g, 1lb2oz, cooked beetroots (beets) in natural juices – diced

750ml, 1.3 pints, 3.3 cups, vegetable stock

1½ tablespoon Thai fish sauce

Juice of 1 lime

Pepper

To serve:

Natural yogurt

1 spring onion (scallion), chopped

1.Place the coconut oil in a large sauce pan over a low heat. Add the spring onions, ginger, garlic, chillies, lemon grass and the stalks of the coriander to the pan. Stir and cook gently for about 5-7 minutes, until softened but not browned.

2.Add the beetroots and hot stock to the sauce pan. Remove the pan from the heat. Add the coriander leaves to the pan. Either blend until smooth using a stick blender, or - after having cooled the soup - use an ordinary blender and then return the soup to the pan.

3.Add the fish sauce and lime juice to the soup, season with some black pepper and re-heat the soup. Taste and check the seasoning before serving. If you find that this Asian-style beetroot soup is too thick for your liking, simply add some water.

Chickpea and Tomato Gazpacho

If you are looking for a recipe for a chilled soup, try this super-delicious chilled chickpea and tomato gazpacho served with an avocado salsa. It is easy and relatively quick to make – you just need to leave it to "mature" for a while once you've made it.

I have cooked a lot of buffet-style lunches in my job as a cook and this cold chickpea and tomato gazpacho soup is always popular whenever I serve it on a summer buffet.

Apart from being mega-tasty, it is also a light and healthy soup!

Chickpeas are high in saponins which help lower cholesterol. They are also rich in something called fructo-oligosaccharides which feed the immune system-boosting probiotic bacteria in the gut.

Avocados are rich in Vitamin E and heart-healthy monounsaturated fat.

Red chillies contain high levels of beta-carotene, a powerful antioxidant, and also contain vitamin A, E and C, dietary fibre, potassium and iron.

And on and on the list of the health benefits goes.

For the chickpea and tomato gazpacho:

400g (14oz) tin/can cooked chickpeas – I buy an organic variety – rinsed

400g (14oz) tin/can chopped tomatoes

125ml (4floz, just over ½ cup) natural Greek-style yogurt

2 garlic cloves, crushed

1 heaped teaspoon ground cumin

1 heaped teaspoon finely grated ginger

1 red chilli, deseeded and finely chopped

1 tablespoon lemon juice

2 tablespoons olive oil

½ teaspoon salt and some black pepper

For the avocado salsa:

1 ripe avocado

½ medium red onion, finely chopped

1 tablespoon finely chopped fresh mint

1 tablespoon lemon juice

1 tablespoon olive oil

A pinch of salt and black pepper

Extra yogurt for serving (optional)

1.Place all the ingredients for the soup in a food processor or blender and pulse to a smooth purée. Transfer to a pitcher and gradually add some cold water to adjust the soup's thickness to a consistency you are happy with – I like this soup to be quite thick.

2.Check the seasoning to see if you want to add any more salt and/or pepper. Cover and refrigerate for at least 30 minutes to allow flavours to blend.

3.Halve, de-stone, peel and dice the avocado - mix with all the other ingredients for the salsa.

Serve the soup in cups, or glasses - with a dollop of yoghurt (if you are using it) and a dollop of salsa on top.

Salad Recipes

Crispy Kale Salad

©www.light-food-full-of-flavour.com

While kale is an exceedingly healthy vegetable – it is super-rich in vitamins, minerals and fibre - it can be somewhat challenging taste-wise.

Like most vegetables, kale is best eaten raw or steamed. I sometimes use raw kale together with basil, walnuts, garlic and parmesan to make pesto and find it really tasty. Or I add it to a soup at the very end of cooking time and then use a hand blender to make a smooth soup.

To make this crispy kale salad though, I toss the kale (I use curly kale) with some olive oil and oven-roast it for 10 minutes, until it is really crispy and quite brittle.

Kale is a very good source of vitamin K (said to be good for bone density and to help lower blood pressure) and dietary fat like olive oil enhances the absorption of vitamin K.

Chickpeas are rich in protein and fibre which help you to feel full on less. They are also a good source of different minerals and can help to lower cholesterol levels.

This salad will give you chickpeas two ways as I add both fried chickpeas with cumin (they are great as a snack on their own) and hummus.

And to top it all off I add healthy beetroot as well. I love the contrast between the crispy kale, fried chickpeas and earthy and juicy beetroot.

As I use cooked beetroot in natural juices I can get this salad ready reasonably quickly. You can serve this as a side dish, or as a light meal together with toasted pita bread.

For 2 as a light meal, or 4 as a side dish:

100g, 3 ½oz, 1 ¼ cup, prepared curly kale (pull the leaves off the stem and tear into smaller pieces)

½ tablespoon olive oil

400g, 14oz, 2 ½ cup cooked chickpeas – rinsed and left to dry

1 tablespoon olive oil

2 teaspoons ground cumin

Sea salt and pepper

2-3 cooked beetroots, diced

Hummus

1.Pre-heat the oven to 200C/Fan/180C/400F/gas mark 6. Cover a baking tray with baking parchment. Place the kale on the tray, drizzle over half a tablespoon of olive oil and toss. Once the oven is hot, place the tray in the oven and roast for 10-12 minutes until the kale is really crisp.

2.While the kale is roasting, add one tablespoon olive oil to a large frying pan over a medium-hot heat. Once the oil is hot, add the chickpeas and cumin to the pan and stir. Season with sea salt and black pepper and stir every now and then for about 2-3 minutes. Take the pan off the heat.

3.Divide the roasted kale between 2-4 plates and top with the cumin-fried chickpeas, chopped beetroot and a dollop of hummus.

Quinoa and Chickpea Salad

I'm bringing in the heavy artillery with this quinoa and chickpea salad as it is more of a meal than just a salad.

I have never been a fan of my native country's (Sweden) tradition of smorgasbord - long tables laden with all kinds of food. I simply don't like to mix different meat dishes with different fish dishes with different vegetable dishes and so on.

But this does not apply to a vegetarian smorgasbord. Put me in front of a table filled with different vegetarian dishes and I can barely contain myself. This quinoa and chickpea salad recipe would fit in well on a vegetarian buffet.

For 4-6 people:

75g, 2¾oz, ½ cup, quinoa

600ml, 20floz, 2½ cups, vegetable stock

1 large red onion, halved and finely sliced

2 tablespoons olive oil

10 small tomatoes, quartered

1½ teaspoon ground cumin

1 teaspoon ground coriander

1 ½ teaspoon ground paprika

400g, 14oz, 2½ cups, tin of cooked chickpeas, drained and rinsed

Salt and pepper

1 red pepper (bell pepper), chopped

3 spring onions (scallions), sliced

100g, 3½oz, baby spinach

A small handful parsley, chopped

1 tablespoon lemon juice

100g, 3½oz, 2/3 cup, feta cheese, crumbled

1. Get the stock boiling, add the quinoa, stir and simmer without a lid for 15 minutes. Drain in a colander.

2. While the quinoa is cooking, fry the red onion in the olive oil over a medium heat for 5 minutes until the onions start to caramelize. Add the spices, stir and then add the tomatoes

and season with salt and pepper. Cook for 2-3 minutes until the tomatoes start to soften, then add the chickpeas, stir and continue to cook a little longer until the chickpeas are warmed through.

3. In a bowl, mix together the quinoa and onion, tomato and chickpea mix with all the other ingredients.

You can eat this quinoa and chickpea salad warm or cold.

Orange and Tomato Salad

As far as salad goes, this orange and tomato salad is a real favourite of mine. It is as beautiful to look at as it is delicious and healthy.

It is such a fresh salad and it will fit in nicely on a buffet table. I have served it alongside lots of different kind of food and it has always been a big hit.

I like to use really sweet and juicy oranges and ripe and tasty tomatoes for the salad. This is then combined to perfection with the acidity of the balsamic vinegar in the dressing.

The crunchiness in this salad comes from the celery.

Celery is a very good source of different vitamins and minerals. This low-calorie vegetable also contains two powerful antioxidants - apigenin and luteolin - which can reduce inflammation and help treat a range of inflammatory diseases.

I love the taste and texture of celery and I like adding it to salads. But I do prefer to cut it finely rather than having big chunks of it in a salad like this one.

To be honest, I'm not one for serving big chunks of any vegetable, in any kind of salad. I actually think it tastes better when the vegetables are cut into smaller pieces.

For 4 people as a side dish:

2 large oranges

200g, 7oz, 1¼ cups, small tomatoes, like cherry or plum tomatoes, halved

4 celery stalks, trimmed and sliced finely

4 spring onions (scallions), sliced

3-4 tablespoons pomegranate seeds

100g, 3½oz lettuce, I prefer a mix of lettuce leaves

1½ tablespoon balsamic vinegar

1 tablespoon olive oil

1 teaspoon runny honey

10 mint leaves, shredded

Salt and pepper

1. Cut away the peel and pith from the oranges over a bowl so that you catch the juices. Cut each side of each

membrane to remove the individual segments. Squeeze what's left of the orange into the bowl to get as much juice as possible from the oranges.

2. Place the orange segments in another bowl and mix them with the tomatoes, celery, spring onion (scallion), pomegranate seeds and shredded mint.

3. Add the balsamic vinegar, olive oil, honey and a pinch of salt and pepper to the orange juice and whisk until well combined. Place the lettuce leaves on either a large plate or in salad bowl, place the orange, tomato and celery mix on top and drizzle all of the dressing over it.

Warm Chicken Salad

I really like a warm salad - like this sensationally tasty warm chicken salad which I serve with a rocket (arugula) and mustard dressing and Parmesan cheese shavings.

I always have a piece of really good Parmesan cheese in my fridge. The darker the parmesan cheese is, the longer it has been matured and the tastier it is. And yes, more expensive as well!

The taste is so intense though, that you don't need to use a lot. It's the same with good balsamic vinegar – a little bit goes a long way.

With my big appetite, there's no way I could eat nothing but this warm chicken salad and be content. As the salad is very green, I like to serve it with fried tomatoes on sourdough or some other good bread.

What I do is cut ripe, small tomatoes into quarters. I then fry them for a couple of minutes in a little bit of olive oil, add a good splash of balsamic vinegar and some salt and pepper and fry it all for a further couple of minutes. I serve it on toasted bread with some shredded basil leaves and some of the lovely Parmesan cheese shavings on top.

Simple but super-yummy!

For 4 people:

4 skinless chicken breasts, each cut into strips, approximately the thickness of your little finger

1 tablespoon olive oil

Salt and pepper

150g, 3½oz, 1½ cups, fine green beans, trimmed and halved

200g, 7oz, mix of lettuce leaves

Parmesan cheese shavings (use a vegetable peeler to make the shavings)

For the dressing:

2 anchovy fillets in olive oil, drained

1 heaped teaspoon wholegrain or Dijon mustard

1 clove of garlic, finely chopped

A good handful of rocket (arugula) leaves

A good handful of parsley, leaves only

1 tablespoon red wine vinegar

3 tablespoons olive oil

Some freshly ground pepper

1. Preheat the oven to 200C/fan180C/400F/gas mark 6. Start by making the dressing. Place all the ingredients for the dressing in a food processor and whizz together.

2. Toss the chicken strips with the tablespoon of olive oil and some salt and pepper in a bowl. Brown the chicken strips on both sides in a frying pan over quite a high heat – you will have to do this in batches – and transfer to a roasting tray when done. Once all the chicken is done, place the roasting tray in the oven and cook for 5-7 minutes, or until the chicken is cooked through.

3. While the chicken is cooking in the oven, get some water boiling in a pan, add fine green beans and simmer for 4-5 minutes, then drain.

4. Toss the hot beans and chicken with the dressing in a bowl. Divide the lettuce between four plates, Place the warm chicken and beans on top and scatter over the Parmesan shavings. Serve the warm chicken salad straight away.

Prawn and Grapefruit Salad

I can't do this prawn and grapefruit salad justice with my words alone. You've just got to try it. It is a fantastically fresh and delicious salad.

Now, I call it a prawn and grapefruit salad but I often use crayfish (crawfish) tails, which I find enhances this salad even more. Crayfish is a big thing in Sweden and I was lucky enough to eat crayfish that we caught ourselves when I grew up.

I do buy cooked and peeled crayfish tails as raw ones are hard to come by. But I buy raw prawns and cook them myself. Cooked prawns have usually been cooked to death to give them a longer sell-by date. It's so quick and easy to cook raw prawns and the taste is 100% better than the taste of pre-cooked ones.

If you are using raw, peeled prawns, add a bit of oil (rapeseed, canola or olive oil) to a large frying pan over a medium high heat. Once the oil is hot, add the prawns to the frying pan. Fry them for about 1 ½ minutes – turning them over half-way through - until they are pink and cooked through. Remove the prawns from the pan with a slotted spoon and place them on a plate covered with kitchen towel. Season the prawns with a bit of salt.

I am using pea shoots in this salad. If you can't find it, you can replace the pea shoots with lamb's lettuce (mâche or corn salad).

For 4 people:

2 grapefruits

250g, 9oz, 1½ cups, small tomatoes, halved

2 avocados

400g, 14oz, cooked prawns (shrimp) or crayfish (crawfish) tails

100g, 3½oz, pea shoots, or use lamb's lettuce (mâche or corn salad)

100g, 3½oz, baby spinach

For the dressing:

5 tablespoons grapefruit juice (from juice you will get when peeling the grapefruits

1 teaspoon honey

1 tablespoon olive oil

1 tablespoon balsamic vinegar

Pinch of salt and pepper

1.Cut away the peel and pith from the grapefruits over a bowl so that you catch the juices. Cut each side of each membrane to remove the individual segments. Squeeze what's left of the grapefruit into the bowl. Place the grapefruit segments in another bowl.

2.Whisk together 5 tablespoons of the grapefruit juice with the honey, oil and balsamic vinegar.

3.Halve, de-stone, peel and slice the avocado. Mix the pea shoots and baby spinach in a salad bowl or on a large plate. Top with the grapefruit segments, tomatoes, avocado slices and the prawns or crayfish (crawfish) tails. Drizzle the dressing over the prawn and grapefruit salad.

Avocado and Bean salad

I could easily eat all of this immensely tasty and very healthy avocado and bean salad on my own. I just love it.

There are so many types of food that I simply adore – beans of all different kinds being one of them. I am using broad (fava) beans in this salad.

Broad beans (fava beans) are a good vegetable source of protein and fibre and they are rich in folate and b-vitamins. They do require a bit of work - double podding if still in their pods - but they are well worth the effort.

As for salad dressing - I do not drown my salads in it but simply sprinkle some on top. I would not use all of the dressing in the recipe for this avocado and bean salad – any left-overs of the dressing will keep for a couple of days.

200g, 7oz, 7 cups, mixed leaves – I like to use a mix of watercress, rocket (arugula) and spinach

75g, 2¾oz, broad beans (fava beans) - fresh or frozen

1 avocado

Juice of ½ a lemon

1 tablespoon sunflower and pumpkin seeds

Shavings of Parmesan cheese (use a potato peeler to make the cheese shavings)

Dressing:

1 heaped teaspoon Dijon mustard

black pepper

1 tablespoon red or white wine vinegar

1 ½ tablespoon hemp or linseed oil (or use 3 tablespoons olive oil)

1 ½ tablespoon olive oil

2 teaspoons water

1. If the beans are still in their pods, open up the pods and remove the beans. Cook the broad beans in a pan of simmering water for 2-3 minutes if fresh, 4 minutes if from frozen, and then drain. Once the beans are cool enough to handle, peel off the skin of each bean (the skin slips off easily when you pinch the ends).

2. Place the sunflower and pumpkin seeds in a non-stick frying pan and dry-roast them over a moderate heat, stirring every now and then, for about a minute until the seeds start to brown a little. Be careful that they don't burn. Once done, transfer the seeds to a plate and let them cool down.

3. Make the dressing by placing the mustard, pepper and the vinegar in a bowl. Whisk the ingredients together and keep on whisking while very slowly adding the oil. Add the water and whisk again.

4. Halve, peel and take out the stone from the avocado. Cut the avocado into cubes on a cutting board and squeeze over the lemon juice. Place the lettuce leaves in a bowl and add the avocado and broad beans. Sprinkle over the sunflower and pumpkin seeds and drizzle over some of the dressing. Scatter the cheese shavings on top of the salad.

Asian-Style Carrot Salad

An Asian-style carrot salad which is packed full of flavour and yet really easy to make.

I cook a lot of Asian-style food and I find that this type of food requires a different style of salad to accompany all the fragrant, sharp and hot flavours.

What you want is the combination of hot, sweet, sour and salty flavours - flavours that you typically find in Southeast Asian food.

This carrot salad is such a fresh-tasting one. I admit that it it's not very spicy - you could add some chopped chillies to the salad if you wish. Personally I find that it's enough with the sharpness from the spring onions (scallions).

I found the recipe for this Asian-style carrot salad in a Swedish cook book at a friend's house. I don't remember the exact recipe but this is pretty similar. There's no need to be exact with something like this anyway.

For 4 people:

4 large carrots, grated

5 spring onions (scallions), chopped

25g, 1oz, ¼ cup, fresh coriander (cilantro), both leaves and stalks chopped

4 Little Gem hearts (or some other crispy lettuce), leaves separated

2 tablespoons light olive oil

1 tablespoon Thai fish sauce

Juice of 1 lime

1. Lay out the Gem lettuce leaves in a salad bowl.

2. Mix together the oil, fish sauce and lime juice.

3. Place the grated carrots, chopped spring onions (scallions) and coriander in another bowl. Pour over the dressing and mix well. Place the mixture on top of the lettuce leaves in the salad bowl.

Crunchy Thai Salad

I made this crunchy Thai salad today for a friend from the Philippines and she immediately asked for the recipe.

I am adding sesame oil to the dressing - a really tasty and mild sesame oil though. Until recently, I have only come across sesame oils with a very strong taste and a tendency to take over the whole show. The kind of sesame oil you mostly find in a supermarket.

The one I am using now is an organic, unrefined, first cold pressing sesame oil. Sounds expensive, doesn't it - a bit posh? But it is less expensive than any olive oil I have ever bought. And the taste is sublime.

Look out for this kind of sesame oil in delicatessens, health food shops or shops specialising in Asian food.

I am using a tablespoon of this mild sesame oil. If you have got sesame oil with a very strong taste, you might be better off just using one teaspoon of this and adding a tablespoon of coconut oil or vegetable oil as well to the dressing.

Crunchy Thai Salad:

For the dressing:

Juice of 1 lime

1 tablespoon mild sesame oil (see above)

1½ tablespoon Tamari soy sauce (gluten-free) – or use light soy sauce

1 tablespoon Thai fish sauce

2 teaspoons finely grated fresh ginger

1 garlic clove, crushed/minced

2 teaspoons honey

For the salad:

Half a small pointed cabbage (hispi/sweetheart) – finely shredded

2 medium-sized carrots – coarsely grated

½ cucumber – halved and finely sliced

1 large red pepper (bell pepper) – I buy the pointed variety – finely sliced

2-3 spring onions (scallions) – sliced

A large handful of fresh coriander, leaves and stalks –
coarsely chopped

A small handful of fresh mint leaves – roughly chopped

A large red chilli, deseeded and finely sliced (optional – the
dressing has got enough attitude to not need the chilli in my
opinion, but this is Thai food!)

Mix together all the ingredients for the dressing. Add the
salad ingredients to a large bowl and pour over the dressing.
Mix the salad well and allow it to rest for at least 30 minutes -
the flavours will intensify if you leave it for longer. Toss
before serving.

Chicken and Mango Salad

What a beauty – a light, fresh and delicious chicken and mango salad!

Fruit and chicken are tasty together. In this salad the sweetness of the mango is combined with a kick from a chilli sauce that you toss the chicken in. Add to this crunchy sugar snap peas and velvety avocado and you are in for a treat.

Mangoes are low in fat and a great source of beta-carotene.

Avocados are full of heart-healthy monounsaturated fat and rich in vitamin E.

Sugar snap peas are low in fat and have a high fibre content that helps to make you feel fuller for longer. They also contain a lot of different vitamins and are rich in iron.

For 4 people:

Chilli sauce:

2 red chillies, deseeded and finely chopped

2 garlic cloves, finely chopped

1 lemongrass stalk - cut off the thin top, leaving you with the thicker "bulb" at the bottom, discard tough outer layer and cut off the root, cut the "bulb" in half and slice very finely

3 teaspoons fish sauce

2 level teaspoons honey

2 tablespoons vegetable or groundnut oil

4 chicken breasts, cubed

1 large ripe mango (or 2 small ones), peeled and cubed

2 avocados

2 un-waxed limes, zest of 1 and juice of 2 (If you can only get hold of waxed limes, make sure you scrub them really well with a clean scrubbing brush.)

200g, 7oz, 1 cup, sugar snap peas

2 spring onions (scallions), sliced

A bunch of fresh coriander

300g, 10½oz, 1¼ cups, natural, plain yogurt

Note: Don't be too forceful when grating the zest of citrus fruit. You only want the very outer layer of the fruit, not the bitter pith, the inner white part. I find that it's worth investing in some really good graters with different coarseness. You want a fine grater for citrus fruit.

1.Bash the chopped chilli and garlic into a paste in a pestle and mortar. Mix in the sliced lemongrass, fish sauce, honey and oil.

2.Add the grated zest of 1 lime to the yogurt. Leave to the side. Put a pan with some salted water on to boil for the sugar snap peas.

3.Add a bit of oil to a large frying pan over a medium-high heat – I use coconut oil. Season the cubed chicken with some salt and black pepper and fry until nicely browned and cooked through. Remove from the heat and add the chilli sauce to the pan, tossing the chicken until all the pieces are coated with the sauce.

4.Add the sugar snap peas to the boiling water. Reduce the heat and simmer the sugar snap peas for 2 minutes. Remove the pan from the heat and rinse the sugar snap peas under cold water to stop them from cooking any further.

5.Add the lime juice to a bowl. Halve, de-stone, peel and dice the avocados. Add the diced avocado to the bowl with lime juice and toss. Place the cubed chicken, mango, avocado, sugar snap peas, spring onions (scallions) and fresh coriander in a salad bowl and mix together gently.

Serve the chicken and mango salad with the yogurt with lime zest.

Asparagus Salad with Green Beans and Poached Eggs

Here is a recipe for a delicious asparagus salad with green beans and poached eggs.

Asparagus is a nutritional powerhouse. It is a good source of vitamin C (particularly green asparagus), folic acid and potassium. It is also high in antioxidants, packed with fibre and protein and contains anti-cancer properties.

Green beans are rich in silica - silica is important for keeping bones strong – and also contain folic acid and vitamin C.

I use watercress and baby spinach in most of my salads. Both are incredibly nutritious, and in my view also very tasty.

It is easy to think that all types of lettuce leaves are really nutritious, but this is not the case. Iceberg lettuce contains 96% water and ranks the lowest in nutritional value (it is nearly devoid of all nutrition). The darker the lettuce leaf is, the more nutrients it contains.

I do recommend adding spinach to your salads, and watercress if it is available (which it is in Britain).

I top this asparagus salad with poached eggs to make it more of a meal – and I and my big appetite will have two eggs, thank you very much!

I eat it with sourdough bread topped with avocado and red pepper (bell pepper), or sourdough bread with tomatoes and garlic. And eaten like this, it becomes a light, mega-healthy and utterly tasty meal!

You can use nothing but olive oil for the dressing - 3 tablespoons - if you don't have any flax or hemp oil.

For 4 people:

200g, 7oz, slightly less than a cup, asparagus, cut off and discard the woody ends (if the stalks are quite thick, cut in half)

200g, 7oz, slightly less than a cup, fine green beans

100g, 3½oz, 3½ cups, spinach

100g, 3½oz, 3 cups, of either watercress/romaine/red leaf/rocket

Small handful of mint leaves, shredded

Grated zest of 1 un-waxed lemon

Shavings of Parmesan (use a vegetable peeler), or crumbled feta cheese

1-2 eggs per person – poached, or boiled (add the eggs to a pan of simmering water and boil for 5½ minutes, then rinse under cold water to stop them for cooking any further)

For the dressing:

1 teaspoon Dijon mustard

A pinch of salt and black pepper

1 tablespoon red or white wine vinegar

1 ½ hemp or flax (linseed) oil

1 ½ tablespoon olive oil

1 teaspoon water

1.Put a pan with some salted water on to boil for the asparagus and beans, and another one - without the salt - for the eggs. Make the dressing by placing the mustard, pinch of salt and pepper and the vinegar in a bowl. Whisk the ingredients together and keep on whisking while slowly adding the hemp or flax oil and olive oil. Add the water and whisk again.

2.For the asparagus salad, place the asparagus and beans in the pan with simmering salted water and simmer for 4-5 minutes (depending on how al-dente you like your vegetables). Drain in a sieve.

3.While the vegetables are cooking, poach or boil the eggs. Divide the spinach and whatever other leaves you are using between 4 plates. Scatter some shredded mint leaves over each plate. Divide the asparagus and beans between the plates and top with poached or boiled, peeled and halved eggs.

4.Add the lemon zest to the mustard dressing and sprinkle some dressing over each plate, followed by either Parmesan shavings or crumbled feta cheese.

Carrot and Quinoa Salad

I absolutely adore this carrot and quinoa salad of mine - it's bursting with flavour, filling, healthy and low in calories. It's a perfect salad to take with you to work.

It is full of protein-rich ingredients – soybeans, quinoa and chickpeas – which all make you feel full without having to eat too much.

What you need to be aware of though, is that the iron in vegetables and grains – called non-heme iron - is less easily absorbed by the body than iron from meat, poultry, fish and shellfish.

A good way to increase the amount of iron you absorb from vegetables and grains – if you are not eating it together with animal-based protein - is to eat it together with food rich in vitamin C.

The watercress that I add to this salad is rich in vitamin C. Other vegetables rich in vitamin C are broccoli, green peas and sweet red peppers (bell peppers) and these vegetables could all be added to the salad.

You could stir-fry broccoli together with the carrot batons, or add cooked peas and/or raw red peppers (bell peppers) to this carrot and quinoa salad.

For 4 people:

50g, 1¾oz, ¼ cup, quinoa

400ml, 1¾ cup, vegetable stock

1 tablespoon rapeseed or olive oil

½ teaspoon yellow mustard seeds

2 heaped teaspoons ground cumin

½ teaspoon ground turmeric

¼ teaspoon ground cinnamon

1 large carrot, or 2 medium-sized carrots, cut into matchstick-sized batons

Salt and pepper

400g, 14oz, 2½ cups, can of cooked chickpeas, drained and rinsed

100g, 3½oz, 1 cup, cooked edamame beans - immature green soya beans (soybeans)

3 spring onions (scallions), sliced

1 tablespoon chopped fresh chives

2-3 tablespoons pomegranate seeds

100g, 3½oz, 3½ cups, watercress – or use a mix of rocket (arugula) leaves and spinach

For the dressing:

1½ tablespoon juice from an orange

1 tablespoon lemon juice

1 teaspoon white wine vinegar

1 tablespoon olive oil

1 level teaspoon runny honey

¼ teaspoon ground cinnamon

Pinch of salt and black pepper

1.Start by getting the vegetable stock to a boil in a pot. Add the quinoa, return the stock to a boil, stir well and then lower the heat to a simmer. Cook for 15 minutes, drain in a colander before tipping the quinoa back into the pot. Allow to stand for a few minutes before fluffing with a fork.

2.Add frozen soya beans (soybeans) to a pot with boiling water. As soon as the water comes back to a simmer, cover with a lid and cook the beans for 4-5 minutes.

3.Add 1 tablespoon of oil to a wok or large frying pan over a medium high heat. Place the mustard seeds in the wok or pan and as soon as the mustard seeds start to "crackle and pop", add the cumin, turmeric and cinnamon and fry for about 30 seconds before adding the chopped carrot. Season

with salt and black pepper. Stir-fry for about 2 -3 minutes –
the carrots should still be crunchy. Add the chickpeas and
give everything a good stir.

4.Take the wok or pan off the heat. Stir in the quinoa, soya
beans, spring onions (scallions) and chopped chives.

5.Whisk together all the ingredients for the dressing. Place
the watercress at the bottom of a salad bowl or spread it out
on a large plate. Place the carrot and quinoa mix on top of
the watercress, drizzle the dressing over the carrot and
quinoa salad and scatter pomegranate seeds on top.

Lentil and Chickpea Salad

This is a filling, really tasty and healthy salad - a warm lentil and chickpea salad which is bursting with flavour and is filled with nutritious ingredients.

Pulses are low in fat whilst packed with protein and fibre - as well as a variety of minerals.

All pulses have a low GI and help to slow down the absorption of sugar into the blood, making your sugar level stay even and making you feel full for longer.

I must admit that to feel fully satisfied I often crave some kind of animal protein to accompany my vegetables. But since I've been eating more pulses, it seems to have reduced my craving for animal protein.

I am using Puy lentils which I personally think is much tastier than green lentils - but either will do, of course.

For 4 people:

150g, 5½oz, 0.7cups Puy lentils – or use green lentils

1 tablespoon olive oil

1 small red onion, finely chopped

Thumb-size piece of ginger, finely grated

3 garlic cloves, finely chopped

2 heaped teaspoons ground cumin

Pinch of chilli flakes

200g, 7oz, ripe small tomatoes, quartered

Salt and pepper

2 medium-sized carrots, coarsely grated

400g, 14oz, tin/can of cooked chickpeas, rinsed

Fresh coriander (cilantro)/parsley/chives

1.Rinse the lentils under plenty of cold water and cook according to pack instructions.

2.While the lentils are cooking, place the oil and chopped onion in a medium-sized pot over a low heat. Stir and cook for 5 minutes. Add the ginger, garlic, cumin and chilli flakes and cook for a further minute before adding the tomatoes. Season with some salt and pepper. Continue to cook for about 10 minutes, until the tomatoes have broken down.

3.Add the grated carrots to the pot and cook for a further minute before adding the chickpeas. Heat through before turning off the heat.

4.Drain the lentils and add them to the pot along with a couple of handfuls of chopped herbs - such as coriander (cilantro), parsley and chives (I personally add all three). Serve immediately.

Oven-Roasted Cauliflower Salad with Chickpeas and Quinoa

I recently made this oven-roasted cauliflower salad with chickpeas and quinoa.

How taste can change. I didn't use to like cauliflower. But then cauliflower seemed to pop up all over the place – in one interesting recipe after another. Now I am hooked.

It is all in the cooking as far as I am concerned.

Cauliflower is part of the super-healthy cruciferous family – broccoli, cabbage, Brussels sprouts, kale and cress are some of the other members. These vegetables are rich in vitamins, minerals and fibre and also contain powerful phytochemicals which can help to reduce the risk for cancer.

I am using healthy and tasty coconut oil in this recipe but you can replace it with olive oil.

1 tablespoons coconut oil

1 medium-sized head of cauliflower – cut into florets first and then into smaller pieces

2 teaspoons ground coriander (cilantro)

Salt and pepper

2 tablespoons of coconut oil

1 small red onion, chopped

1 garlic clove, crushed/minced

2 teaspoons ground cumin

½ teaspoon ground allspice

¼ teaspoon crushed chilli flakes

Salt and pepper

400g, 14oz, 2 cups, cooked chickpeas – if you buy them cooked, rinse well under cold water

150g, 5½oz, 0.8 cup, quinoa

100g watercress, or spinach

1.Preheat the oven to 200C/fan 180C/400F/gas mark 6. In a roasting pan, toss together the cauliflower pieces, ground coriander (cilantro) and coconut oil. Season with some salt and pepper and place the roasting pan in the oven for 30 minutes.

2.Rinse the quinoa under cold water, drain and then place in a pot with 400ml, 13½floz, 1.6 cups water. Cover the pot with a lid. Bring to a boil, then lower the heat and simmer for 15 minutes, until the water has been absorbed.

3.While the quinoa is cooking, place 2 tablespoons of coconut oil in frying pan over a low heat. Add the chopped onions and fry for about 5 minutes. Add the crushed garlic and fry for a further minute before adding the cumin, allspice and chilli flakes. Fry for one more minute.

4.Season the onion mixture with some salt and pepper and add the cooked chickpeas to the frying pan. As soon as the chickpeas are heated through, take the pan off the heat. Add the quinoa and roasted cauliflower to the pan and mix together.

5.Divide the watercress or spinach between four bowls or plates and top with the cauliflower mixture.

You could also add some crumbled feta cheese to each portion, and/or some pumpkin seeds.

Asian Coleslaw

A delicious, full-flavoured Asian coleslaw which is both healthy and kind to your waistline.

It requires a bit of preparation and soaking but once finished it will easily keep for several days in the fridge. The taste will improve when the coleslaw is left to stand for a while.

The inspiration for this coleslaw comes from Japanese and Korean cuisines. Both Japanese and Korean food often includes a fair amount of sugar though. I only add a small amount of raw, untreated honey in place of sugar in any type of Asian-style food where sugar is otherwise used.

When it comes to cabbage, my favourite type is sweet pointed cabbage. I love adding finely shredded pointed cabbage to my salads – love that sweet crunch you get when biting into it!

Cabbage is also super-good for you – containing among other things highly potent anti-cancer and liver-friendly nutrients.

Asian Coleslaw:

1 small pointed cabbage - finely shredded (I use a sharp knife rather than a grater)

2 medium-sized carrots, coarsely grated

2 green apples, coarsely grated

3 spring onions (scallions), chopped

50ml, 2floz, ¼ cup, cider vinegar

½ tsp natural salt – such as sea salt or Himalayan rock salt

Dressing:

1½ tablespoon fresh lime juice

1½ tablespoon Tamari soy sauce (which is gluten-free) – or use light soy sauce

1 teaspoon pure sesame oil

1 level teaspoon raw honey

1 garlic clove, crushed/minced

½ teaspoon ground ginger

1 tablespoon sesame seeds – dry-roasted for 1 minute (optional)

1.Place the shredded cabbage, grated carrots, apples and chopped spring onions (scallions) in a non-metallic bowl. Add the cider vinegar and salt and mix thoroughly. Leave to stand for 1 hour – stirring the mixture every now and then.

2.After an hour, put a lid or a plate on top of the coleslaw and pour off the liquid. Mix together the lime juice, soy sauce, sesame oil, honey, garlic and ginger, season with some black pepper and add to the coleslaw together with the sesame seeds. Mix thoroughly.

Pastry for Quiche

Not only do I think it's easy to make pastry for quiche, I also find the whole process therapeutic.

Most recipes tell you to add 1-2 tablespoons of water to the pastry dough. I use either cottage cheese, yogurt or crème fraiche instead. Cottage cheese will make the least calorific pastry, and whatever dairy product I put in the pastry, I also add to the filling of the quiche.

And then there is flour. These days in the UK you can get your hands on really good stone-ground, organic flour from specialist mills in the bigger supermarkets.

You pay a little bit more for these types of flour but here's the deal – in mass produced flour most of the nutrients have been removed while a wide variety of additives have been added.

I used to make my pastry for quiche with a mix of wholemeal (whole-wheat) flour, spelt and white flour for my pastry. Of course, if you use more white flour, you'll get a lighter pastry. But increasing the other types of flour will make the pastry much more interesting taste-wise, and healthier.

Lately though, I've made my pastry for quiche with only wholegrain spelt flour and this has produced the tastiest pastry ever.

I stick to the same measurements when using nothing but wholegrain spelt flour, even though I end up with a pastry dough that is a little bit stickier. As I press out the pastry with my hands (see below), this is not a problem.

It is necessary to blind-bake the pastry first to stop the pastry from collapsing. This is done by covering the pastry with baking parchment and then adding some kind of baking beans on top.

There is no need to buy ceramic baking beans – use a bag of dried beans instead, or something like it. You can re-use these over and over again. Just make sure you have enough to cover the base of the pie dish and up the sides.

I use my hands to make my pastry for quiche. There are no machines involved. I find that I can use less flour this way and get a really flaky pastry that melts in your mouth.

And instead of chilling the dough before pressing it out in the pie dish, I chill it afterwards. Trust me - it works!

110g, 3¾oz, 1 stick, lightly salted butter, cut into cubes

165g, 6oz, 1.2 cups flour

1 tablespoon of plain cottage cheese, or crème fraiche/ natural yogurt

Pie dish, approximately 23cm/9in in diameter

Baking parchment and baking beans (see above)

1. Put the butter and most of the flour into a large bowl. With your hands, quickly work the ingredients into a dough. Flatten out the dough in the bowl and place the tablespoon of whatever dairy product you are using in the middle of the dough. Fold in the sides, then add the rest of the flour to the bowl and quickly work it all together. You should end up with a very soft, but not sticky dough.

2. Once again, flatten out the dough and place it in the middle of your pie dish. With your fingers, keep pushing out the dough from the middle towards and then up the sides of the dish until it looks reasonably even (see three first photos below). Place the pie dish in the fridge for 30 minutes

3. Heat the oven to 200C/fan180C/400F/gas mark 6. Take out the pie dish and use a fork to prick the pastry all over the bottom of the pie dish (this is done to prevent the pastry from rising in the middle). Cover the pastry with baking parchment, place whatever baking beans you are using on top (last photo below) and bake in the oven for 15 minutes.

4. Take out the pie dish and carefully remove the baking parchment and the baking beans. If the sides have collapsed a bit, then take a teaspoon and gently press the back of the spoon all around the edge of the pie dish to make the sides rise a bit. But hey, don't fret if the pastry is a bit uneven – that rustic look is what might convince people that you actually made it!

5. Return the pie dish to the oven for another 5 minutes until the pastry starts to brown a little. Take it out of the oven.

You've now got a gloriously tasty pastry for quiche, a pastry-case ready to be filled.

One of the best things with quiches is that they tend to taste even better the next day. This makes them excellent food to make in advance. Bring on that party!

Leek and Courgette Quiche

I often make quiches with whatever ingredients I happen to have at hand.

This leek and courgette quiche came about when I was visiting a friend recently. She asked me if I could make something from the vegetables she had at home.

This friend of mine, although as thin as a beanpole, loves quiche and eats it quite often. But she eats tiny portions of it. Actually, she eats small portions of most things that she eats.

I do unfortunately have a much bigger appetite - which is why I eat a huge portion of salad whenever I have quiche and attack the salad before eating the quiche.

I like being asked to create a dish from whatever is at hand. This time I found a lot of green vegetables that I felt would go well together, so set about creating the following quiche.

For the pastry, see **Pastry for Quiche (page 441)**. (I used cottage cheese in the pastry.)

1 medium sized leek, properly rinsed, halved and sliced

1 medium sized zucchini (courgette), halved and sliced

A couple of sprigs each of thyme and rosemary (optional), stalks removed and leaves chopped

2 tablespoons olive

100g, 3½oz, 3½ cups, fresh spinach

2 spring onions (scallions), chopped

3 eggs, organic or at least free range

175g, 6oz, ¾ cup, cottage cheese (or use natural yogurt or crème fraiche instead)

100g, 3½oz, 1 cup, Parmesan cheese, grated

Salt and pepper

1. While the pastry case is cooking in the oven (200C/fan/180C/400F/gas mark 6), gently fry the leek and zucchini (courgette) together with the thyme and rosemary, if using, in the oil in a large frying pan for about 10 minutes.

2. Add the spinach to the frying pan and stir until the spinach has wilted. Take the pan off the heat and add the spring

onion (scallion). Let the vegetable mix cool down to room temperature.

3. In a bowl, mix the eggs, cottage cheese and Parmesan together. Add the vegetable mix to the bowl and season with some salt and pepper. Taste and check the seasoning. When the pastry case is ready, pour the mixture into the case and bake in the oven for approximately 25 minutes – until the filling is set and nicely browned on top.

Serve this leek and courgette quiche together with a salad containing lots of different coloured vegetables to make the meal healthier, tastier and full of texture.

Butternut Squash Quiche

I never follow a recipe when making quiche. I usually just make them up at the spur of the moment - as was the case with this butternut squash quiche that turned out to be one of the most delicious ones I've ever made.

Take care not to overdo the dried herbs that I add to this recipe as it can easily overpower the whole thing.

I used nothing but wholegrain spelt flour for the pastry, and what a winner that was. It gave the pastry a wonderfully nutty taste. I actually got hold of this organic stoneground flour in a supermarket. If you can't find something like it in a supermarket near you, try a health food shop.

I stuck to my usual pastry measures and resisted adding any more flour even though the dough was a little sticky. It was still easy to press it out and up the sides of my pie dish.

Use a heaped tablespoon of the cottage cheese in this recipe for the pastry.

Butternut squash quiche for 6 people:

For the pastry, see **Pastry for Quiche (page 441)**

A small butternut squash, about 700g, 1½lb, 3 cups peeled, halved, deseeded and cut into bite-size pieces.

1 tablespoon olive oil

1 red onion, peeled, quartered and each quarter finely sliced

1 red pepper (bell pepper), halved and sliced

2 tablespoons balsamic vinegar

3 eggs, preferably organic or at least free-range

300g, 10½, 1¼ cups, cottage cheese

½ teaspoon mixed dry herbs

Salt and pepper

1. Preheat the oven to 200C/400F/gas mark 6. Make the pastry for the quiche. Push it out with your fingers into your pie dish and place it in the fridge to chill for 30 minutes.

2. Toss the butternut squash pieces with the olive oil and spread them out in a roasting tray and sprinkle some salt on top. Place the tray in the oven and roast for 25-30 minutes – stir midway through - until tender. Set aside.

3. While the butternut squash is roasting, add 1 tablespoon of olive oil to a frying pan and fry the red onion over a

medium heat for 5 minutes. Add the balsamic vinegar and a little bit of salt and fry for another minute. Add the sliced red pepper (bell pepper) to the frying pan and fry for a further minute. Set aside.

4. Take out the pie dish from the fridge, prick the bottom with a fork, cover with baking parchment and add whatever baking beans you are using. Bake in the oven for 15 minutes.

5. Take out the pie dish and carefully remove the baking parchment and the baking beans. If the sides have collapsed a bit, then take a teaspoon and gently press the back of the spoon all around the edge of the pie dish to make the sides rise more. Return the pie dish to the oven for another 5-7 minutes until the pastry starts to brown and the bottom of the pastry is properly baked through and dry. Take it out of the oven.

6. Mix together eggs, the rest of the cottage cheese, the dry mixed herbs and season with salt and pepper.

7. Mix together the butternut squash, red onion and red pepper. When the pastry case is ready, add this mix to the pastry case and pour over the egg and cottage cheese mix. Return the pie dish to the oven and bake for about 25 minutes, until the top of this butternut squash quiche starts to brown a little.

Broccoli and Spinach Quiche

Lately I have been hooked on using wholegrain spelt flour for my quiche pastry. It makes a wonderfully tasty pastry that really enhances a quiche like this broccoli and spinach quiche

I've also chosen to use strong-tasting cheese for the filling of this quiche. I love blue cheese and I think it goes really well with the broccoli and spinach. But if you're not a fan of this kind of cheese, chose another strong-tasting cheese like mature or extra mature Cheddar or Gruyère cheese.

I stick to my usual measurements for the pastry even though this produces a slightly sticky pastry dough when using nothing but wholegrain spelt flour. This is not a problem though, as I use my hands to push out the pastry into the pie dish (see pastry for quiche below).

The end result is a really flaky pastry with a delicious nutty flavour.

For 4-6 people:

For the pastry, see **Pastry for Quiche (page 441)**

350g, 12oz, 5 cups broccoli, cut into small florets, stem sliced

200g, 7oz, 7 cups, fresh spinach

3 eggs – organic or at least free-range

400g, 14oz, 1.6 cups plain, full-fat cottage cheese

75g, 2¾oz, 0.3 cups blue cheese, crumbled - or other strong-tasting cheese, grated

Pinch of freshly grated nutmeg

Salt and pepper

1.Preheat the oven to 200C/400F/gas mark 6. Make the pastry for the quiche. Push it out with your fingers into your pie dish and place it in the fridge to chill for 30 minutes.

2.Put a pan with salted water on to boil for the broccoli. When the water is boiling, place the broccoli in the pan, cover with a lid and leave to simmer for 2 minutes only. Drain the broccoli in a colander and leave to cool down.

3.Take out the pie dish from the fridge, prick the bottom with a fork, cover with baking parchment and add whatever baking beans you are using. Bake in the oven for 15 minutes.

4.Put the fresh spinach in a large colander and slowly pour over a kettle of boiled water to wilt the spinach. When the spinach is cold enough to handle, squeeze out as much water as possible with your hands. Finely chop the spinach and leave to the side.

5.Take out the pie dish and carefully remove the baking parchment and the baking beans. Return the pie dish to the oven for another 5-7 minutes until the pastry starts to brown and the bottom of the pastry is properly baked through and dry.

6.Mix together the eggs, cottage cheese, crumbled or grated cheese and a pinch of grated nutmeg. Season with salt and pepper. Spread out the chopped spinach in the pastry case, place the broccoli on top and pour over the egg and cheese mixture. Bake in the oven for around 30 minutes, until the broccoli and spinach quiche is nicely browned.

Tomato and Basil Quiche

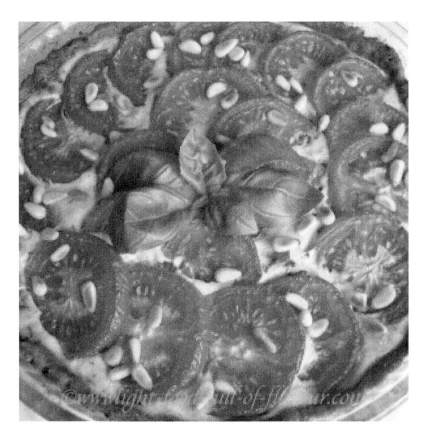

My quiches are mostly vegetarian and here is another one – a delicious tomato and basil quiche with a pastry made with spelt flour.

Tomatoes and basil are made for each other. I am personally very picky about the tomatoes I buy – I like my tomatoes to be really fragrant.

I am only using spelt flour for my quiche pastry these days. As I wanted to make the pastry for this quiche a bit lighter, I used about 2/3 of white spelt flour and 1/3 wholegrain spelt flour.

I stick to my usual measurements for the pastry even though this produces a slightly sticky pastry dough when using nothing but spelt flour.

This is not a problem though, as I use my hands to push out the pastry into the pie dish (see pastry for quiche recipe below).

The end result is a really flaky pastry with a delicious nutty flavour.

Tomato and basil quiche:

For the pastry, see **Pastry for Quiche (page 441)**

5-6 ripe medium-sized tomatoes, sliced

2 handfuls of basil, chopped

100g, 3½oz, 3½ cup, fresh spinach

3 large eggs – preferably organic or free-range

300g, 10½oz, 1½ cups, full-fat cottage cheese (use 1 tablespoon for the pastry)

½ teaspoon dried oregano

4-5 heaped tablespoons grated Parmesan cheese

1 teaspoon sea salt

¼ teaspoon black pepper

1 tablespoon dry-roasted pine nuts (optional)

1.Preheat the oven to 200C/400F/gas mark 6. Make the pastry for the quiche. Push it out with your fingers into your pie dish and place it in the fridge to chill for 30 minutes.

2.Take out the pie dish from the fridge, prick the bottom with a fork, cover with baking parchment and add whatever baking beans you are using. Bake in the oven for 15 minutes.

3.Put the fresh spinach in a large colander and slowly pour over a kettle of boiled water to wilt the spinach. When the spinach is cold enough to handle, squeeze out as much water as possible with your hands and chop the spinach on a cutting board.

4.Take out the pie dish and carefully remove the baking parchment and the baking beans. Return the pie dish to the oven for another 5-7 minutes until the pastry starts to brown and the bottom of the pastry is properly baked through and dry.

5.Mix together the eggs, cottage cheese, oregano, Parmesan cheese, salt and pepper. Add the chopped basil and spinach to the mix and pour this mixture into the pastry case. Place the tomato slices on top in a wheel-like pattern. Place the quiche in the preheated oven and bake for around 30 minutes, until the egg mixture has set and the tomato and basil quiche is nicely browned.

Scatter the pine nuts over the quiche before serving.

Beetroot Quiche

Beetroots (beets) and goat's cheese are a perfect match. I use both in this beetroot quiche.

Beetroots are a rich source of antioxidants and a wide range of nutrients. Several studies have also shown that eating beetroots or drinking beetroot juice can lower blood pressure and increase stamina.

To make my pastry healthier, I use wholegrain spelt flour. This makes a more robust and really tasty quiche pastry which I think matches the earthy taste of beetroots perfectly.

If you want a lighter pastry for this beetroot quiche, use a mix of white and wholegrain spelt flour.

I tend to make mostly vegetarian quiches when I'm cooking at home.

When cooking on a job, I often make quiches with smoked salmon or crayfish (crawfish) tails, and a lighter pastry. As tasty as these more refined quiches are, I still prefer the taste of a quiche with different vegetables.

And all quiches, in my opinion, taste even better the next day!

I serve this quiche with a large mixed salad.

For 6 people:

For the pastry, see **Pastry for Quiche (page 441)**

4 large raw beetroots (beets), peeled and coarsely grated

3 eggs

300g, 10½oz, 1½ cups, cottage cheese – use 1 tablespoon for the pastry

100g, 3½oz, 0.8 cup, soft goat's cheese

Salt and pepper

1.Preheat the oven to 200C/400F/gas mark 6. Make the pastry for the quiche. Push it out with your fingers into your pie dish and place it in the fridge to chill for 30 minutes.

2.Take out the pie dish from the fridge, prick the bottom with a fork, cover with baking parchment and add whatever baking beans you are using. Bake in the oven for 15 minutes.

3.While the pastry is in the oven, mix together the eggs, cottage cheese and goat's cheese in a bowl. Add the grated beetroot (beets), season with salt and pepper and mix it all together

4.Take out the pie dish and carefully remove the baking parchment and the baking beans. Return the pie dish to the oven for another 5-7 minutes until the pastry starts to brown and the bottom of the pastry is properly baked through and dry.

5.Pour the beetroot mixture into the pastry case and return the pie dish to the oven. Cook the quiche for about 30-35 minutes – until the beetroot mixture has set.

Smoked Salmon Quiche

My smoked salmon quiche is a more festive one compared to other quiches that I make.

This is a quiche that I often make at work - especially as part of a buffet-style lunch where I might also serve a vegetarian quiche.

I make a lighter pastry for this one, using only white organic spelt flour, butter and usually crème fraiche. The end result is incredibly flaky pastry.

You can use cooked crayfish (crawfish) tails instead of smoked salmon – I sometimes do this and it makes for an equally super-tasty quiche. The same goes for cured salmon in place of smoked salmon.

I add either chopped fresh dill, spring onion (scallion) and/or chives to the filling. Be careful when adding salt to the filling as both smoked and cured salmon and cooked crayfish are already quite salty.

Smoked Salmon Quiche:

For the pastry, see Pastry for Quiche (page 441)

For the filling:

3 large, or 4 small-medium sized organic or free-range eggs

300g, 10½oz, 1.3 cups, crème fraiche (use 1 heaped tablespoon for the pastry)

250g, 9oz, smoked salmon, chopped – or use cured salmon or crayfish (crawfish) tails.

A small handful of dill, chopped – or use 2-3 spring onions, or a handful of chopped chives

Salt and pepper

1.Preheat the oven to 200C/fan 180C/400F/gas mark 6. Make the pastry for the quiche. Push it out with your fingers into your pie dish and place it in the fridge to chill for 30 minutes.

2.Take out the pie dish from the fridge, prick the bottom with a fork, cover with baking parchment and add whatever baking beans you are using. Bake in the oven for 15 minutes.

3.Take out the pie dish and carefully remove the baking parchment and the baking beans. Return the pie dish to the oven for another 5-7 minutes until the pastry starts to brown and the bottom of the pastry is properly baked through and dry.

4.In a bowl, mix together the eggs and crème fraiche and season with a bit of salt and pepper. Add the salmon and dill and stir it into the mixture. Taste to check the seasoning.

5.Pour the filling into the pastry case. Place the quiche in the pre-heated oven and bake for around 30 minutes, until the mixture has set and the quiche is nicely browned.

Gluten-Free Quinoa Quiche with Mushrooms and Zucchini

I had request for a gluten-free quinoa quiche and I made this gluten-free quinoa quiche with mushrooms and zucchini.

I used a recipe from a cook book called "Super grains and seeds" by Amy Ruth Finegold and made some changes to it.

As per usual, I make my pastry by hand. It worked really well with the ingredients I used for this recipe. I was happy to see that the pastry case didn't need any blind-baking (this is when you cover the case with baking parchment and baking beans). It held its' shape beautifully without doing this.

The person I made this for only eats dairy products made from goat's milk. I used goat's yogurt in the pastry and the filling – plus goat's cheese in the filling. You can swap the goat's yogurt for ordinary yogurt or crème fraiche – and the goat's cheese for feta cheese or parmesan cheese.

For the gluten-free quinoa quiche pastry:

125g, 4½oz, 2/3 cup quinoa flour

40g, 1½oz, 1/3 cup corn starch

35g, 1¼oz, ¼ cup ground flax seeds (linseeds)

110g, 3¾oz, 1 stick (8 tablespoons) lightly salted butter, cubed

2 tablespoons goat's yogurt

For the filling:

2 tablespoons olive oil

1 large red onion, finely chopped

1 garlic clove, crushed/minced

200g, 7oz, 3 cups, sliced mushrooms – like chestnut mushrooms

1 medium-sized courgette-zucchini, halved and thinly sliced

1 teaspoon fresh thyme leaves – or ¼ teaspoon dried thyme

100g, 3½oz, 4 cups fresh spinach

3 large eggs – or 4 medium

100g, 3½oz, 0.4 cup soft goat's cheese

5 tablespoons goat's yogurt

Salt and pepper

Pie dish, approximately 23cm/9in in diameter

1.Pre-heat the oven to 200C/fan 180C/400F/gas mark6. To make the pastry - in a bowl, mix together the quinoa flour, corn starch and ground flax seeds. Add the cubed butter to the bowl and with your hands, quickly work the ingredients together. Add the goat's yogurt and work this in as well. You should end up with a quite soft dough.

2.Flatten out the dough and place it in the middle of your pie dish. With your fingers, keep pushing out the dough from the middle towards and then up the sides of the dish until it looks reasonably even. Place the pie dish in the fridge for 30 minutes.

3.While the pastry is in the fridge, add the oil and chopped onion to a large frying pan over a medium high heat and fry for five minutes. Add the garlic, mushrooms, courgette and thyme to the pan and continue to stir and cook for a further 10 minutes. Add the spinach and keep stirring until the spinach has wilted – it should only take a minute or two. Season with some salt and pepper and remove the pan from the heat. Drain any excess liquid from the vegetable mixture and leave to cool down.

4.Remove the pie dish from the fridge and use a fork to prick the pastry all over the bottom. Place it in the oven and bake for 15-17 minutes, until the pastry starts to brown and the bottom of the pastry is properly baked through and dry. Take it out of the oven and leave it to cool down a bit.

5.In a bowl, mix together the eggs, soft goat's cheese and goat's yogurt. Season with some salt and pepper and add the cooked vegetable mix to the bowl. Pour the mix in to the pastry case and bake in the oven for about 25 minutes, until the top is slightly golden.

Salsa and Sauce Recipes

Tomato Chilli Jam

As much as I like to try new recipes, some things are really worth repeating. This tomato chilli jam is a side dish that I cook a lot.

It has the wow-factor in abundance and can jazz up the humblest vegetable and give a kick to many a different dish.

Serve it together with oven-roasted vegetables, falafels, some good sausages or your home-made burgers to name but a few.

It's simple to make and freezes well - but to get anything left to freeze you will probably need to double up on the amount you make as this is seriously moreish. I've had many a person wanting to lick the bowl for the last bits of it.

1kg, 2¼lb, 6 cups, very ripe tomatoes cut into even-sized chunks

3 red chillies, deseeded and finely chopped

1 large red onion, peeled, halved and finely sliced

3 garlic cloves, peeled and finely chopped

Thumb-sized piece of ginger, peeled and finely chopped

4 tablespoons balsamic vinegar

1 tablespoon olive oil

25g, 1oz, 1/7 cup, soft brown sugar

Salt and pepper

1. Heat the oven to 200C/fan 180C/400F/gas mark 6. Place all the ingredients in a roasting tin and mix well.

2. Roast for 40 minutes – stir the mixture once after 20 minutes - until the tomatoes are browned and the onion caramelised. Eat hot or cold. It will keep in the fridge for up to a week. You can also freeze it.

Let me give you an example of how easy it would be to create a tasty, healthy, low-calorie meal with this spicy jam.

1. Roast a mixture of sweet potatoes (cut into large chunks) and butternut squash (smaller chunks) tossed in a bit of olive oil and seasoned with salt and pepper in the oven.

2. Place some boneless and skinless chicken-thighs on a roasting tray covered with baking parchment. Brush the chicken with a bit of olive oil, season with salt and pepper and place this in the oven as well.

3. During the last ten minutes, chuck in some small tomatoes together with the sweet potatoes and butternut squash. Towards the end – steam or boil some broccoli and/or sugar snaps or other beans.

4. Serve it all with the tomato chilli jam.

Olive and Red Pepper (Bell Pepper) Dip

I don't like olives on their own but I can't get enough of this super delicious olive and red pepper (bell pepper) dip.

It's easy to make, really healthy and you can use it in so many ways. Add a dollop to a salad, top oat biscuits or bread with a spoonful, stir it through pasta.

The other day I made myself toasted rye bread topped with hummus, avocado, poached egg and this olive dip. It was So Tasty!

The dip is also a nutritional goldmine.

Olives are a good source of vitamin E, and other important antioxidants, and healthy monounsaturated fats.

Red peppers are low in calories and a very good source of vitamin A and C.

Walnuts are like all nuts a very good source of essential fats, vitamins and minerals.

Nutritional yeast flakes are an incredibly good source of different B-vitamins (which are vital for body's energy production) and fibre. Nutritional yeast has a cheesy taste and can be found in health food shops and well-stocked supermarkets.

All the different types of fat in the dip are of the healthy and essential variety - the kind of fats your body need - but it's still fat and it's best to not eat too much of it.

For the dip:

100g, 1 1/2oz, half a cup of pitted olives (any colour)

1 large red pepper (bell pepper), de-seeded and roughly chopped

50g, 1 3/4oz, half a cup, walnut halves

1 heaped tablespoon nutritional yeast

2 tablespoons Extra virgin olive oil

1 tablespoon balsamic vinegar

1/4 teaspoon black pepper

Place all the ingredients in a food processor and pulse for about 30 seconds.

Sweet Chilli Sauce

I want to show that it is possible to make savoury jams without loads of sugar. This is an incredibly tasty sweet chilli sauce - made with very little sugar.

I am forever trying to either eliminate, or at least reduce, sugar used in savoury food. At times I cannot understand why it has even been added to a recipe. Other times I find that you can get an absolutely delicious result with just a tiny bit of sugar, or honey – as is the case in this Not-So-Sweet Chilli Sauce.

I only added two teaspoons of honey to start with (I use raw, untreated honey) but ended up adding two teaspoons of soft brown sugar as well. Though compare that to 150g of sugar used in other recipes like this.

This chilli sauce is simply stunningly tasty and such a versatile thing to have to hand - any left-overs can be frozen. I smother some over salmon fillets and bake the salmon in the oven. Or I add some to fried scallops, or falafels to name but a few things.

You could add it to a stir-fry as well - either a vegetable stir-fry or one where you also add thinly sliced chicken, or prawns.

I tend to blend it to a smooth sauce, but you could just as well leave the sauce as it is once it has cooked.

Sweet chilli sauce:

1 tablespoon groundnut or vegetable oil

1 red onion, peeled and finely chopped

3 large red chillies, deseeded and finely chopped

3 teaspoons grated fresh ginger

2 teaspoons honey

2 teaspoons soft brown sugar

2 teaspoon fish sauce

185ml, 6floz, ¾ cup, cider or white wine vinegar

60ml, 2floz, ¼ cup, water

Juice of ½ a lime

1. Add the oil, onion, chilli and ginger to a sauce pan and cook over a medium heat for about 4 minutes, stirring every now and then.

2. Add the remaining ingredients, bring to a simmer and stir until the sugar has dissolved. Leave to simmer for 35-40 minutes, until it's quite thick and most of the liquid has evaporated. Check the seasoning - you might want to add some more fish sauce, or some salt.

3. Remove from the heat and cool down to room temperature. Either leave it as it is, or use either a stick blender or a food processor/blender to mix until you get a smooth sauce.

This sauce will easily keep for several days if it's covered and kept in the fridge.

Beetroot and Walnut Dip with Pomegranate Molasses

I am a huge fan of beetroot (beets) and this beetroot and walnut dip with pomegranate molasses is both easy to make and super tasty. Oh, and it is healthy as well!

Beetroot is a rich source of antioxidants and it contains potassium, magnesium, iron, vitamins A, B6 and C and folic acid, as well as protein, carbohydrates and soluble fibre.

It also contains betaine, which is important for cardiovascular health.

Beetroot has been shown to lower blood pressure and other studies have shown the positive effect beetroot can have on human exercise and performances. The theory is the nitrates in beetroot are converted into nitric oxide by the body. The nitric oxide dilates the blood vessels. The result is improved oxygen delivery - and that gave a performance boost.

I use beets in a lot of different ways and buy both raw ones as well as pre-cooked ones, as long as they are vacuum-packed in natural juices.

This beetroot and walnut dip is perfect to serve as part of a buffet. I tend to serve it as a light, vegetarian lunch buffet together with hummus, avocado, feta cheese, red peppers (bell peppers), toasted wholemeal pitta bread and a large salad.

But it will also make an awesome side dish to food like roasted vegetables, oven-roasted salmon or chicken to name but a few.

As it is so quick to whip up, add some to a lunch box with raw carrot sticks, sliced cucumber, dark lettuce leaves, hummus and some oat cakes. This would be a really healthy lunch to bring to work.

The walnuts add a lot of extra nutrients to the dip. Apart from being rich in essential fats, walnuts (like all nuts and seeds) are rich in certain vitamins and minerals.

Nutritional yeast flakes are an incredibly nutrient-rich food product - rich in fibre, vitamins and minerals. It has a wonderfully cheesy and nutty flavour. Here in the U.K. you can find it in well-stocked supermarkets and also in health food stores.

Pomegranate molasses is simply a syrup which is made from reduced pomegranate juice. You can sometimes find it in well stocked supermarkets – or look for it in health food shops or shops that specializes in Middle Eastern food.

I bought mine in my local health food shop.

Beetroot and walnut dip:

300g, 10½oz, cooked beetroots in natural juices – roughly chopped

1 large red pepper (bell pepper) – sliced

50g, 1¾oz, walnuts

1 heaped tablespoon nutritional yeast flakes

1 tablespoon pomegranate molasses

1 tablespoon balsamic vinegar

1 tablespoon olive oil

½ teaspoon sea salt (I use Himalayan crystal salt)

¼ teaspoon black pepper

a pinch of cayenne pepper

Place all the ingredients in a food processor and blitz for about 20-30 seconds, until you have a quite smooth mixture.

Mango Salsa

I Love Asian-style food and this gorgeous mango salsa is so full of flavour and such a great accompaniment to many Asian-style main courses.

It's a really fresh-tasting salsa and the perfect combination is to serve it on crisp lettuce leaves, like little gem lettuce leaves – making it into a divine salad.

It has that perfect combination of sweet and sour, spicy and salty which you find in Asian food. If the mango you use isn't that sweet, you could mix a little honey into the dressing as well.

This is such a good example of how amazingly tasty food can still be really low in calories and healthy. Mangoes are a great source of beta-carotene. Chillies are super-healthy and may also help to speed up your metabolism.

Another benefit is of course that it's easy and quick to make. Do make it a little bit ahead of time though - the taste of this mango salsa improves if you leave it to "mature" for a short while before serving it.

It has proved to be a hugely popular side dish whenever I have served it, and I've had people who are otherwise not massively keen on salads falling head over heels with this one.

For 4 people as a side dish:

1 large, ripe mango, peeled and cut into cubes

1 small red onion, peeled and finely chopped

½ cucumber, deseeded and diced

1 red chilli, deseeded and finely chopped

A small handful of mint leaves roughly chopped

For the dressing:

1 tablespoon fresh lime juice

1 tablespoon oil – rapeseed, groundnut or vegetable oil (I prefer to use rapeseed oil)

1 teaspoon Thai fish sauce

1 teaspoon honey (optional)

2 heads of little gem lettuce, leaves separated

1. Place the mango, red onion, cucumber, chilli and mint in a bowl. Mix together the lime juice, oil, fish sauce and honey (if using), pour it over the salsa ingredients and toss everything together. Leave to stand for a while - about 30 minutes.

2. Place the gem lettuce leaves on a large plate, give the salsa a stir and add a dollop of the salsa to each lettuce leaf.

Beetroot Jam

My quest for ways to cut out sugar in savoury food continues. I've only added a bit of honey to this beetroot jam (beet jam) and it tastes amazing.

A savoury jam usually has a fair amount of vinegar in it. Combine that with the punchy and naturally sweet taste of beetroot and red onion and there is simply no need for sweetening it with loads of sugar.

You must obviously be a beetroot lover if you've clicked on this recipe. Those who claim to hate this vegetable are missing out on a LOT of health benefits – apart from the glorious taste of course!

Beetroots are a rich source of potent antioxidants and nutrients. Several studies have also shown that eating beetroots or drinking beetroot juice can lower blood pressure and increase stamina.

This jam will go well with things like falafels, lamb chops, lamb burgers or sausages. And it is also very nice to eat with a bit of goat's cheese, blue cheese or feta cheese.

I made a sandwich for myself the other day with toasted sourdough bread topped with Gruyère cheese, cooked and sliced chicken breast and beetroot jam. Yum!

I am using cooked beetroots in natural juice for this jam - you can find some really good organic varieties in the U.K. If you are not as lazy as I am, you can of course use raw beetroots. Cook them until they are almost done before continuing with my recipe below.

For the jam:

2 tablespoons olive oil

1 red onion, peeled, halved and finely sliced

250g, 9oz, 1¼ cup (chopped), cooked beetroot (beets) in natural juice, drained and diced

50ml, 2floz, ¼ cup, red wine vinegar

2 tablespoons balsamic vinegar

2-3 teaspoons honey

80ml, 3floz, 1/3 cup, water

1 teaspoon sea salt

1.Heat the oil in a sauce pan, add the sliced onion and cook over a low heat for about 10-12 minutes – stirring every now and then to make sure the onion doesn't burn - until the onion is soft. Add the diced beetroots, red wine vinegar, balsamic vinegar, honey, water and salt to the sauce pan and stir.

2.Bring to a boil, lower the heat and simmer for about 10 minutes - until most of the liquid has evaporated. Take the sauce pan off the heat and let the jam cool down.

This beetroot jam will easily keep for a week if well covered and stored in the fridge.

Red Pepper Salsa

You can't go wrong with a red pepper salsa (bell pepper salsa) as tasty as this one. It is perfect to serve as a dip with toasted pitta bread and it would also fit in very well as part of a mezze-style meal.

Or brush toasted slices of sourdough bread with a little olive oil and top with some goat's cheese or feta cheese and a dollop of the salsa. Swap the cheese for slices of stir-fried chicken and add a dollop of yogurt along with the salsa.

It will definitely liven up a soup and it will add pizzazz to oven-roasted vegetables and many other dishes as well.

I buy the pointed variety of peppers (bell peppers) as I find that they are usually much tastier than normal peppers (which can be frightfully bland in taste).

This red pepper salsa is also quite healthy with only a one teaspoon of honey added to it. Peppers are obviously healthiest eaten raw and as I love them so much, I eat raw ones on a daily basis.

For the red pepper salsa:

2 tablespoons olive oil

1 medium-sized red onion, finely chopped

3 garlic cloves, finely chopped

1 teaspoon ground cumin

A good pinch of chilli flakes

3 red peppers (bell peppers), deseeded and finely chopped

1 tablespoon tomato purée

1 teaspoon honey

1 tablespoon red wine vinegar

200ml, 7floz, 0.9 cup water

Salt and pepper

1.Place the olive oil in a pot over a low heat and add the chopped red onion and garlic to the pan. Stir and cook for 5 minutes – taking care that the onion and garlic don't burn – until the onion starts to soften.

2.Add the ground cumin, chilli flakes and chopped red pepper (bell pepper) to the pan and continue to cook for a further couple of minutes. Add the tomato puree, honey, red wine vinegar and water to the pan. Season with salt and pepper, stir and bring to a simmer.

3.Allow to simmer for about 15 minutes – until most of the liquid has evaporated and the salsa has become syrupy.

It will easily keep in the fridge for a good five days, if covered properly. I haven't tried to freeze it myself – there has been nothing left to freeze – but I do think you could freeze it as well.

Pea Aioli

Aioli is really a garlic mayonnaise so weight-wise it is not the best thing to overindulge in. But a dollop of this gorgeous pea aioli won't do much harm.

That is pretty much my food philosophy anyway. I believe you can eat a bit of everything and still be healthy and maintain a weight you are happy with. The trick is to eat much more of the good stuff and only a small amount of the un-healthier food – and preferably only occasionally.

What's the fun in completely denying yourself something that you really like?

Calories aside, this pea aioli actually contains some pretty healthy ingredients – egg yolk (which is the most nutrient-dense part of the egg), olive oil, garlic and peas. All of these are all full of nutrients that are really good for our bodies.

Green peas – which make up the biggest part of this aioli - are high in fibre, protein, vitamins, minerals and lutein. They are loaded with antioxidants and anti-inflammatory nutrients, have a relatively low GI and are an extremely low-fat food.

To avoid losing a lot of those nutrients through cooking, I place frozen peas in a pot, pour over boiling water from a kettle, cover the pot with a lid and just before the peas come up to a boil, I pour off the water and rinse the peas under cold water.

This pea aioli makes a great accompaniment to things like asparagus, crudités, roasted vegetables and prawns and scallops – and either of these, or perhaps a mix of them, will make a great starter or as part of a buffet.

As the peas are quite sweet, I think this aioli needs a fair amount of black pepper and a really good pinch of cayenne pepper.

225g frozen peas, cooked as per above

2 garlic cloves, crushed/minced

1 egg yolk – as you are eating this raw, use an organic or free-range egg yolk

100ml, 3½floz, slightly less than ½ cup, olive oil

Salt, black pepper

A pinch of cayenne pepper

1.Place the peas and 1 tablespoon of water to a food processor and blitz to a puree.

2.Add the egg yolk and garlic to a bowl and whisk together. Keep whisking while very slowly adding the oil, drop by drop to start with, until the sauce emulsifies and thickens. Once you have incorporated all the oil, stir in the pea puree and season with salt, black pepper and a pinch of cayenne pepper.

Roasted Carrot Chickpea Hummus

I love hummus – like this roasted carrot chickpea hummus.

Carrots are actually healthier when cooked. Cooked carrots release more beta carotene than raw. Tomatoes are also healthier when cooked as processing or cooking makes the health-boasting lycopene in tomatoes more easily absorbed.

I am adding whole garlic cloves to the roasting tin, with their skin left on though. The garlic becomes really sweet when oven-roasted like this. You just open up the skin and squeeze out the garlic once roasted.

Chickpeas, like all other pulses, are low in fat and saturates whilst being packed with both insoluble and soluble fibre, protein and a variety of minerals.

A daily portion of pulses provides good amounts of both protein and fibre, and these two nutrients prevent food to leave the stomach too quickly, helping us to feel fuller for longer.

2 large carrots – cut into batons

3 whole, large garlic cloves, with the skin left on

3 tablespoons olive oil

2 heaped teaspoons ground cumin

½ teaspoon ground paprika

Salt and pepper

400g, 14oz, 2½ cups, cooked chickpeas

2 tablespoons tahini

Water

1.Pre-heat the oven to 200C/fan 180C/400F/gas mark 6. Place the carrot batons and garlic cloves in a roasting tin. Add the olive oil, ground cumin, paprika and season with salt and pepper - mix well.

2.Place the tin in the oven and cook for around 30 minutes – tossing the vegetables half-way through.

3.Add the chickpeas to the tin and mix well. Return the roasting tin to the oven for a further 5 minutes.

4.Let the vegetables cool down. Squeeze out the garlic from their skins and place everything in the roasting tin and the two tablespoons of tahini in a food processor. With the motor running, add 5 tablespoons of water to start with. If you find that it still too thick, add some more water.

5.Once it is smooth enough, check the seasoning - you might even want to add some more cumin (I am a huge cumin fan myself).

For a roasted carrot chickpea hummus with more of a kick – sprinkle over some cayenne pepper before serving. You could also add a squeeze of lemon juice.

Hummus is great to have as a snack if you are watching your weight. Eat it on some oatcakes (preferably oatcakes without any sugar), or with some raw vegetables – like carrots, cucumber or cauliflower.

Cake Recipes

Double chocolate cakes

A chocolate lover's dream - double chocolate cakes!

I used to bake quite regularly some years ago – I even baked and sold cakes at a market - and I was constantly trying to make the ultimate chocolate cake.

These double chocolate cakes ended my trials – they are simply stunning! And they are gluten-free!

First of all, I want to talk about the chocolate that I use (there's a lot) – part a good quality 70% dark chocolate and part a good quality milk chocolate with quite a high cocoa percentage, around 37-42%.

I have been able to find milk chocolate with a high cocoa percentage in well-stocked supermarkets.

These double chocolate cakes are rich and obviously calorie-laden **but I make them very small**, small enough to not affect your weight very much.

I melt the dark chocolate but chop the lighter chocolate and add the chopped chocolate pieces as the last thing to the batter. I also add a fresh raspberry to each cake – hidden in the middle and not revealed until you bite into the cakes.

These days I normally use xylitol in place of sugar when I am baking. Xylitol is a vegetable sugar which is similar to fructose in fruit and has a very low GI. It looks and tastes like sugar but has very little effect on raising your blood sugar.

What xylitol hasn't got is the preserving factor that normal sugar has. Made with ordinary sugar, these double chocolate cakes will keep for up to a week in the fridge. Unless I'm baking for a lot of people – knowing that they will be eaten in a couple of days – I use ordinary sugar.

This will make 24 small double chocolate cakes:

110g, 3¾oz, 70% dark chocolate

110g, 3¾oz, 1 stick, lightly salted butter

2 eggs – preferably organic or free-range

140g, 4¾oz, 0.7 cup, caster (superfine) sugar

70g, 2½oz, ½ cup, ground almonds

110g, 3¾oz, milk chocolate with a high cocoa content – 37-42% - roughly chopped

24 raspberries

1.Preheat the oven to 200C/fan 180C/400F/gas mark 6. You can use individual, **small** muffin cases, or silicon trays - place whatever you chose on a baking tray.

2.Place the butter and dark chocolate in a bowl over a pot with simmering water (the bowl must not touch the water) and stir until melted. Remove the bowl from the heat and leave to cool down slightly.

3.Place the eggs and sugar in another bowl and use an electric whisk, or whisk by hand, to beat the butter and sugar together until pale and light. Add the melted dark chocolate and butter mix to the bowl and use a large spoon to mix together.

4.Add the ground almonds and mix it in. Add the chopped milk chocolate and mix together once more. Add enough chocolate mixture to just cover the base of each muffin case, place a raspberry on top and divide the rest of the mixture between the mini muffin cases.

5.Place the tray in the oven and bake for about 18-20 minutes – the cakes should still be quite soft in the middle. Leave to cool down completely before removing from the tray.

Almond Lemon Drizzle Cakes

I am not going to hold back - these almond lemon drizzle cakes are a total taste sensation. Bite into the cakes, and you get an explosion of sharp lemon mixed with the slightly gooey and sweet taste of the almonds.

A lot of the cakes I bake contain ground almonds and not so much flour. These very moist, very lemony cakes are no exception.

I am also using xylitol in place of ordinary sugar. Xylitol looks and tastes like sugar but has very little effect on raising your blood sugar. It is a vegetable sugar which is similar to fructose in fruit and has a very low GI.

I'm not sure if it's sold in super-markets. I bought it in a health food shop.

Note: if like me you want to get rid of those bingo-wings – whisk by hand when whisking is required.

To make 12 small cupcakes (I use silicone miniature muffin trays):

110g, 3¾oz, 1 stick, butter, melted

110g, 3¾oz, slightly more than ½ cup xylitol - or use caster sugar (superfine sugar)

60g, 2oz, ½ cup ground almonds

Grated zest of 2 un-waxed lemons, juice of 1 ½ (the juice is used for the lemon drizzle)

2 large eggs at room temperature

60g, 2oz, 0.4 cup self-rising flour

40g, 1½oz, 0.3 cup icing sugar (confectioner's sugar) - for the lemon drizzle

1. Pre-heat the oven to 180C/350F/ gas mark 4. Either line a 12-hole cupcake tin with foil or paper cases or use a silicone miniature muffin tray.

2. Place the butter and sugar in a bowl. Use an electric whisk, or whisk by hand, to beat the butter and sugar together until pale and light. Use a large spoon and mix in first the ground almonds and the lemon zest, followed by one egg at a time. Sieve the flour into the bowl and mix it in quite quickly.

3. Divide the mixture between the cupcake cases and bake in the oven for 18-20 minutes, until nicely browned and springy.

4. While the cakes are baking, prepare the lemon drizzle by whisking together the lemon juice and the icing sugar. When the cakes are ready, prick them all over with a tooth-pick or a fork and then divide the lemon drizzle over the hot cakes. Leave to cool in the tin.

These little almond lemon drizzle cakes are perfect both as an afternoon treat with a cup of tea or coffee, and as something to round off a meal with.

Swedish Apple Cake

Not only does this Swedish apple cake bring back wonderful childhood memories - it is also one of my absolute favourite cakes.

In British apple cake-recipes they always seem to use cooking apples. I don't. I use apples such as Gala or Pink Lady or any other juicy eating apple that I have to hand. I add the juice of a lemon to a big bowl of cold water and add the apple slices to the water while preparing the rest of the cake.

When it comes to vanilla, I will only use vanilla pods or a good vanilla extract – not some fabricated vanilla essence. It is a bit expensive but you don't need to use much to get a lovely vanilla flavour.

I am using xylitol in place of sugar these days. Xylitol looks and tastes like sugar but has very little effect on raising your blood sugar. You can use caster (superfine) sugar instead.

Swedish apple cake:

150g, 5½oz, 11½ tablespoons (0.7 cup), unsalted butter, melted

3 eggs

200g, 7oz, 1 cup, xylitol - or use caster (superfine) sugar

1 teaspoon vanilla extract

175g, 6oz, 1¼ cup, plain flour

1 teaspoon baking powder

7-8 apples, depending on size, peeled, cored, halved, sliced to a medium thickness and placed in a bowl with lemon water (see above)

Cinnamon

1. Heat the oven to 180C/350F/gas mark 4. Line a baking tray (approximately L14" x W11" x H1.5" – L36cm x W26cm x H4cm) with baking parchment).

2. Place the sugar, eggs and vanilla extract in a bowl. Use an electric whisk, or whisk by hand, and beat until you've got quite a thick and pale mixture.

3. Add the melted butter to the sugar and eggs and mix it in with the help of a large metal spoon. Mix the flour with the

baking powder and sift it into the bowl. Gently fold in the flour until just combined.

4. Spoon the cake mixture into the prepared baking tray. Transfer the apple slices to a colander and shake off any access water. Here comes the tedious part – you have to stick the apple slices into the cake mixture, one by one and very close together (see first photo below).

5. Once that is done, dust the cake with a fair amount of cinnamon (second photo below) and bake in the preheated oven for around 30 minutes but check a bit before. As the cake is so thin, you really need to keep an eye on it so that it doesn't over-bake.

Once it is ready, cut the Swedish apple cake into pieces and serve warm or cold - either as it is or with vanilla sauce or a bit of whipped cream.

French Chocolate Cake

There is no doubt about it - this is a French chocolate cake recipe fit for a chocolate lover. And it is gluten-free!

I have come across people who don't like chocolate - and all the chocolate lovers I talk to don't believe me when I tell them this – but to me it seems they are few and far between.

This French chocolate cake is **very rich and truly divine**. You'll find that most people will be perfectly satisfied with only a small piece. Though I do go the whole hog with this cake and serve it with a bit of whipped cream and either fresh raspberries or a raspberry coulis.

To make the cake even more special, you can add finely grated zest from one orange. Just make sure that you scrub the orange first if it is waxed.

French chocolate cake for 8-10 people:

150g, 5½oz, 0.7 cup, unsalted butter, melted

180g, 6oz, 0.9 cup, caster sugar (superfine sugar)

150g, 5½oz, 0.9 cup, good quality, 70% dark chocolate

4 large eggs, yolks and egg whites separated

60g, 2oz, ½ cup ground almonds

Grated zest of an orange (optional) - scrub the orange first if it is waxed

Frosting

100g, 3½oz, 0.6 cup, good quality, 70% dark chocolate

1 tablespoon butter

1. Pre-heat the oven to 180C/350F/gas mark 4. Prepare a round cake tin by lining it with baking parchment, or if you have them, a round tin liner. Start by melting the chocolate. Break it up and place it in a bowl over a pot with simmering water. The bowl should not touch the water. Once the chocolate has melted, remove the bowl and put it to one side.

2. Whisk the butter and sugar until pale and light. Using a metal spoon, add the egg yolks and mix well. Add the melted chocolate and mix it in. Add the ground almonds (plus the grated zest of an orange if using) and mix well.

3. In a separate bowl, whisk the egg whites until stiff. Add half of the egg whites to the rest of ingredients and using

quite big movements, carefully mix it in to loosen up the chocolate mixture but without breaking up the stiff egg whites too much. Add the rest of the egg whites and carefully fold it in as well.

4. Spoon the mixture into the prepared cake tin and place the tin in the oven. Bake in the oven 25-30 minutes. Check after 25 minutes as this cake should still be quite soft in the middle and not properly baked through like a normal cake. Take out the cake and let it cool down.

5. Once the cake has cooled down, remove from the cake tin and place it on a large plate. For the frosting, melt the chocolate and the butter in a glass bowl on top of a pot with simmering water. Remove the bowl from the heat, stir the mixture and let it cool down a little before spooning it over the cake. Use a spatula to spread the frosting over the cakes and down the sides. Cool before serving.

This French chocolate cake makes a wonderful dessert. It will keep for quite a few days should you get any left-overs.

Devon Apple Cakes

Last time I baked these Devon apple cakes I thought they had to be my favourite cakes. But then I say the same thing about a lot of other cakes that I bake.

Once again I choose to bake smaller cakes rather than one big cake. I do personally find it easier to control my cake intake when they are this size.

To make 20 small cakes:

225g, 8oz, 1cup, butter, melted

500g, 1lb 2oz, apples

Juice of 1 lemon

200g, 7oz, 1cup, caster sugar (superfine sugar)

3 large organic or free-range eggs

225g, 8oz, 1.6 cup, self-rising flour (or use 225g plain flour and add an extra teaspoon baking powder)

2 teaspoons baking powder

25g, 1oz, ¼ cup, ground almonds

For the topping:

25g, 1oz, 2 tablespoons, butter

10g, ¼oz, 1 tablespoon, dark brown soft sugar

30g, 1¼oz, ¼ cup, roasted chopped hazelnuts

30g, 1¼oz, 0.3 cup, flaked almonds

1 teaspoon cinnamon

1.Pre-heat the oven to 190C/fan 170C/375F/gas mark 5. You can use individual muffin cases (chose smaller sized cases) or silicon trays - place whatever you chose on a baking tray.

2.Mix together the ingredients for the topping. Divide the mixture into 20 portions.

3.Add the lemon juice to a bowl. Peel and core the apples, cut them into cubes and toss the cubes in the lemon juice.

4.Place the butter and sugar in another bowl and whisk together, using either an electric hand whisk or an ordinary whisk, until the mixture becomes pale and fluffy. Beat in the eggs, one at a time, adding a little flour with each egg to prevent the mixture from curdling.

5.Mix together the remaining flour with the baking powder and sift into the bowl, add the ground almonds and using a large metal spoon, gently fold the flour and ground almonds into the butter mixture. Stir in the apple pieces and lemon juice.

6.Divide the mixture between the muffin cases, filling each about 2/3 full. Crumble a portion of the nut and cinnamon topping over each case and press it down lightly with your fingers. Bake the Devon apple cakes in the pre-heated oven for around 22-25 minutes – or until each cake is well risen and brown.

Raw Chocolate Truffles

Can you call chocolate healthy? My raw chocolate truffles are rich in healthy ingredients and are also really easy to make.

On top of that these chocolate truffles are gluten-free, dairy-free and suitable for vegans.

Raw cacao nibs are broken up pieces from the cocoa bean, once the bean has been roasted and the husk has been removed. Raw cacao (nibs or powder) is rich in antioxidants, different minerals and fibre - but is also a stimulant as it contains theobromine, which can have a similar effect on your body to caffeine.

But hey, as long as you eat them in moderation.

I have combined raw cacao powder with coconut oil, walnuts and raw organic honey to make these raw chocolate truffles.

Coconut and coconut products, like coconut milk and coconut oil, has high levels of vitamins C, E and B and is also rich in magnesium, potassium and iron. Coconut has a high level of dietary fibre which makes you feel fuller quicker.

It does contain saturated fat but coconut is rich in medium-chain fatty acids which the body processes differently than other saturated fats. These medium-chain fatty acids promote weight maintenance without raising cholesterol levels.

Walnuts are apparently the healthiest of all nuts as they contain the highest level of antioxidants compared to other nuts. These nuts are also rich in several minerals, including calcium and magnesium which are both really important for the health of our bones.

The honey I'm using is a raw organic honey – a lovely orange blossom honey at the moment. It is still a type of sugar but, unlike runny honey, a sugar that is full of minerals.

Once my raw chocolate truffles have firmed up, I dust them with raw cacao powder.

To make 12 raw chocolate truffles:

25g, 0.9oz, coconut oil

50g, 1¾oz raw honey

50g, 1¾oz raw cacao powder

50g, 1¾oz walnut halves

Raw cacao powder for dusting

1.Add the walnut halves to a food processor and pulse for about 30 seconds.

2.Place the coconut oil in a pot over a low heat and stir until melted – it won't take long. Remove the pot from the heat and stir in the honey, chocolate and the grated walnuts and mix well. Place this mixture in a bowl and place the bowl in the fridge for about 15 minutes.

3.Remove the bowl from the fridge and form 12 truffles with your hands. Place the truffles on a plate and put this plate in the freezer for a further 15-20 minutes. Remove the truffles from the freezer and dust them with raw cacao powder. Store the truffles in an air-tight container in the fridge.

Lime and Almond Cake

I serve this divine lime and almond cake either as a dessert after a meal – with lots of berries and mango - or as an afternoon cake with a cup of tea or coffee.

There is lots of ground almond and very little flour in this cake - I use organic white spelt flour. It's a cake so there is butter and sugar involved, but almonds are good for you and organic spelt flour is so much better than the ordinary plain flour sold in supermarkets.

And I am using xylitol in place of sugar. Xylitol is a vegetable sugar which is similar to fructose in fruit and has a very low

GI. I'm not sure if it's sold in super-markets. I bought it in a health food shop.

You can use caster sugar, superfine sugar instead xylitol.

Tip: If you can only get hold of waxed lime fruits, make sure you scrub them really well with a clean scrubbing brush. And don't be too forceful when grating the zest. You only want the very outer layer of the fruit, not the bitter pith, the inner white part.

For 8 people:

3 medium-sized eggs

160g, 5¾oz, 0.8 cup, xylitol - or use caster sugar (super-fine sugar)

½ teaspoon good-quality vanilla extract

125g, 4½oz, 9 tablespoons, unsalted butter, melted

200g, 7oz, 1¾ cups, ground almonds

60g, 2oz, ½ cup, white spelt flour - or use plain white flour

2 teaspoons baking powder

Grated zest of 2 un-waxed limes

1.Pre-heat the oven to 180C/350F/ gas mark 4. Line a 20cm-diameter cake tin with a cake tin liner, or lightly grease the tin with butter and dust with a bit of ground almonds. Place the eggs, sugar and vanilla extract in a bowl. Use an electric whisk, or whisk by hand, to beat the eggs and sugar together until pale and light. Use a large spoon and mix in the butter.

2.Place the ground almonds in another bowl and sieve the spelt flour and baking powder into the bowl. Add the lime zest, mix together and add this to the bowl with the eggs, sugar and butter. Mix it all together quite quickly.

3.Pour the mixture into the prepared tin and place the tin in the oven. Bake the lime and almond cake for approximately 30 minutes, until nicely browned. Allow the cake to cool in the tin.

Banana and Chocolate Cakes

Several versions and too many cakes later (well, I've got to try them), I have finally created a recipe for what I think are utterly delicious banana and chocolate cakes.

You can bake it as one big cake or you can make little cupcakes. I prefer to make cupcakes as I find it easier to control my cake-intake this way. (The photo is of a slice of a big cake solely because it was more photogenic than the cupcakes!)

Apart from the butter and sugar – they are cakes after all – these banana and chocolate cakes are almost good for you. Wishful thinking perhaps but they contain lots of healthy bananas, nuts and a bit of dark chocolate. Oh yes, a little bit of antioxidant-rich dark chocolate is good for you – as long as you stick to "a little bit.

I'm using very little flour in these banana and chocolate cakes, and the flour I use is organic white spelt flour (dinkel wheat flour). Spelt is an ancient type of wheat which is becoming more and more popular. People with wheat intolerance often find that they can eat bread or cakes made with spelt.

This will make 24 banana and chocolate small cakes:

2 large eggs

200g, 7oz, 1cup, caster sugar (superfine sugar)

150g, 5½oz, 0.7 cup (1.4stick) unsalted butter, melted

3 large ripe bananas, mashed (use a fork to mash the bananas)

50g,1¾oz, 1/3 cup 70% dark chocolate, chopped

50g 1¾oz, 1/2 cup walnuts, roughly chopped

200g, 7oz, 1¾ cups, ground almonds

70g, 2¼oz, 1/2 cup, plain white spelt flour - or use ordinary plain white flour

2 teaspoons baking powder

1 teaspoon bicarbonate of soda

1.Pre-heat the oven to 180C/fan 160C/350F/gas mark 4. You can use individual muffin cases or silicon trays - place whichever you choose on a baking tray. Place the eggs and sugar in a bowl and whisk together, using either an electric whisk or an ordinary whisk, until the mixture becomes pale and fluffy.

2.Add the melted butter to the bowl and mix it in using a large metal spoon. Add the mashed bananas, chopped chocolate and walnuts to the bowl and mix everything together.

3.Place the ground almonds in a separate bowl. Sieve the flour, baking powder and bicarbonate of soda into the ground almonds. Mix well and then add this to the other bowl, mixing it all together quite quickly.

4.Divide the mixture between the cupcake cases, filling each about 2/3 full. Bake the cakes in the pre-heated oven for around 20 - 22 minutes – until each cake is well risen and nicely browned. (If you choose to bake one big cake, you will need to leave it in the oven for around 40 minutes and cover it with baking parchment about half-way through to protect the top from browning too much.)

Carrot Cakes

Every time I bake theses carrot cakes, I'm stunned by how incredibly delicious they are. Simply irresistible!

There is a fair deal of sugar and sunflower oil in these cakes. As per usual though, I make my cakes small - so small in fact that the amount of sugar and oil in each cake is relatively low.

I make the topping slightly sour and it is a perfect match for the cakes.

You can, of course, make one big cake. You need to bake it for around 50 minutes (possibly a bit longer) and cover it with baking parchment about half-way through to protect the top from browning too much.

I use miniature muffin silicone trays with 11 holes - this recipe will make 33 small carrot cakes.

250g, 9oz, 1¼ cup, caster sugar (superfine sugar)

200ml, 7floz, 0.9 cup, sunflower oil

3 organic or free-range eggs

300g, 10½oz, 2.8 cups coarsely grated carrot

100g, 3½oz, 0.8 cup, chopped walnuts

190g, 6¾oz, 1.3 cup, plain (all-purpose) white flour

1 teaspoon baking powder

1 teaspoon bicarbonate of soda (baking soda)

1 teaspoon ground cinnamon

½ teaspoon salt

For the topping:

150g, 5½oz, 3/5 cup, Philadelphia cream cheese

2 tablespoons lemon juice

2 level tablespoons icing sugar (confectioner's sugar)

1.Pre-heat the oven to 180C/fan160C/350F/gas mark4. Prepare whatever cake tin or tray you are using (if you haven't got silicone trays, use mini-muffin cases). Place the sugar and sunflower oil in a bowl and whisk together until fluffy. Add the eggs to the bowl and use a large metal spoon to mix them in. Add the grated carrot and chopped walnuts and stir to mix them in.

2.Place the flour in another bowl and add the baking powder, bicarbonate of soda, cinnamon and salt and mix together. Sieve the flour mix into the bowl with the sugar, oil and eggs. Mix everything together quite quickly.

3.Divide the mixture between the trays - or muffin cases - filling each hole in the tray about 2/3 full. Bake the cakes in the pre-heated oven for around 25 minutes – until each cake is well risen and nicely browned.

4.Mix together the ingredients for the topping and once the cakes have cooled down, place a small amount of topping on each cake.

Chocolate and Raspberry Brownies

Can cakes ever be good for you?

These miniature chocolate and raspberry brownies are made with antioxidant-rich dark chocolate, nutritious almonds, spelt flour and xylitol - which looks and tastes like sugar but has very little effect on raising your blood sugar.

I read about xylitol a while ago and finally got around to try it. And now that I have, I won't use sugar again. Xylitol is a vegetable sugar which is similar to fructose in fruit and has a very low GI.

I'm not sure if it is sold in supermarkets. I buy it from health food shops. And you can of course use caster sugar (superfine sugar) instead of xylitol.

The one thing to keep in mind when using xylitol is that it hasn't got the preserving factor that normal sugar has. I have tried making things like quince jelly using xylitol in place of sugar. It didn't work.

The only really naughty thing in these cakes is the butter – but considering how small I make these brownies they won't affect your weight too much if you eat no more than one or two.

Some weight-friendly advice: As these cakes will not last for that many days if you use xylitol, make sure you've got plenty of friends and family around when baking them!

To make 22 miniature chocolate and raspberry brownies:

100g, 3½oz, slightly less than a stick, unsalted butter

100g, 3½oz, 70% dark chocolate

2 eggs, organic or at least free-range

140g, 5¼oz, 0.7 cup xylitol – or use caster (super-fine) sugar

60g, 2oz, ½ cup, ground almonds

60g, 2oz, 0.4 cup white spelt flour – or use plain white flour

1 teaspoon baking powder

22 raspberries

1.Pre-heat the oven to 180C/fan 160C/350F/gas mark 4. You can use individual small muffin cases or silicon trays - place whatever you chose on a baking tray.

2.Place the butter and chocolate in a bowl over a pot with simmering water (the bowl must not touch the water) and stir until melted. Remove the bowl from the heat and leave to cool down slightly.

3.Add the eggs, sugar and ground almonds to the bowl and mix together. Mix together the flour and baking powder and sieve the mixture into the bowl. Stir everything together quite quickly.

4.Divide the mixture between the miniature muffin cases and push a raspberry into each. Place the baking tray in the oven and bake the brownies for 16-17 minutes (they should still be soft in the middle). Allow to cool before serving.

Gluten-Free Blueberry Cakes

Believe it or not but these very moist and delicious gluten-free blueberry cakes are on the verge of being healthy!

Does it sound too good to be true? Well…

Blueberries are bursting with vitamins C and E - one large handful of the berries provides as many antioxidants as five servings of carrots, broccoli or apples. Berries in general contain many phytonutrients that boost your immune system.

(Ok, I'm not going to deny that for best effect berries should be eaten on their own and raw, but they will do some good in a cake as well.)

Fresh berries also have the lowest sugar content of all fruit – you can eat a big serving of berries without it affecting your weight very much.

Almonds are known to lower bad cholesterol (I use ground almonds in this recipe). These nuts are a rich source of vitamin E and they also contain high quality protein and are rich in dietary fibre, B vitamins, essential minerals and monounsaturated fat.

The sugar I sometimes use these days is xylitol. It is a vegetable sugar that looks and tastes like sugar but which has very little effect on raising your blood sugar. Xylitol has a really low GI – half that of fructose in fruit. I buy it in a health food shop.

And when it comes to butter, well, nowadays a lot of health experts are saying that a little bit of butter in your diet does no harm and is much better for you than most manufactured spreads.

I rest my case!

This will make 10 gluten-free blueberry cakes:

100g, 3½oz, 0.9 stick, unsalted butter – softened

100g, 3½oz, ½ cup, xylitol (or use caster/superfine sugar)

2 large eggs, organic or at least free-range

125g, 4½oz, 1.1 cups, ground almonds

1 teaspoon baking powder

4 tablespoons milk

100g, 7oz, 0.7 cup, blueberries

1.Pre-heat the oven to 180C/fan 160C/350F/gas mark 4. Line the holes of a muffin tin with medium-sized paper cases.

2.Place the butter and sugar in a bowl and using a whisk, cream together until light and fluffy. Add the eggs one at a time, whisking well after each egg. Mix together the ground almonds and baking powder and using a large spoon, fold it into the bowl with the butter, sugar and eggs. Stir in the milk, followed by the blueberries.

3.Divide the mixture between the paper cases and place the muffin tin in the oven. Bake for about 25 minutes. Leave the cakes to cool in the tin.

Gluten-Free Raspberry Muffins

Gluten-free raspberry muffins made with ground almonds and shredded coconut which are also lactose-free and, if you leave out the honey, even sugar-free.

I admit that I rarely take on cook jobs where the clients can't or won't eat a huge number of different types of food as I'm not sure I'll be able to be creative enough.

But I am forever curious when it comes to food, and I want to constantly try new things – new recipes, new methods, new ingredients. My curiosity was definitely awoken when I saw recipes for gluten, lactose and sugar-free cakes in a magazine and I had to come up with a recipe myself.

Look, I'm not trying to kid either myself or anyone else that these muffins are comparable to a cake full of sugar and butter, but they are tasty. Why wouldn't they be – they are full of tasty ingredients.

They are also full of healthy ingredients with a natural sweetness - ground almonds, coconut and raspberries. I've flavoured these gluten-free raspberry muffins with vanilla extract and you can also add 1-2 teaspoons of honey if you wish.

On the subject of honey, raw unpasteurized (untreated) honey is rich in beneficial enzymes, vitamins and antioxidants.

Runny honey is made by heating up raw honey to make it more liquid so that it can be cleaned up and put into jars or plastic bottles.

The heat turns honey's natural sugar into another fast-releasing sugar – pretty much like ordinary sugar – and removes all the health benefits of honey.

To make 9, medium-sized muffins:

125g, 4½oz, 1.1 cups, ground almonds

50g, 1¾oz, 0.45 cup, shredded coconut

1 teaspoon baking powder

1 teaspoon vanilla extract

1-2 teaspoons honey (optional)

3 eggs – organic or free-range

250g, 9oz, raspberries

1.Pre-heat the oven to 200C, fan 180C, 400F, gas mark 6. Line the holes of a muffin tin with 9 medium-sized muffin cases. In a bowl, mix together the ground almonds, shredded coconut and baking powder.

2.Break the eggs into another bowl and add the vanilla extract and honey, if using. Whisk together lightly with a fork.

3.Add the egg mixture to the dry ingredients and mix together. Carefully fold in the raspberries. Divide the mixture between the muffin cases and place the muffin tray in the oven. Bake the muffins for 18-20 minutes, until they have a nice brown colour. Allow the gluten-free raspberry muffins to cool in the tin.

Lemon Tart

I sometimes cheat when I'm cooking – not with ingredients but with methods. This super-delicious lemon tart is a prime example.

One reason is that when I am on a job, I am always short of time. Another reason is that I am a severely impatient person.

In many cake recipes, for example, it says that you should add the eggs one at a time and mix carefully in between adding the eggs. I add all the eggs at the same time and you know what, my cakes still come out really beautiful and yummy.

This lemon tart recipe is from Raymond Blanc, a self-taught French chef with a Michelin-star restaurant in England. I have made this many times when working and I made it again the other night while out on my current job on the West-coast of Scotland.

While I more or less use the same ingredients as this chef does, I really simplify the way I make the pastry. I haven't tasted his lemon tart – which I am sure is absolutely amazing – but my version never fails to wow either. It is incredibly tasty!

Normally I do try to find enough time to blind-bake the pastry – this is when you cover the pastry with baking parchment and some kind of baking beans. The reason for blind-baking is to make sure that the pastry case doesn't collapse along the sides.

As time really wasn't on my side the other night I even skipped this process. (And to be quite honest, I often skip blind-baking when I am making quiche outside of work. I obviously still have to bake the pastry case first - I just skip the baking parchment and baking beans and bake the case in one go until it is ready and can be filled and finished off in the oven.)

What I did though was to press the pastry slightly up and above the edge of the tart dish and fold it over. Once the tart was ready, I simply used a knife and trimmed the edge.

Note: I use xylitol instead of sugar. It is a vegetable sugar that looks and tastes like sugar but which has very little effect on raising your blood sugar. Xylitol has a really low GI – half that of fructose in fruit. I buy it in health food shops.

For 6-8 people:

Pastry:

120g, 4oz, ½ cup, unsalted butter, slightly softened

80g, 2oz, 0.6 cup icing (confectioner's) sugar, sifted

2 medium organic or free-range egg yolks

250g, 9oz, 1.8 cups plain flour, sifted

1 tablespoon cold water

For the filling:

5 medium organic or free-range eggs

150g, 5½oz, 0.75 cup xylitol – or use caster sugar (super-fine sugar)

140ml, 5floz, 0.6 cup double cream

Grated zest of 3 lemons and the juice of 4 (or do what I do when I am in a hurry, skip the zest and just add the juice of about 4½ - 5 lemons – simply taste the filling until you think it is sour enough)

1 organic or free-range egg, beaten, for glazing

1.Pre-heat the oven to 180C/ fan 160C/350F/gas mark4.

2.To make the pastry (my way), add all the ingredients to a bowl and work it together with your hands until you've got a smooth pastry. Using your hands, press out the pastry in a 21cm, 8½ inch tart tin. Place the pastry case in the fridge to chill for 30 minutes.

3.Take out the pastry tin from the fridge, prick the bottom with a fork, cover with baking parchment and add whatever baking beans you are using. Bake in the oven for 15 minutes.

4.Carefully remove the baking beans and baking parchment, return the pastry case to the oven for about 5 more minutes, until the pastry is golden. Brush the pastry case with the beaten egg and return it to the oven for 1 more minute.

5.For the filling, whisk the eggs and sugar together, gently whisk in the cream, lemon juice and zest until just combined and pour it into the case. Cook for about 25 minutes. Remove the tart from the oven and let it cool for an hour.

Low-GL Carbohydrates

Your body needs carbohydrates. It is by far the safest "fuel" for your body to run on. Some carbohydrates though, are better for your health and weight than others.

The best way to lose weight - and to stay healthy - is to keep your blood sugar levels on an even keel. And the best way to achieve this is by eating carbohydrates which slowly releases the sugar into to your body, and avoid those that goes straight into your blood stream causing your blood sugar to shoot up.

But it doesn't end there. Most foods don't consist of solely one thing. While meat is mostly protein and fat, other types of food contain a mixture of carbohydrates, protein and fat.

The GI, the glycemic index, only tells you if a carbohydrate is fast or slow releasing. The GL is a measure of the amount of carbohydrates in the food multiplied with the GI of the carbohydrates.

Watermelon, for example, has a relatively high GI score but it contains very few carbohydrates so it has a low GL score. Sweet potatoes, on the other hand, have a low GI score but they contain a high percentage of carbohydrates so have a high GL score.

The lower the GL score of a food item, the more you can eat of that food without gaining much weight.

Low-GL Carbohydrates

The carbohydrates with the lowest GL are non-starchy vegetables:

Asparagus

Aubergine

Beansprouts

Broccoli

Brussels sprouts

Cabbage

Cauliflower

Celery

Courgette (zucchini)

Cucumber

Endive

Fennel

Kale

Lettuce

Mangetout

Mushrooms

Onions

Peppers

Radish

Rocket

Runner beans

Spinach

Spring Onion

Tenderstem broccoli (broccolini)

Tomatoes

Watercress

It is a good idea to fill up half of your plate with vegetables from this low-GL carbohydrates group – as a salad or lightly steamed/cooked.

You can make them all the more delicious by drizzling some dressing over your salad, and toss your lightly cooked vegetables with some olive oil, lemon juice/zest and season with a little salt and some more black pepper. You could also add some crushed/minced garlic, herbs or some grated Parmesan cheese.

Starchy Vegetables, Grains, Rice and Pasta

Squash

Carrots

Swede

Beetroots

These vegetables have a higher GL than non-starchy vegetables but a much lower GL than

Sweet potatoes

Parsnips

Potatoes

It is better to eat more of the first four and less of the last three if you are watching your weight.

But don't cut out sweet potatoes from your diet as they are incredibly nutritious. When I cook something like a vegetarian casserole or curry, I add twice as much squash as sweet potatoes. I do adore both of these vegetables and I use them a lot.

When it comes to grains and rice, quinoa is by far the most nutritious and the kindest to your waistline. You can eat nearly twice the amount of quinoa compared to brown rice for the same effect on your blood sugar.

Apart from being really nutritious, quinoa also contains a high amount of protein – which gives it a low GL score (see pulses below).

Of the different types of rice, brown basmati rice has the lowest GL.

For pasta, your best choice is wholegrain pasta or pasta made from pulses.

Oats are great to use for breakfast. Of the fibres in grains, oat fibre is the best at controlling blood sugar – oats subsequently have a low GL score.

Pulses/Legumes

Pulses/Legumes - beans, peas, chickpeas and lentils - are the best foods for both balancing your blood sugar and giving you the right mixture of carbohydrates and protein. This perfect balance gives all pulses a low-GL carbohydrates score.

Pulses are also low in fat and saturates whilst being packed with both insoluble and soluble fibre and a variety of minerals.

Fruit

Fruit contains a simple sugar called fructose and fructose needs to be converted to glucose before it can be used as fuel for your body. This makes fructose a slow-releasing carbohydrate.

But, and it is a big but, some fruit contain pure glucose as well – like grapes and dates – and eating these fruits will cause your blood sugar to shoot up.

Bananas contain both glucose and fructose and are therefore faster releasing than apples - which contain mainly fructose and are slow-releasing.

Berries, apples, pears and plums are your best choice of fruit when it comes to GL points.

Berries have the lowest sugar content of all fruit and are also really nutritious. Notice the difference - one single date has the same effect on your blood sugar level as a large punnet of strawberries!

Dried fruit has a high sugar content – as does fruit juice – and a high GL score.

The "bad guys"

And then there are the carbohydrates that it is best to avoid or at least cut down on – refined carbohydrates.

Refined carbohydrates like white bread, white rice and refined cereals have a similar effect to sugar on your blood sugar. It will make your blood sugar shoot up only to come crushing down not long afterwards – making you crave more food not long afterwards.

These blood sugar spikes and troughs are also really bad for your health as they damage your arteries.

A plate full

Finally - and this is important - eating low-GL carbohydrates together with some protein (vegetable or

animal-based) and some fat (seed and nut oils, olive oil and coconut oil) will further lower the GL score of carbohydrates. And fibre-rich food will lower it even more.

Weight Loss Tips

If you want to lose weight and keep the weight off, these weight loss tips show you that certain foods are good to include in your daily food intake, while you need to be more restrictive with others.

Avoid "light-versions" of food. They may have less fat but this is usually replaced by a very high sugar content to improve flavour. High sugar consumption is bad news for both your health and your weight.

Flavoured yogurts – low-fat or not – contain a lot of sugar. Buy full-fat natural yogurt, or soya or coconut yogurt, and add fresh berries instead.

Fruit is nutritionally really good for us but also contains a fair amount of sugar. It is best to be somewhat restrictive with your fruit intake if you are trying to lose weight. Berries have the lowest amount of sugar, are packed with antioxidants and are a good choice of fruit for anyone watching their weight - followed by apples, plums and pears, which are also good choices. **All dried fruit and fruit juices have a high sugar content.**

Avoid white bread and pasta made with refined white flour as much as you possibly can. All refined food, including white rice, are bad news for both your weight and health. It's a good idea to cut down on bread altogether. The types of bread that will affect your weight the least are pumpernickel bread, followed by sourdough bread.

Bread will make you put on weight much more than pasta. Again, choose wholegrain pasta over white pasta. I buy a wholegrain spelt pasta which is so delicious. It's not going to do you any good, of course, if you cover your pasta with a cream & cheese sauce. Try my Oven-roasted tomato sauce (vegetarian recipes), it is delicious and also healthy.

If you are looking for information about how to lose belly fat, some of the following weight loss tips are especially good for you.

1.Fill up with vegetables and fruit that are packed with high levels of antioxidants, such as berries, dark green leafy vegetables and tomatoes. Studies by Fujita Health University in Japan found the lower your antioxidant levels, the higher your levels of tummy fat

2.Soya food also helps to reduce tummy fat. In trials from University of Virginia, women given just one soya drink a day after menopause lost tummy fat while women denied the soya didn't.

3.Eat chillies to increase your metabolism. Chillies are incredibly healthy. They contain high levels of beta-carotene - a powerful antioxidant - and also vitamin C, potassium, dietary fibre and iron. And capsaicin, the basic compound in chillies, may speed up your metabolism and your ability to burn calories.

4.Pomegranates can also help to reduce tummy fat. Scientists at Edinburgh University found that people who drink pomegranate juice every day developed less tummy fat cells compared to those who don't. And according to scientists in Israel, drinking 120ml of pomegranate juice a day for a year decreases the size of fatty cholesterol build-ups in the heart arteries.

5.Eating a grapefruit at every meal appears to boost weight loss. Scientists attribute this to its ability to reduce insulin levels, which in turn helps to reduce appetite and calorie intake.

6.Chickpeas have been found to be good at helping with weight control. In a recent study, adults who ate 100g of chickpeas each day for four weeks ate fewer processed snack foods and felt fuller than when they didn't include chickpeas in their diet.

7.The fatty acids in olive oil can make your body burn food faster in the period after you have eaten it, according to dieticians at McGill University in Quebec. Olive oil encourages the body to raise its metabolism and expend calories.

8.Japanese researchers report that vinegar helps us to burn fat. It seems that the acetic acid in vinegar switches on genes that make fat-burning enzymes spring into action, boosting the metabolic rate and helping to suppress the accumulation of body fat. Other studies have shown that vinegar-taking mice also had lower cholesterol levels and blood pressure. Add a tablespoon of cider vinegar to a small glass of water and/or make a delicious vinegar and olive oil dressing to add to your salad.

9.**Eating plenty of low-GL (glycemic load) carbohydrates will help you lose weight - see Low GL Carbohydrates.**

10.Drink a cup of black or green tea with a meal containing carbohydrates. These teas interfere with the enzymes that break down carbohydrates, slowing their digestion and reducing insulin levels, but also cutting the calories you absorb from them by up to a quarter.

Index

Almond lemon drizzle cakes 495

Banana and chocolate cakes 513

Carrot cakes 516

Chocolate and raspberry brownies 519

Devon apple cakes with a nut a cinnamon topping 504

Double chocolate cakes 492

French chocolate cake 501

Gluten-free blueberry cakes – friands 522

Gluten-free raspberry muffins 525

Lemon tart 528

Lime and almond cake 510

Raw chocolate truffles 507

Swedish apple cake 498

Chicken

Chicken and broad beans in a sherry, mustard and tarragon sauce 255

Chicken burger 281

Chicken curry with lemongrass and tomatoes 251

Chicken curry with miso 288

Chicken pasanda 269

Chicken stir-fry 244

Chicken with harissa and squash tagine 237

Dukka marinated chicken with lentils and roasted vegetables 301

Ginger and soy chicken 295

Lemon and garlic chicken with quinoa and pesto 277

Marinated chicken with chilli, coriander and lime 234

Mexican chicken and guacamole with tomato salsa 274

Moroccan-style chicken casserole 241

Parmesan breaded chicken with a tomato basil sauce 262

Piri-piri chicken with roasted squash 298

Poached chicken in an Asian-style broth 258

Saffron chicken casserole 266

Spicy pomegranate marinated chicken thighs 292

Tarragon chicken with a vermouth sauce 248

Vietnamese chicken meatballs 284

Fish

Asian-style trout with roasted vegetables 205

Cured salmon two ways 181

Fish tagine 218

Ginger-glazed salmon with citrus couscous 174

Halibut on spicy mash with samphire 139

Lemon sole with capers and mushy peas 142

Lightly smoked salmon with mushy peas 163

Lime-marinated salmon with a mango chutney sauce 191

Marinated mackerel fillets 202

Miso-marinated salmon with sweet potato mash 160

Pan-fried salmon with an anchovy and walnut vinaigrette 188

Poached salmon and vegetables 154

Rolled crepes canapés 221

Salmon and noodles in an Asian-style broth 209

Salmon and quinoa kedgeree 228

Salmon, sweet potato and chilli fishcakes 146

Swedish seafood casserole with saffron 166

Lamb

Herb-crusted lamb chops on a bed of vegetables 333

Indian lamb mince pie 352

Lamb and beetroot burger with feta and garlic sauce 314

Lamb biryani with saffron rice 345

Lamb kofta in a tomato sauce 321

Lebanese-style lamb in pitta bread 318

Moroccan lamb meatballs in an aromatic sauce 337

Tomato and basil quiche 454

Salads

Asian coleslaw 438

Asian-style carrot salad 416

Asparagus salad 424

Avocado and bean salad 413

Carrot and quinoa salad with chickpeas and soy beans 428

Chicken and mango salad 421

Crispy kale salad with chickpeas, beetroot and hummus 398

Crunchy Thai salad 418

Lentil and chickpea salad 432

Orange and tomato salad 404

Oven-roasted cauliflower salad 435

Prawn and grapefruit salad with avocado and pea shoots 410

Quinoa and chickpea salad 401

Warm chicken salad 407

Salsas sauces and dips

Beetroot and walnut dip with pomegranate molasses 474

Beetroot jam 480

Mango salsa 477

Olive and red pepper dip 469

Pea aioli 486

Red pepper salsa 483

Roasted carrot and chickpea hummus 489

Sweet chilli sauce 471

Tomato chilli jam 466

Scallops with spicy mash and tomato salsa 215

Soups

Asian-style beetroot soup 392

Asian-style salmon soup 368

Avocado and spinach soup 383

Carrot and watercress soup 389

Chicken and noodle soup 359

Chickpea and tomato gazpacho 395

French fish soup 365

Lentil and carrot soup 375

Minestrone soup 386

Pea soup two ways 377

Spicy sweet potato soup 371

Thai-style chicken soup 380

Traditional Spanish gazpacho 362

Watercress and spinach soup 356

Thai-style mussels 231

Vegetarian Recipes

Aubergine and green bean tagine 110

Aubergine (eggplant) tomato and chilli Lasagne 78

Beans in tomato sauce (fasolia) 119

Beetroot and chickpea burger 84

Broad (fava) beans and poached eggs on bread 81

Buckwheat sweet potato crepes 100

Carrot and soy bean fritters 113

Cauliflower rice with lime and coriander 97

Coconut dhal 107

Courgette and pesto lasagne 51

Gluten-free socca pancakes with vegetable stir-fry 54

Indian dal with aubergine, squash and carrots 135

Indian falafels 90

Oven-roasted tomato sauce/soup 62

Puy lentils with roasted beetroot and sweet potatoes 65

Sourdough bread with tomatoes and garlic 129

Spicy Indian fritters (pakoras) 87

Spinach tomato ricotta bake 104

Margareta Wiklund asserts her right to be identified as the author of this work.

Copyright © 2012-2019 www.light-food-full-of-flavour.com. All rights reserved.

No part of this publication may be reproduced, stored in a retrieval system, or transmitted in any form or by any means, electronic, mechanical, photocopying, recording or otherwise, without prior permission of the author.

Disclaimer: The techniques and advice described in this book represent the opinions of the author based on her experience. The author expressly disclaims any responsibility for any liability, loss or risk, personal or otherwise, which is incurred as a result of using any of the techniques, recipes or recommendations suggested here. If in any doubt, or if requiring medical advice, please contact the appropriate health professional.

Printed in Great Britain
by Amazon

84440250R00315